FIVE EVANGELICAL LEADERS

JOHN STOTT

MARTYN LLOYD-JONES

FRANCIS SCHAEFFER

JAMES I. PACKER

BILLY GRAHAM

Christopher Catherwood

HAROLD SHAW PUBLISHERS
WHEATON, ILLINOIS

To the memory of:

Martyn Lloyd-Jones 1899–1981
Francis Schaeffer 1912–1984

Two great giants of the faith,
to whom, under God,
we all owe so much.

ISBN 0-87788-257-6, cloth
ISBN 0-87788-274-6, trade paper

Library of Congress Cataloging in Publication Data

Catherwood, Christopher.
  Five evangelical leaders.

  1. Evangelicalism—Biography.   I. Title.
II. Title: 5 Evangelical leaders.
BR1643.A1C37   1985   280'.4'0922 [B]   85-1928
ISBN 0-87788-257-6

95 94 93 92 91 90 89 88 87 86 85 6 5 4 3 2 1

CONTENTS

ACKNOWLEDGMENTS

First of all, my warmest thanks to my parents, and to my agent Edward England for conceiving the idea that led to this book. Without all the support and encouragement of these three people, this book would never have been possible. They can take credit for the strong points, but any faults are mine. I should add here, at the request of the living subjects of this book, that the views expressed in it are my own.

I would also like to express deep gratitude to Harold Shaw for publishing the U.S. edition that you have before you. I am honored by his commitment to the book, which he accepted both before it was written and prior to its publication by Hodder and Stoughton in Great Britain. Without the generosity of Harold Shaw Publishers, the overseas research in the U.S. with Billy Graham and his team and at L'Abri in Switzerland with Francis Schaeffer in 1983 would not have been possible. I am also grateful to Luci Shaw, for her editorical advice and encouragement, and for helping a British author write for an American readership. I am also indebted to Managing Editor Megs Singer, for her detailed work across a distance of many thousands of miles.

Many people helped me during the course of my research in 1982–84 when four of the subjects were alive. Dr. Graham arranged for my accommodation with his team in 1983, an immense help in writing that chapter. I saw Dr. Packer on one of his visits to Britain, and I spent three sessions with Dr. Stott in his study near All Souls. My visit with the late Francis Schaeffer is described in the book, and the day I spent with him discussing his life by the fireside in Chalet le Chardonnet is one that I shall never forget. As for the late Dr. Martyn Lloyd-Jones, he was my maternal grandfather, to whom I was very close for the twenty-six years when I was with him, and no more need be said.

Of the other people whom I interviewed, the following deserve special mention: Dr. Oliver Barclay, former chairman of IFES, Chua Wee-hian, its general secretary, and Robert Horn, of *Evangelical Times*, advised me on more than one chapter. On the Stott chapter, I am grateful to John Eddison for allowing me to quote from John Stott's chapter in *Bash: A Study in Power*, to Mark Labberton, Stott's former study assistant, for the quotation from his thesis, and to Robert Howarth, formerly on the staff of All Souls, and Frances Whitehead, Dr. Stott's secretary, for checking all the facts in the chapter.

With the Schaeffer chapter, I would like to convey special thanks to Susan Schaeffer Macaulay and her husband Ranald Macaulay. My stay with them in the English L'Abri at Greatham was one of the most enjoyable experiences that I had in researching this book. My gratitude to the staffs at both L'Abris. Os Guinness, Deirdre Ducker, Steve Turner, the Diamonds, and Joe Martin all gave me valuable time.

In the Graham chapter, Russ Busby, Billy Graham's photographer and longstanding team associate, helped me both personally and in sharing with me his considerable collection of Graham material. Roger Palms of *Decision* and Don Bailey, Dr. Graham's press assistant, each gave me the same kind of help. Many members of the Graham team gave me interviews, among them being Cliff Barrows, Grady and "T.W." Wilson, Howard Jones, Sterling Huston, Lewis Drummond, Henry Holley, and Dr. John Wesley White. Maurice Rowlandson of British BGEA facilitated things from the English end. Stanislav Svek supplied valuable information on Billy Graham's trip to Czechoslovakia, as did Keston College about his first visit to the U.S.S.R.

With the chapter on James Packer, I am indebted to Dr. Raymond Johnston of CARE, Professor Don Carson of Trinity, Deerfield, and to Dr. Dick France of London Bible College. Both Dick Lucas and David Jackman provided advice and hospitality for my interviews with Dr. Packer.

To spend time with five giants of Christian faith, their friends, and relatives, was a profound spiritual experience. I can only hope that the sense of God alive and at work through these five men in this book comes through as vividly to the reader as it did to me.

INTRODUCTION

Evangelicalism in Britain and North America has come alive since the Second World War. Evangelicals have come out of the ghetto in which they had incarcerated themselves since the turn of the nineteenth century. The growth of biblical, evangelical Christianity has been a work of God, as is always the case. But, as we know from Scripture, and from Christian biography, God often chooses to bring about his purposes by raising up faithful, God-honoring men and women to do his will on earth.

The Pauline picture of the Christian life is that of a battle. In an army, each type of soldier has a different and vital task to perform—some are infantrymen, some man the heavy artillery, others serve in the cavalry. Each division fights a different part of the battle, but all share a common purpose, a common motive and, above all, each soldier has been enlisted through the same leader, Christ himself. This book aims to look at five of the men whom God has raised up in this century to be his lieutenants in the battle.

Though each man is different from the others, all five have preached the same gospel and served the same living Savior.

To Martyn Lloyd-Jones, preaching was logic on fire, eloquent reason, theology coming through human zeal. He revolutionized the place of preaching in Evangelicalism, restoring its power and relevance to the ordinary Christian. He resurrected much solid, biblically-based theology, but also gave the thoughts of an earlier generation a new life and vigor. In helping to establish the International Fellowship of Evangelical Students, he founded a Christian movement of international visioin perhaps unique in the world.

Billy Graham has transformed the face of evangelism. He has shown that the gospel is both alive and relevant in every country on earth. His stand on the truth of Jesus Christ has been a witness from the cities of America to the jungles of Asia, and the way in which he has cleaned up evangelism and used it as a means of racial reconciliation has been a potent factor in the spread of the gospel.

Francis Schaeffer has demonstrated that, in an age of skepticism and doubt, the message of Jesus Christ is still absolutely true. He has translated the eternal gospel into a language that can be understood even by those whose minds have been twisted by humanistic, relativistic thinking. He showed at L'Abri that Christians have nothing to fear from the twentieth century, and that it is they alone who, in Christ, have the answers to today's questions.

Jim Packer has done much the same in the field of theology. He has demonstrated the bankruptcy of liberal thinking, and shown that theology is not only a live and fascinating subject but also a vitally important one for Christians of all abilities.

Last, John Stott has not just made clear the importance of biblical, expository preaching, but also illustrated that it is possible for Christians to be conservative in their theology—guardians of the gospel—and radical in their application—people who care about the world in which God put them and creators of his new society.

Why these five? Each one has influenced me in many ways. Martyn Lloyd-Jones, my maternal grandfather, was someone with whom I enjoyed the warmest and most formative relationships of my conscious life. Francis Schaeffer, too, has greatly shaped the way in which I think and view the world—both Schaeffer and my grandfather molded me in many ways. My student career was enhanced by hearing Stott and Packer speak on many occasions, and their books provided discussion till the early hours of many mornings. In 1979 I was part of the Overseas Student Outreach Team at Cambridge, and took many students from all over the world to hear Billy Graham's sermons in the CICCU Mission. Each of these men fascinated me long before I came to write their stories.

But it can also be said that the growth of evangelical Christianity in Britain and North America cannot in human terms be understood without these five men. They have, in their very different ways, been at the heart of the movement, and have profoundly influenced its direction. Their zeal for the gospel, their resolute reliance on Scripture as God's true and living Word has set the course. In an age in which men and women have ceased to hope, they have demonstrated without apology the certainty and hope that is only to be found in Jesus Christ the risen Savior. Where scientific and materialistic humanism has failed, each of these five has been able to preach the Good News with a renewed power and confidence. Each has done so in a unique way, and often to totally dissimilar audiences, but the basic message has been consistently the same.

The five have not always agreed with each other on methods, or particular emphases, however, and it would have been impossible to write this book in a way which suggested that all of them were right in every detail. I have given my own interpretation of their respective roles and impact, and of their contributions to the battle. For example, four are Calvinists in theory and practice, one in theory only. Two are Anglicans, two separated Free Churchmen, and one indifferent to such labels. Three have been active with Third World Christians, two less so. Inevitably, great men attract disciples who often argue their masters' cases more vigorously than the masters themselves. Not everyone reading this book will therefore agree with everything expressed in it.

But all five have been unashamedly Evangelical, proof of the power of God at work today. My grandfather Lloyd-Jones used to say that he could forgive a preacher almost anything if he gave him a sense of the presence of God. It is my hope that this book will convey just such a sense of the acts of almighty God through the lives of these his five children.

Balsham,
Cambridgeshire,
June 1984

JOHN STOTT
1921–

John Stott

J ohn Stott was born on April 27, 1921, the only son of a leading Harley Street physician, Sir Arnold Stott, and his wife Emily. His father, like Martyn Lloyd-Jones who knew him, trained at Bart's and went on to become a consultant at the Westminster Hospital. He was a major general in the Army Medical Corps during the Second World War. As a childhood friend of John Stott's told me, he was not always a very sympathetic man, but this lack was balanced by the warmth and kindness of his wife. They were, nonetheless, a very united family. Sir Arnold was an agnostic and very much a part of the secularist, scientific world, while Lady Stott was a Lutheran. Young John's first words, he once joked to his Californian study assistant Mark Labberton, were "coronary thrombosis," and this was indicative of the kind of atmosphere in which he was raised.

He was brought up in the parish of All Souls, Langham Place, strategically located near Harley Street, the BBC headquarters and all the major department stores of Oxford Street and Regent Street. Little John would sometimes sit up in the gallery, and as he told me with a mischievous twinkle in his eye, would occasionally throw paper pellets onto the congregation below.

Even as a small boy, his deeply felt need for the underprivileged and for social justice was one of his main characteristics. One year he spent his summer holidays near Tenby in South Wales, the same region where he now has his country cottage. On nearby Cauldy Island was a monastery, whose monks had their mail delivered by local fishermen. Little John saw one of the boatmen open and read a monk's letter. This outraged him, he told me, and upset him for two to three days afterwards. Even then he had a "God-given sense of fair play."

Life at school

At thirteen he went to his father's old school, Rugby, well known as a result of its portrayal in the novel *Tom Brown's Schooldays*. Under its distinguished headmaster, Dr. Arnold, it became known for founding not only the popular sport named after it, but also the public school tradition of the "stiff upper lip," the scorning of emotion, and the cultivation of the gentlemanly image that so long marked the English middle and upper classes. Needless to say, as one older man has recalled, such a school was far from sympathetic to evangelical Christianity.

Stott, despite having a "scientific secularist" father, had been taught the Christian faith by his mother. He and his sisters had gone to church, read their Bibles, and said their prayers. But, he has written, he did this "more out of affectionate loyalty to her, and out of routine, than as a personally meaningful discipline."

He had, however, as he told me many years later, high ideals as an adolescent. (At the age of fifteen he founded the ABC Society—to give tramps a good bath. Whether ABC stood for *Always Be a Christian* or *Association for the Benefit of the Community* he cannot now remember.) In spite of high ideals, he realized that he was weak-willed—an admission that brought home to him his own alienation and defeat.

He became convinced, he has since written, "that there was more to religion than I had so far discovered. I used on half holiday afternoons to creep into the memorial chapel by myself, in order to read religious books, absorb the atmosphere of mystery, and seek for God. But he continued to elude me." He went to the Christian Union which had become, according to a contemporary, a rather secretive affair, as a result of the official disapproval of school authorities. (Needless to say, this added to its appeal for quite a few boys, including Stott himself.)

He had been attending this group for several months when it was visited by Rev. Eric Nash, known to generations of schoolboys as "Bash." Nash had founded a "Varsity and Public School" camp (or "Bash"), at Iwerne Minster. It was geared exclusively to evangelize public school boys—the sons of the socially elite. Many outsiders, especially in the Free churches, disliked their strong emphasis on sports, their distrust of the intellect, and the fact that they were socially so exclusive. But scores of boys were converted through them over the years and still are today. For all his faults, Nash was an effective evangelist—one with great spiritual vision for reaching young men with the Good News.

Conversion

At a meeting organized in February, 1938 by the Christian Union leader, John Bridger, Nash spoke on Pilate's question: "What then shall I do with Jesus, who is called the Christ?" Rugby was the school at which "muscular Christianity" had begun—an unthinking, nominal, and very English kind of belief having more to do with "being a good chap" than having a personal relationship with Jesus Christ as Savior. When young Stott saw Nash, he recalled, "He was nothing much to look at, and certainly no ambassador for muscular Christianity. Yet as he spoke I was riveted."

"That I needed to *do* anything with Jesus," Stott recorded of the meeting, "was an entirely novel idea to me, for I had imagined that somehow he had done whatever needed to be done, and that my part was only to acquiesce." Nash, however, made clear to them that neutrality was impossible—either they must imitate Pilate and weakly reject him, or actively accept him and follow him.

As Stott later told me, Nash was wise enough not to press for decisions there and then; there was no altar call. But he saw that the young seventeen-year-old was a seeking soul, and clearly one who had never been personally challenged in such a way before. He took him for a drive in his car, and in response to John Stott's questions, explained to him the way of salvation. "To my astonishment," Stott has written, "his presentation of Christ crucified and risen exactly corresponded with the needs of which I was aware."

Significantly, however, Nash did not even then press for a decision. "He had the sensitivity and wisdom," Stott remembers, "to let me go, so that I could 'open the door' to Christ by myself, which I did that very night by my bedside in the dormitory while the other boys were in bed and asleep."

John Stott thereupon became very active in evangelism—a "mirror image of Bash," a contemporary has told me, diligently leading several of his fellow students to faith in Christ. When Bridger left for Cambridge, Stott took over the leadership of the Christian Union. He also became the school's head boy despite his Christian activities and—this was 1939—despite the fact that he had become a pacifist.

When war broke out in September, 1939, those pacifists who wished to escape the draft as conscientious objectors had to register before a tribunal which decided whether or not their pacifism was genuine. Since clergy were exempt from military service, those conscientious objectors who could prove that their wish to be ordained predated the outbreak of war were excused from appearing before the tribunal. Fortunately for Stott, he had told his headmaster as early as 1938 of his pacifist convictions and of his wish to enter the ministry. He felt at the time that to take part in war was against the teaching of the Sermon on the Mount. (Years later in his study in London, he told me that in retrospect he had not thought out his position as thoroughly then as he has now. While he calls himself a "nuclear pacifist," he no longer embraces the total pacifist position.)

In 1939 he went to Trinity College in Cambridge, where he initially studied modern languages, a subject requiring considerable self-discipline and rigorous logic, two characteristics that many people feel have been hallmarks of his subsequent preaching style. As with Martyn Lloyd-Jones and his medical studies, his early secular studies were thus far from wasted. Translation involves close study of the text, and a former colleague of his believes that the close attention that Stott pays today to what the biblical text actually says, and its effect on his preaching, can be traced back to those days.

Although he was very active in evangelism of his fellow students, Stott was not officially involved with the Cambridge Inter-Collegiate Christian Union. This was partly because, on top of his academic studies, he acted as Nash's camp secretary, helping to run the camps. After Stott's conversion, Nash wrote to him once a week for over five years. These letters were a mix of theology (in neat paragraphs and section headings) and pastoral advice—how to pray, how to read the Bible, and "how to practice the presence of Christ each day" in the real world.

Nash's expectations, Stott has written, "for all those whom he led to Christ were extremely high. He could be easily disappointed. His letters to me often contained rebuke, for I was a wayward young Christian and needed to be disciplined. In fact, so frequent were his admonitions at one period that, whenever I saw his familiar writing on an envelope, I needed to pray and prepare myself for half an hour before I felt ready to open it."

For all Nash's single-mindedness and concern for the young Christian, he remained deeply suspicious of theology and of the intellect. Many of his former campers would enter the Anglican ministry, but, as one Cambridge student once told me, Nash's approach often resulted in their inability to cope with or confront the liberal theology of their lecturers. They would go to classes, put their feet up, and read copies of the *Times*. Derek Kidner, now well known as a Bible commentator, helped change this at Cambridge. He became president of the CICCU—and also obtained a First Class degree. Another Cambridge student was the scientist Oliver Barclay, later to become general secretary of the InterVarsity Fellowship and chairman of IFES. He was, during the war, the exact contemporary at Trinity of John Stott.

In his Weymouth Street flat, Stott recalled to me that the two were soon close friends as undergraduates, and would go for long walks, discussing Christian faith and issues. It was a significant friendship. For if Stott was Nash's "right-hand man," Barclay fulfilled that role for Douglas Johnson, general secretary of IVF. As seen in a later chapter in this book, Martyn Lloyd-Jones was in the process of transforming the IVF into a more vigorous organization in which Christians would be unafraid to exercise their minds and express their enthusiasms—the exact opposite, in many ways, of the very simple, stiff-upper-lip Christianity that Nash represented.

"God had given me," Stott has said, "an enquiring mind." This was shown in the First Class degree he obtained in the Language Tripos at Cambridge. He then transferred to theology, and, as Oliver Barclay told me, decided to take it seriously. (Nash, he recalls, never tried to stop him.) There was, he told me, "practically no help" for evangelical theology students at the time, but he was determined to bridge the gap between Evangelicals and the intellectual world, while at the same time retaining his Christian commitment and evangelistic zeal.

Ridley Hall, Cambridge, where he and the other ordinands studied, was then at its nadir. Stott's arrival, Oliver Barclay told me, altered the situation. The principal was a liberal theologian of vague beliefs. On one occasion, at a lecture, he informed students that there was no evidence in the New Testament for a certain major doctrine. Stott therefore asked him to explain a biblical passage that spelled the doctrine out with great clarity. The principal turned to him, and admitted, "You probably know the New Testament better than I do." Many of the evangelical students at Ridley beavered quietly away with their work, never raising the issues, whereas others openly confronted liberal teaching. Stott mixed the two by organizing a quiet revolution. Others recognized the success of this approach, and one of the effects this had was a substantial increase in the number of CICCU men who received honors in their courses.

"Bash," John Stott once reminded me, "had given me a great love for the Bible"; but he had now advanced considerably beyond the rather basic kind of Christianity represented by Nash (which, to the more doctrinal Evangelical, seemed rather too pietistic in approach and divorced from reality), while fully retaining his evangelical faith. He was much more in the vigorous, thoughtful, IVF mold, which, under Martyn Lloyd-Jones's influence, enabled one to maintain intellectual integrity while being fully committed to evangelical Christianity.

Nevertheless, the firm foundations planted by Nash were to place Stott in good standing in later years. This has been well summarized by his former study assistant, Mark Labberton, an American who wrote that "single-minded commitment to Christ, passionate concern for sharing the gospel, disciplined devotion to the Word, simple and direct preaching were all hallmarks of Bash's influence on Stott and on many other . . . evangelical leaders in the Church of England." From the beginning Bash created a climate of thought and behavioral aspects of which Stott "has certainly passed far beyond, but the fundamentals of which have not been left behind."

Nash concentrated only on the few, those from privileged backgrounds. But, as Stott has written, what "motivated him was not snobbery but strategy. He believed that God had called him to work in these schools, and that the reason for his divine call was that the future leadership of church and state was to be found there." This was certainly very true of Stott's own generation. Many leading Anglicans such as Stott himself, Michael Green of Oxford, Mark Ruston of Cambridge, and Dick Lucas of London are former Bash campers, as are several influential non-Anglican Christian laymen, such as two successive chairmen of the IVF (now UCCF): Fred Catherwood, the industrialist and politician, and John Marsh, the surgeon, both of whom were also Cambridge contemporaries of John Stott.

Single-mindedness

Several former Bash campers, emulating the model set by Nash himself, remained bachelors. John Stott has never married, and many have attributed this partly to the influence of Nash, whose ideal of the celibate clergyman, giving his whole life to Christian service without the distraction of family, motivated several deliberately to remain single. Christ, in Matthew 19, refers to those who do not marry for the kingdom of heaven's sake. Needless to say, many women deeply resented these eligible bachelors who refused to make themselves available, and at Oxford Martyn Lloyd-Jones's daughter led the fight against the kind of influence that Nash was felt to have at Cambridge. (By one of the ironies of life, she married one of those Bash camp leaders who decided neither to enter the Church of England nor to stay single—Fred Catherwood. Had he followed Nash's advice, you would not now be reading this book!)

Not everyone who remained unmarried for this reason was able to cope. One clergyman eventually had to resign his job, and subsequently became an artist, living in the United States. But John Stott, as he once told Martyn Lloyd-Jones (who strongly favored marriage), felt that it was God who had called him to be single and had given him a gift for it. There is little doubt that he would not have been able to do many of the things that he has done had he been married, with a wife and family to look after. He has been able to devote himself in a single-minded way to study and to pastoral ministry. In particular, he has been able to travel extensively, often to the Third World, without any of the usual problems of family separation suffered by married men. While some (mainly women) feel that he would have seen some issues either more clearly or sooner had he had a wife to advise him, his life has, in human terms, been strengthened by his singleness.

Certainly, as Mark Labberton has written in a paper for Fuller Seminary, the "pains of loneliness, the feelings of being in the battle alone, the emotional constrictions of a background that teaches one always to keep 'the stiff upper lip' and of the many other circumstances he has experienced have all had their impact," especially, Labberton feels, in helping Stott develop pastorally and as a preacher.

All Souls

Sir Arnold Stott had always hoped that his son would join the Diplomatic Service, and many see John Stott's role as that of a diplomat in evangelical gatherings such as the Lausanne Congress of

1974 (more on this later). But young Stott was ordained into the Church of England instead, to the parish of All Souls, Langham Place—where he has remained ever since. The rector at the time, Rev. Harold Earnshaw-Smith, was in frail health, and his curate found himself immediately saddled with a considerable number of responsibilities.

All Souls is very strategically placed. Many of the congregation are students and professional people. London University, some of the major hospitals, Harley Street, and the BBC are all short walking distances away. Some have commented that All Souls does not represent a broad cross-section of society, but the same critics are usually the most enthusiastic supporters of the local church principle, and the students and professional people who come to All Souls make it a varied, highly intelligent congregation.

There were, however, in Stott's early days, some working class areas (which still exist), whose inhabitants were reached through the All Souls school and subsequent All Souls Club House, a Christian community center. An old friend told me how on several occasions John Stott and several of the local children went charging off to Kent by car for a picnic. Another particular feature of the area is the proximity of some of London's top department stores. At one period, one of the curates was specially delegated to look after this vital area of witness.

On his arrival at All Souls, Stott used many of the methods he had learned in Bash Camp and at Cambridge. As we chatted in his book-lined study, he reminded me that he had been giving Bible readings since the age of nineteen, warmly encouraged by Nash. The love for the Bible that the camps had instilled in him naturally led him to give preaching the highest priority. As Oliver Barclay pointed out to me, it was the preaching ministry of All Souls that brought the church to people's attention. Stott was at the height of his preaching powers at Westminster Chapel. The chapel was to remain London's main preaching center for some time to come. But in Anglican circles, expository sermons such as were now being given at All Souls were a new phenomenon because of the sad decline of preaching in the Church of England that had continued since the end of the nineteenth century.

Earnshaw-Smith had a major heart attack in 1946, six months after Stott's arrival, and a second one not long after. As a result, his curate was, in Stott's own words to me, "thrown in the deep end." Any thought of transferring to another parish, as was quite usual for a young curate to do after two or three years, was thus rendered impossible. Stott was offered chaplaincies at Eton, the world-famous school, and, by contrast, at the Mayflower, the Christian family center in the heart of London's East End. Earnshaw-Smith's state of health led him to refuse both.

Had he accepted either of the above posts, he would not have been in place when Earnshaw-Smith suffered his final—and fatal— third coronary. The congregation took the unprecedented step of petitioning King George VI, who was technically responsible for the new appointment, that the curate be appointed as rector. The appeal succeeded, and John Stott became rector of All Souls (and also of the associated church of St. Peter's Vere Street) at the unusually early age of twenty-nine.

A new man meant new methods. As well as the concentration on regular, biblically-based expository preaching (which will be examined in more detail later), came some innovations. Evangelism, especially at the new monthly guest services, was increased, and thus a regular flow of conversions began. (Stott gained the idea from the weekly evangelistic addresses run by CICCU in his Cambridge days.) Follow-up by members of the laity also became increasingly vital, especially after the lay training school was set up in 1961.

Above all, the church had confidence in God. "Ultimately," Stott wrote, "evangelism is not a technique. It is the Lord of the church who reserves to himself his sovereign right to add to his church. We need to humble ourselves before God and seek his face. Then, if we are expectant in faith he will add to his church, not from mission to mission or even month to month but daily, such as are being saved."

Stott did not limit himself to church activities, even in these early days. He was soon recruited as a missioner at the first post-war university missions, along with Martyn Lloyd-Jones. Between them they altered the nature of missions. Hitherto these had often been rather simplistic affairs, largely lacking in appeal for the more intellectual type of student. The new style was, as Oliver Barclay once told me, "thoughtful, expository preaching," and to one university professor at Oxford, Stott became a "new phenomenon" in Anglican Evangelicalism by introducing a "scholarly evangelism."

This gave new heart to many in the university Christian unions; they realized for the first time that a Christian did not have to be anti-intellectual to survive. The new respect demonstrated by outsiders for the Christian gospel increased Christian morale and helped their own confidence and effectiveness in evangelism. A student could be a committed Christian and an intellectual, someone who did not have to unscrew his or her head in order to prove zeal for the Lord.

Many young people, especially new converts, were deeply influenced by hearing expository preaching—the thorough, careful discussion of the biblical text that was characteristic of both Stott and Lloyd-Jones. As a result, many of these men went into the ministry themselves, deliberately adopting the same style of doctrinal yet challenging preaching through which they themselves had become Christians or had had their Christian lives changed. An example of the effectiveness of this approach is seen in St. Helen's Bishopsgate, a church where, through the expository preaching ministry of Dick Lucas, a formerly struggling church now draws over 1200 to its Tuesday lunchtime evangelistic meetings, through which scores of people have been converted over the years.

Dick Lucas is one of many clergy who have been influenced by another group in which John Stott was active in the 1950s—the Eclectic Society. This was initiated by John Stott together with other members of staff from All Souls. Stott told me that the group was based on common acceptance of biblical authority—it was for conservative Evangelicals only—but one in which there was mutual acceptance and openness for radical application of biblical principles, as well as complete freedom of speech. Many of the members were curates (the upper age limit was forty), and some served under very liberal vicars who were either unsympathetic to or even strongly opposed to the evangelical faith of their young assistants. This created numerous problems for the curates. Questions of faith and intellect, doubts as to whether a truly evangelical Anglican church was possible frequently confronted members of the Eclectic Society.

The existence of the Eclectic Society showed to many of these men what was possible and how to accomplish it. It showed that one could be an Evangelical and have an "outstanding mind," as one former eclectic put it to me. It was, one has recalled, "a very great thing when it started," an organization whose meetings were a liberation to its often hard-pressed membership. The clergy at other churches saw in All Souls a church that was both intellectual and evangelistic, Anglican and Evangelical, a place which adhered to the Prayer Book and was also thoroughly contemporary. At a time when liberals in the Church of England often gave the impression that to be Evangelical was to be a suspect Anglican, All Souls showed that to be an Evangelical was to be truly Anglican, loyal to the principles on which the Church of England was founded.

Wider horizons

John Stott once told me that he was "by temperament an activist," and the list of organizations in which he has been involved, or which he has established, is a very long one. (Often, he initiates an organization and later hands it over to others.) Some of these have been purely Anglican in scope, such as EFAC (Evangelical Fellowship in the Anglican Communion), whose group member, the Church of England Evangelical Council, encouraged the growing influence of Evangelicals within the Church of England in recent years; or the EFAC bursary scheme which has helped many Anglicans from the Third World to receive the kind of thorough evangelical training in the West that would not otherwise have been possible.

Some specialist groups which have not always been specifically Anglican have also been brought together by John Stott. (Many Free

Church Evangelicals have expressed regret that John Stott has been so active in several purely Anglican concerns.) These have either been subject-oriented—for Christian doctors or educators, for example—or ad hoc gatherings of specialists in many fields, to think through the issues in an interdisciplinary but thoroughly biblical way. Such groups have often given John Stott valuable advice, enabled him to see the different sides to an argument, and supplied him with accurate data when speaking on a specific topic in a sermon or public debate. These specialists have included people from Stott's Cambridge days, such as Fred Catherwood, or younger men, such as the writer Os Guinness.

But two of his involvements are worth mentioning in more detail—the first because it is part of his life on a wider front, the second because it is his current main activity. These are his international work at All Souls and his directorship of the London Institute for Contemporary Christianity, which is based at St. Peter's Vere Street.

The idea for the All Souls International Fellowship (ASIF) began in 1961. Like Nash, Stott was able to spot areas from which future national leaders would come—and in the case of the Third World, this was often from the ranks of those who had been educated in the West. By the early sixties there were nearly 50,000 overseas students in Britain, about 35,000 in London (constituting a quarter of the entire London student population), of whom 5,000 were attached to the British Council Overseas Student Center in Portland Place, right next to All Souls itself. But, as John Stott wrote to Lorne Sanny, director of the Navigators in the United States, "There is still no one working full-time in this field so far as I know."

In 1963 John Stott went on a mission to Royal College in Nairobi (now Nairobi University). Ever since Cambridge days ornithology has been his hobby, and on a bird-watching safari in Kenya, he asked Robert Howarth, an ex-All Souls student then working in Africa for the Navigators, to establish an overseas student fellowship. Howarth and his wife began work in London with ASIF in August, 1963.

As Stott wrote at the time, students from other countries should be the concern of local Christians for two main reasons. First, they were strangers in a strange land—and Christians should be people "given to hospitality." Second, it was an opportunity to reach out with the gospel. Some foreign students, already Christians, were under the illusion that Britain was a Christian country, and it was important to nurture them in the faith, so that instead of becoming disillusioned they would return to their home countries with a stronger Christian faith. Others were from lands where the preaching of Christianity was restricted and many would naturally become interested in the gospel while in Britain.

"Here," he wrote, "is a mission field on our doorstep, with potential leaders of the future brought to our shores without our needing to cross the seas to find them." Stott was emphatic that it was an international, not an overseas fellowship. It was not to be "English Christians entertaining overseas visitors. It is a fellowship of all nations, with several nationalities represented on the committee." During his first ten years as rector, the number of overseas visitors had been steadily increasing.

"Come to All Souls on any Sunday," he wrote, "and you will see, in nave, side aisles and galleries, men and women of every race and color. It is to us a joy and privilege to welcome them. After the service, on the portico steps, members of many nations linger to greet one another, and join in animated and happy conversation. There can be no racial barriers in Christian fellowship."

By the end of the first year, Howarth has recalled for me, 400 had registered on the ASIF, representing fifty countries. Thirty-seven professed faith in the first ten months. Stott himself was very active, always attending the monthly visitors buffet lunch, the international carol service, and the ASIF Christmas party. He would preach simply, so that those with limited English could understand, and, indeed, was so involved that one British former member of staff remembers English people in the congregation muttering that the rector "concentrated too much on overseas members!" However, many British and American students in London were deeply challenged by meeting fellow students from the Third World on equal terms.

Several international students lived in the rectory on Weymouth Street. (It was known by the irreverent as "The Wreckage" or "The

Monastery" because of its bachelor inhabitants. The current rector of All Souls is married, and now, to get to John Stott's "pad" one has to risk bumping into bicycles in the hall.) One of the former residents is Professor George Kinoti, now chairman of the department of zoology at Nairobi University in Kenya, who shared some of his memories with me. He had known Stott since 1959, when he showed him around Makerere University during one of his early visits to Africa. Several future prominent African Christian leaders were befriended by Stott, including Bishop Gitari of Kenya and Bishop Misaeri Kauma of Uganda. He also knew the late Archbishop of Uganda, Janani Luwum, who was brutally executed under Idi Amin.

Stott visited Africa on a number of occasions, and, as Professor Kinoti recalls, took part in several university missions there. East Africa has seen considerable revival over the years. Recently some of this has been connected with the charismatic movement, and John Stott's emphasis on the "vital importance of a balanced, biblical Christianity" has influenced ministers there to avoid some of the excesses that misguided zeal in revival may encourage, especially in areas where knowledge of Scripture is in need of strengthening.

The majority of John Stott's missionary addresses, in Britain and abroad, are now to be found in his book *Basic Christianity*, his best-known work. It is probable that he has become known internationally through his writing. He has always been a very private individual, perhaps all the more so because he has never married. His friendships extend far and wide, and he is a good correspondent. Bishop Gitari of Mount Kenya East wrote to me that his "frequent letters . . . remain a great encouragement." The fact that he is uncompromisingly Evangelical and at the same time deeply concerned over social issues is, in Bishop Gitari's view, one of the reasons why he has been accepted as a teacher in so many Third World and other countries. In America, John Alexander of InterVarsity Christian Fellowship told me that his expository ministry has influenced many young United States and Canadian students, especially through his frequent appearances at the great triennial missionary conferences at Urbana, Illinois, where he often appeared before 17,000 students or more.

Yet the first to disclaim any special personal merit would be John Stott himself. Apart from his innate desire for privacy, he has felt that God should be the focus of attention, not human individuals. Like Martyn Lloyd-Jones, he has not wanted any biography written in his own lifetime. Nevertheless, he agreed to cooperate with this chapter on the basis that it would contain only the biographical information necessary for an understanding of his thought.

I have therefore taken the biographical section of this chapter only as far as Stott felt it was right to go. He does not want this to be an account of his "contribution" to Evangelicalism, either in Britain or further afield. The reader will have to reach his own conclusions on this point. However, he has given me some brief details about his latest activity, the London Institute for Contemporary Christianity, and the rest of this chapter will be an analysis of two of his major lines of thought, preaching and social action, culled from his books and personal conversation. (He has asked that a paragraph such as this be inserted in the chapter.)

The germ of the London Institute began ten years ago, he told me, when he was asked by his friend Dr. James Houston to lecture on the Christian response to contemporary issues at Regent College in Vancouver, Canada during the summer session. Stott became a frequent visitor, enthused with what Regent is trying to do in encouraging Christian thinking on secular issues. He then read Blamires's famous book, *The Christian Mind*, which as he pointed out to me, proved to be a "seminal book for a lot of Evangelicals."

In 1974 he initiated a series of annual lectures by Christian specialists on selected topics, which have, over the years, covered a wide range of subjects. From this beginning arose a more permanent structure—the London Institute for Contemporary Christianity, which began in 1982-83, with John Stott himself as the director. Lectures stimulate the students to think biblically about the world in which they live, to challenge their preconceptions, and to help them better to fulfill their scriptural role as salt of the earth and light of the world in the societies in which they find themselves. Lecturers are from a wide variety of background and opinion, but all are biblically-based Evangelicals.

Students come from all over the world—when I joined John Stott there for lunch one day there were people from many different nationalities clearly in evidence. Sadly, John Stott is "a prophet not without honor save in his own country," for while there are many students from the Third World and the United States (they are often young Americans who have heard him at Urbana), not so many Britons have applied. But the LICC is still in its early days. It is to be hoped that it will assume the place in Europe for thoughtful Christian studies that Regent has become in North America.

Two characteristics mark John Stott's career and thus affect his thought. The first—the high place he has given to sound, doctrinal, expository preaching—has been with him from the beginning, and the love of Scripture was instilled in him early. The second—a demonstration of the fact that one can be biblically conservative and also actively involved in the resolution of social issues—has developed more recently and has caused controversy in some evangelical circles. (The other controversial aspect of Stott's life, an issue felt chiefly among the Free Churches, has been his decision to remain an Anglican, a topic dealt with in detail in the chapter on Jim Packer.)

As a leading, internationally well-known African Christian told me, these two strands of Stott's life—expository preaching and social action—are interwoven, with preaching (and his high view of Scripture) assigned first priority. It is because he is known to be thoroughly conservative theologically that his sometimes radical social views command attention. By showing that it is possible to hold two such sets of views in balance without compromise to either, he has stirred many Christians to think through the biblical basis of their own position.

The expository preacher

John Stott is above all a preacher; it is impossible to understand the man and his impact under God without grasping this. Fortunately he has expressed his views on the subject cogently in *I Believe in*

Preaching. Significantly, it is also the nearest thing to an autobiography in print. It is his high view of preaching that has led him, in the eyes of many, to become the leader that he is today.

"Preaching," he states, "is indispensable to Christianity. Without preaching, a necessary part of its authenticity has been lost. For Christianity is, in its very essence, a religion of the Word of God." Jesus Christ himself was the "Word . . . made flesh," and his disciples continued to preach. When the Reformation came, it "gave centrality to the sermon," and great Christian leaders have continued to preach ever since. "God himself," Stott writes, "speaks to us by the preacher." Tragically, in the twentieth century, preaching has reached a low ebb. "In the Western world, the decline of preaching is a symptom of the decline of the church." When Christ himself showed the importance of preaching, why has it now declined?

Stott has outlined some causes. There is an "anti-authority mood," a sense of relativism in a revolutionary age. Here he feels that Christians should, while recognizing the modern trend, stick by the historic truth. Christianity is a revealed faith, preachers are the "stewards of the mystery of God," whose authority is God himself. It is supremely his Word that the preacher expounds, not human views. The gospel is relevant, relating as it does to the world as it really is.

Then there is the technological revolution—the television age, which has blunted people's ability to concentrate and absorb information. The preacher should, Stott believes, "fight for people's attention"; his consistency of life and practice should assist in holding it. But preaching is still "unique and irreplaceable," God "speaking through his minister to his people" in the power of the Holy Spirit, feeding the flock. "Nothing," he writes, "could ever replace this."

Indeed, in an age in which the joy of worship has been rediscovered by many Christians, Stott reminds us that "acceptable worship is impossible without preaching." Knowledge following exposition draws forth true worship. The basis of the gospel has been forgotten, its basic truths denied, and there is "dialogue rather than proclamation." There needs to be a recovery of Christian morale, a "certainty and full assurance," both in prayer and in preaching the

Good News of Jesus Christ. Doubt is a symptom of "spiritual sickness in our spiritually sick age." There should be persistent and expectant prayer "for grace from the Holy Spirit of truth." Stott believes that this is God's time "to push back the forces of unbelief and to set the pendulum swinging in the direction of faith again," and that the church should therefore "resume the bold proclamation of her unchanging message." In such a time, it is vital to assert the "indispensable and paramount place of preaching in the purpose of God for his church." In Stott's words, it is "a stirring summons."

What is preaching, and how can it be made truly effective? Stott points out that it is not a matter of "mastering certain techniques, but being mastered by certain convictions." The first of these is about God himself, that he is Light, that he has acted and revealed himself above all in Jesus Christ, and that he has spoken—in human language. This is the preacher's authority and leads to the next conviction with regard to Scripture—it is "God's Word written." The responsibility of the preacher is not to give a twentieth century testimony to Christ, but to relay to the twentieth century "the only authoritative witness there is," the Word of God. To Stott, it is shameful that Evangelicals fail to be the preachers they ought to be. The preacher should be the fervent herald of God's message, "a living word to a living people from the Living God." God's Word, in the power of the Holy Spirit, speaks to every generation and changes their lives.

The third conviction is that the "church is the creation of God by his Word," which is his scepter to rule it, and his food to nourish it. "For whenever the Bible is truly and systematically expounded, God uses it to give his people the vision without which they perish." Fourth, the minister is not a priest but a pastor, administering the Word to the flock; he is "essentially the teacher."

In the fifth place, "all true Christian preaching is expository," a conviction that firmly echoes the views of Martyn Lloyd-Jones. The Bible should not be a peg for the preacher, but his master. Exposition establishes the limits and also demands integrity, eliciting the clear, evident, and original meaning without manipulation. It is surely no coincidence that Stott and Lloyd-Jones, two of the most effective preachers of this century, have been expositors. It is, of course, the sovereign power of God that has made them what they are. But it is arguably their solid belief not just in the primacy of preaching, but also in the faithful unfolding of the Scriptures as the best means of accomplishing the task that has, in human terms, given their proclamation its power.

The preacher, as seen already, is many things—herald, steward, ambassador, and so on. But he is also, Stott believes, a bridge-builder. This conviction came later in his career, through the influence of a young New Zealand curate at All Souls named Ted Schroder. He was, as a leading figure at All Souls once told me, a "brash colonial who was quite willing to speak his mind." (The English curates, it seems, tended to be more reserved and in awe of their rector.) Some felt that Stott's preaching, as he himself has put it, was "biblical but not contemporary," whereas Schroder was often "contemporary but not biblical" enough. What was needed was to be both biblical and contemporary. When Christ became man he showed that he identified with the human race without ever losing his divine nature. Similarly, Christian preaching, without losing its clear Christian identity, should be something to which the world can relate.

The tragedy of much preaching today, Stott feels, is that Evangelicals are often conservative and biblical, but ignore contemporary concerns, whereas liberals are radical and "relevant" but not biblical. The real aim should be to "relate God's unchanging Word to our ever-changing world," since the preaching of the Word in the world "is not something optional." A sermon must be understandable; Stott agrees with Martyn Lloyd-Jones in saying that "the business of preaching is to relate the teaching of the Scriptures to what is happening in our own day."

"Above all else," Stott has written, "we must preach Christ . . . and not Christ in a vacuum . . . but rather a contemporary Christ who once lived and died, and now lives to meet human need in all its variety."

This means that the Bible has profound relevance to the society in which God has placed us; it lays down his principles for justice, human dignity, and ethics. While the kingdom of God is not a political unit, but is composed of all his people on earth, it is, Stott points out, "really absurd to say that social amelioration by Christian influence is impossible." John Stott has been actively involved himself with those who seek both to defend the gospel and to proclaim the need for Christians to play their part as salt and light in God's world. But he has shown that for Christians to relate the preaching of ethics to only personal ethics is wrong. The preacher should not play politics from the pulpit, but he should enunciate those clear biblical principles upon which Christians in secular life should base their actions.

The preacher has a duty, he feels, to help "Christians develop a Christian mind." The "systematic exposition of the Bible over the years" should give Christians a "framework of truth"—the "whole counsel of God." The preacher should not be partisan, but expound biblical principles, examine and discuss the conclusions that other biblical Christians have made, state his own position, and then allow members of the congregation to make up their own minds.

Some have questioned whether a minister should preach sermons on unemployment, or on nuclear proliferation, as John Stott has done in All Souls and elsewhere. (His views on nuclear warfare will be examined later.) They feel that a minister should stick to preaching the great doctrines, and provide a doctrinal framework within which lay Christians can work out the details. Some have asserted that Stott used to preach within these constraints until Ted Schroder challenged him. They worry that he has now become controversial for the wrong reasons, feeling that for a minister to be controversial because he unashamedly proclaims the gospel is one thing, and quite acceptable; but for him to arouse ire because he espouses a particular secular cause, such as full employment or the halting of the nuclear arms race, is quite another.

To Stott, the minister who deliberately avoids controversial topics is being "irresponsible." The "absurd polarizations" between conservative and radical Evangelicals, he told me, were all wrong. He now feels that his earlier sermons lacked relevance since he used to omit the application, believing that the Holy Spirit would somehow do it for him. Now he divides principles from policies. For example, in the nuclear warfare debate it seems clear to him that weapons that cause the indiscriminate mass annihilation of innocent non-combatants are immoral and incompatible with biblical principles. He has therefore become a "nuclear pacifist." But he would not call himself a unilateralist. To him, the mechanism of disarmament is a specialist topic beyond the competence of the church. It is a consequential policy to be worked out in detail by those Christians and others able to judge the best technical and political means. But though the *policy* is to be left open to debate, the *principle* is clear.

Furthermore, as all systematic preachers have discovered, if one goes through a book of the Bible in an expository way there are certain crucial verses that cannot be avoided; it becomes impossible to escape a subject if it appears in the text, as John Stott found on several occasions. It would be wrong to omit a topic simply because it was one on which Christians and others have disagreed.

It is surely evident that Christians cannot live in a cocooned world, pretending that the society in which they have been placed does not exist or is beyond their concern. Christians may not be "of this world," but they are to be salt and light within it, with all the responsibilities that such roles confer upon them. The Bible does indeed lay down principles which cover everything that God created; there is nothing to which God's Word, the Bible, is irrelevant, even if Christians differ as to exactly how various verses apply to specific situations.

A question that still exists, though, is whether a minister of the gospel is the best participant in such a debate. All Christians agree that Jesus Christ is the way, the truth, and the life, and that it is only through his death that we are saved. This is indisputable, and any non-Christian hearing this message and rejecting it, rejects truth. The problem arises when contentious issues of a lesser order are proclaimed from the same pulpit, creating confusion. It probably does not worry a non-Christian unduly that a minister believes in inerrancy, or has specific views on baptism or the gift of tongues.

But suppose a Christian in All Souls has a friend for whom he is burdened spiritually and whom he wishes to bring to an evangelistic service at the church. The friend is a United States Air Force colonel at the American nuclear missile base at Greenham Common. Now it may be that the use of such weapons is unbiblical, but the prime need of the colonel is to be converted to faith in Christ. From a sermon on disarmament, all he learns about the preacher is that he is a "nuclear pacifist," which he himself is not. Not all Christians agree with the nuclear pacifist position—some are total pacifists (which Stott is not), and others, such as Francis Schaeffer, feel that the use of nuclear weapons in certain circumstances is entirely compatible with biblical principle.

The result is that a non-Christian is alienated from the gospel for a reason quite extraneous to the gospel itself, one on which Christians disagree. This is surely not right either. But it is not quite so simple. Suppose a slave plantation owner had been taken to William Wilberforce's church—that of the man who gave his whole life to freeing slaves. Slavery was an issue which divided Christians (the great nineteenth-century Bible commentator, Dabney, defended the institution in the southern states of America). No one today would agree that slavery was right, and many would hold that nuclear weapons are just as wrong.

The answer was surely given by the apostle Paul, especially in Philemon. Paul never explicitly denounced slavery, and the gospel, when he preached it, could be heard by owner and slave alike without any previous prejudices on other grounds. Yet the logic of Paul's ethical teaching is abundantly clear, and although it was only implicit on the question of slavery, it created such a climate that Christians later saw that the ownership of one human being by another was incompatible with Christian principles. Christian ministers of the gospel can be like Paul on such issues in our own day.

The lesson could be drawn that Christian laypeople should be far more active than they are at present—then there would be no need for clergy to become embroiled in secular controversies. Furthermore, how are many ministers who claim only to preach the "simple gospel" preparing their congregations to fulfill their God-appointed roles as salt and light in the world which God has created?

While Stott's own involvement in the debate between evangelism and social action will be considered further on, there is no doubt that the division between these two elements of Christian responsibility has been unbiblical, and that while it may not be right for ministers of the gospel to pronounce *directly* on nuclear weapons or unemployment, lay Christians have a very clear biblical mandate to act responsibly on God's earth. Only those who do so have any right to criticize.

The essence of preaching

The best teachers, Stott has written, are "those who remain students all their lives." The study of Scripture is thus a primary responsibility for the preacher. A minister's study of the Bible should always be comprehensive—Stott reads the whole Bible every year, following the Murray McCheyne schedule recommended to him by Martyn Lloyd-Jones. Such study should be open-minded; one's own prejudices should be put aside to receive what the Bible is really saying. It should also be expectant; the Bible can freshen the reader and banish spiritual staleness.

A preacher should also be in touch with the real world; as Stott has said, the best preachers are always diligent pastors. (Some feel that he made a mistake when he left the full-time pastorate of All Souls in 1970.) They should listen to their congregations and ensure that they read widely in contemporary secular literature to see what people around are thinking without in any way compromising themselves with the spirit of the age.

Thus, in 1974 John Stott set up a reading and study group to examine key current topics. He often consults with specialists before preaching on major contemporary issues, to ensure that his facts are correct, and that he is aware of the different sides in the debate. Those who visit his study have seen his filing system, one that is legendary in its thoroughness. He blocks off special time for study (while recognizing that this might not always be so possible for hard-pressed ministers with no pastoral assistance). At All Souls he saw to it that the talents of all his congregation were used, which helped to free him from administrative chores that distracted him from his more important duties. Thirty years ago he bought a cottage in Wales where he goes to read and write, and sometimes to relax with his favorite hobbies—ornithology and photography.

To Stott, in Spurgeon's words, "to be unprepared is unpardonable presumption." In his book, Stott gives details of how a good preacher should prepare himself for the sermon. Personal preparation is essential. He has, he writes, "always found it helpful to do as much of my sermon preparation as possible on my knees, with the Bible open before me, in prayerful study." Then the preacher must meditate on what the text meant then and how it applies today, and what the passage's "dominant thought" is. A sermon, as opposed to a lecture, "aims to convey only one major message." Structure is also essential, as long as it arises naturally from the text. The language of the sermon should be as "simple and clear as possible."

Above all, "he who preaches Christ must know Christ." What one does is as important as what one says; "the practice of preaching cannot be divorced from the person of the preacher," and consistent Christian living, in loyalty to Christ, is the preacher's "prior responsibility." Sincerity is vital, and Stott, especially in his early days, urged lay friends in the congregation to be as honest as possible with him as to the content and effectiveness of his preaching.

As Christians, we should, he believes, "feel what we say." Preaching should involve both mind and heart, and Stott agrees with Martyn Lloyd-Jones that it should be "logic on fire." True "preaching is never a superficial activity, it wells up out of the depths." It should, in Newton's words, "break a hard heart and . . . heal a broken heart." The preacher is a humble man, dependent on the "power of the Holy Spirit . . . Only Jesus Christ by his Holy Spirit can open blind eyes . . . give life to the dead and rescue slaves from satanic bondage." Stott himself discovered this "power through weakness" to be very true when he was preaching in Sydney, Australia, in 1958. He himself was ill and felt that he had not been up to par. But he found out later that many had been converted despite his lackluster delivery.

"Nothing," he concludes, "is better calculated to restore health and vitality to the church or to lead its members into maturity in Christ than a recovery of true, biblical, contemporary preaching." In this he is surely correct. The goal of the preacher should be to convey a sense of the glory of God, and Stott has described his own feelings when such an event occurs. "The most privileged and moving experience a preacher can have is when, in the middle of a sermon, a strange hush descends upon the congregation. The sleepers have woken up, the coughers have stopped coughing, and the fidgeters are sitting still. No eyes or minds are wandering. Everybody is attending, though not to the preacher. For the preacher is forgotten, and the people are face to face with the living God, listening to his still, small voice."

Christ was a preacher, the apostles were preachers, as were the Reformers, and whenever revival has come, the place of preaching has been at its very center. Yet sadly, today it is a neglected art, especially by those who claim to enjoy the fullness of the Holy Spirit's presence among them. The preaching ministry of John Stott and the scriptural case that he makes out for the need for biblical, Christ-centered preaching surely shows that it is as much needed in our own day as it has been throughout the history of the Christian church.

As Stott has written, the "Christian preacher is to be neither a speculator who invents new doctrines which please him nor an editor who excises old doctrines which displease him, but a steward, God's steward, dispensing faithfully to God's household the truths committed to him in the Scriptures, nothing more, nothing less, and nothing else." What need could be more urgent today than for the faithful, expository preaching of the Word of God in Scripture to a church that has lost its sense of direction, and to a world that cries out for a Savior?

Evangelism and social concern

One of the most significant developments of recent years has been the fact that it is again possible to show social concern for the poor and underprivileged and still be a fully committed evangelical Christian. The evil days when compassion for the needy was left to liberals while Evangelicals lived in a pietistic ghetto are now past; faith and action are no longer seen as contradictory.

The reasons for the change have been twofold. First, Christians in the West rediscovered the biblical teaching on the subject and their own heritage of scripturally-based social concern from the past. Second, Evangelicals in the Third World began to play their full and equal role in God's family, a growth that became apparent in the Congress at Lausanne, held in 1974. (The details of how it came into existence are given in detail in the chapter on Billy Graham.) Gottfried Osei-Mensah of the Lausanne Committee for World Evangelization told me that John Stott took part in the earlier congresses in Berlin and in Amsterdam and was on the drafting committee for the Lausanne covenant.

While it is not possible, for the reasons given earlier, to mention the contribution that all those present felt he made, it can be truly said that the final covenant bears his hallmark and can be taken as representing his own views as well as those of the congress. Lausanne has been seen by Christians from all over the world as a major turning point in the history of the evangelical church, both for its reaffirmation of the need to combine social concern with the primary task of proclaiming the gospel and for the way in which it marked the coming of age of the church in the Third World.

The Lausanne preamble gave thanks to God for the way in which he was working throughout the world, with repentance that the church had not done all that it should, but with a resolute desire to affirm the faith and resolve to make disciples of every nation. The covenant itself began with a declaration of continued evangelical belief in the being and purpose of God and in the authority and power of the Bible, which is infallible and without error. "The message of the Bible is addressed to all mankind," for "God's revelation in Christ and Scripture is unchangeable."

In an age of ecumenism and compromise, the 2,700 participants, from over 150 countries (more than half of these being in the Third World), emphatically affirmed their faith in the gospel. There "is only one Savior and only one gospel." They rejected as "derogatory to Christ and to the gospel every kind of syncretism and dialogue which implies that Christ speaks equally through all religions and ideologies. Jesus Christ being himself the only God-man, who gave himself as the only ransom for sinners, is the only mediator between God and man."

This meant that evangelism—the "proclamation of the historical, biblical Christ as Savior and Lord"—is as vital as ever, especially as over "2,700 million people . . . more than two-thirds of mankind, have yet to be evangelized." However, some Christians, while affirming this, had regrettably neglected social concern, regarding it as incompatible with evangelism. "Although reconciliation with man is not reconciliation with God," the covenant states, "nor is social action evangelism, nor is political liberation salvation, nevertheless we affirm that evangelism and socio-political involvement are both part of our Christian duty. For both are necessary expressions of our doctrines of God and man, our love for our neighbor, and our obedience to Jesus Christ."

The covenant goes on to say that the

message of salvation implies also a message of judgment upon every form of alienation, oppression, and discrimination, and we should not be afraid to denounce evil and injustice wherever they exist. When people receive Christ they are born again into his kingdom and must seek not only to exhibit but also to spread its righteousness in the midst of an unrighteous world. The salvation we claim should be transforming us in the totality of our personal and social responsibilities. Faith without works is dead.

As the covenant affirms, Christians "need to break out of our ecclesiastical ghettos and permeate non-Christian society." It makes quite clear that "evangelism is primary," but, by way of balance, it is equally plain that the church must maintain its integrity—"a church which preaches the Cross must itself be marked by the Cross." The church must be scrupulously honest and loving, and not in any way linked with "any particular culture, social or political system, or human ideology." For it is, as Stott has pointed out in his commentary, "the community of God's people. It bears God's name and so puts God's name at risk."

Much of the Lausanne covenant dealt with the fact that the age of Western domination of the Christian church is now over—that we live in an age of a genuinely multiracial, cross-cultural, international body of Christ. Churches now work in equal partnership— Lausanne provided the recognition that the Third World church has come of age. Too often the church had fallen prey to secular mentalities and adopted worldly methods, and this, like the old cultural imperialism of the past, was retrogression rather than advance.

But above all, it set two vital priorities. Delegates to Lausanne were forcefully reminded of the 2,700 million unevangelized people mentioned earlier. But there was now "in many parts of the world" (many of which Stott had himself visited) "an unprecedented receptivity to the Lord Jesus Christ." National churches could take the opportunity, and the congress noted (in a way which vindicated the stand made twenty-five years earlier by Martyn Lloyd-Jones in IFES) that sometimes for an indigenous church to grow in real self-reliance it might be necessary for the number of foreign missionaries to be reduced, which would release them for other ministries.

Controversially, the covenant also stated that the church could not hope to attain the goal of bringing the Good News to every land without sacrifice. "All of us are shocked," it stated, "by the poverty of millions and disturbed by the injustices that cause it. Those of us who live in affluent circumstances accept our duty to develop a simple lifestyle in order to contribute more generously to both relief and evangelism."

This created some division. Some felt that the call to simple lifestyle was in itself simplistic—the idea that restraint among Western Christians could alleviate in any significant way the ocean of poverty in the Third World was to fail to understand the basic causes of that poverty. The radicals, whose name was derived from the Latin word, *radix*, or "root," had failed, in their view, to go to the root of this issue, which was that the cultures of the Third World were fundamentally pagan in structure. As a leading Indian Christian told me, the problem with India was not that it lacked resources, of which it had plenty, but that the prevailing culture was thoroughly Hindu, creating a basic spiritual rot that permeated throughout society, and thus causing the mass of poverty for which India was famous. Christians he knew who had set up a community designed to rid their area of poverty had been persecuted and beaten up by local Hindus.

Others, especially in North America and other parts of the developed world, were innately suspicious of anything to do with radical action. To them, for Christians to become involved in social action was to compromise the gospel itself—even though Lausanne had not ceased to stress the primacy of evangelism.

For the radicals, many of whom came from South America, the covenant had not gone nearly far enough. For them, the simple lifestyle was an article of faith. They felt God was emphatically on the side of the poor, the underprivileged, and the oppressed. Christians therefore had the duty to engage in the struggle for justice and to aid attempts to alter the social structure of the societies in which they lived. Sin was not just an individual matter; it was also corporate—what they called "structural sin."

So Lausanne, far from resolving the matter, stirred up the debate even more. The common ground between all the protagonists, however, was their loyalty to Scripture and their willingness to submit to its authority. It was on this basis that an international gathering representing all viewpoints and many different nationalities was held in Grand Rapids in June, 1982, to discuss the whole issue of "evangelism and social responsibility." The chairman of the drafting committee (and the actual drafter of the report, according to one person closely involved) was John Stott. What was needed was someone who was trusted by the traditionalists for loyalty to evangelism and known devotion to the exposition of the Word of God on the one hand, and an evident concern for the poor and oppressed on the other.

The relationship between these two areas of Christian activity was, the report noted, "Lausanne's unfinished business." All were united on the fact that biblical Christians "who seek to live under the Lordship of Jesus Christ and the authority of Scripture and who pray to be guided by the Holy Spirit, should not be divided on an issue of such importance." Thanks to this desire to come together, and to the exercise of considerable diplomatic skill, the conference was able to produce a united report—although as the drafting committee observed, "we have found it a struggle." All races and nations had their blind spots, each of which was part of the Fall experienced by all humanity.

These were the facts: that there were 2,700 million unevangelized people in the world, and 800 million who were destitute or in some way oppressed. "Only the gospel can change human hearts," the report noted, but Christians could not "stop with verbal proclamation." God was both creator and judge, and the basis of all social action was surely "the character of God himself," shown in Jesus Christ. The first fruit of the Spirit was love.

The report proved that historically, Evangelicalism and social action have been closely linked. (John Stott made this clear in a talk in his own name to mark the Wilberforce anniversary in 1983.) Wilberforce, who helped free the slaves, and Shaftesbury, who put an end to the cruel exploitation of children, both showed in the nineteenth century that one could be a committed Evangelical and care in an active way for the poor and oppressed.

Unfortunately, at the end of that century, some people "confused the kingdom of God . . . and they went on to imagine that by their social programs they could build God's kingdom on earth"—what is called the "social gospel." One result of "an over-reaction to this grave distortion of the gospel" was that "many Evangelicals became suspicious of social involvement." This dichotomy was both unhealthy and unbiblical, since Acts 6 clearly shows that the early church practiced both social action and evangelism without contradiction.

As Stott has pointed out on many occasions, social action can lead to evangelism and also stem from it. The book of James shows that good works are "an indispensable evidence of salvation," and, as Stott himself reminded me one day, 2 Corinthians 8 and 9 demonstrate that those who have abundance should help those who do not. Those who have been evangelized—and born again—will thus naturally have compassion for the poor and wish to do something about their plight.

In addition, "social action can be a bridge to evangelism," opening otherwise closed doors. Evangelism is, of course, the "logical" first priority—people cannot have Christian compassion for the underprivileged unless they become Christians in the first place. Furthermore, "evangelism relates to people's eternal destiny . . . Christians are doing what no one else can do." So Christians can act in two ways—in the unique work of spreading the gospel and in the shared task of social action, carried out by them from a different base than the non-Christian.

Christians are the "new community"—a theme which also runs through John Stott's book on Ephesians, *God's New Society*, and his commentary on the Sermon on the Mount, *Christian Counter-Culture*. The church is the salt of the earth in a fallen world and should act as a "challenge to the old" community. It is the biblical duty of Christian people "simultaneously to permeate the world and to retain their kingdom distinctives."

Many of the participants at Grand Rapids agreed on the principles. The problem remained as to how Christians should act in the social sphere. All were united on the fact that the "Bible lays great emphasis on both justice (or righteousness) and peace," but there was disagreement on how far to go. Social service was one thing, but some interpretations of social action included a degree of radical political involvement that many found difficult to swallow. Some felt that the Christian attitude to the state should be one of outright opposition and rejection. Others believed that Christians should be separate but parallel, while others thought that the church should permeate and transform the secular society in which it found itself. There was also a major difference observed as to the scope of action for Christians in open, democratic states and those living in closed, authoritarian regimes.

John Stott once told me, as we discussed this issue in his study, that he stood between the two extremes—he is neither a materialist nor an ascetic. He believes that Christians should be able to enjoy the good things of creation and that the new community of Jesus Christ should be one in which poverty is abolished. Christians, he feels, should stick to principles and avoid getting bogged down in the technicalities of macroeconomics.

As Stott reminded me, Dives went to hell not because he was rich but because he was scandalously indifferent to the poor around him. It was not a case of cause and effect—Dives was rich, therefore Lazarus was poor—but an indictment of indifference to the suffering of fellow humans. As Paul states, those who have should help those who do not have. One should help not out of guilt, but out of love, out of a Christ-centered compassion for one's fellow (and equal) human beings, and not out of a man-centered asceticism. If more Christians saw the validity of this, many more Evangelicals would be active in social concern than there are at present. In rightly rejecting a liberal social gospel as well as a hyper-spiritual radical asceticism, they have neglected their clear biblical duty to be God's salt and light in society. The right response to any extreme is not to be extremist, but biblical, a message urgently needed today.

John Stott, as the title of his book, *Balanced Christianity* implies, believes deeply in maintaining a biblical balance. In some areas this has meant that he has been attacked by both sides. An example of this is his nuclear pacifist position, a stance that he has developed in recent years.

Nuclear pacifism

On the one hand, there are those—notably Francis Schaeffer in the United States and Jerram Barrs in Britain—who hold that the traditional Christian view of the "just war" can include the use of nuclear weapons. They point out that a Christian has a duty to resist evil, if necessary, by the use of force, as in the Old Testament and as implied by Paul in Romans 13. A country that is attacked has the right to defend its citizens, especially if the opponent is as evil in structure as is the Soviet Union. Justice must be defended, and there are in the real world "totalitarian states which must be resisted." They feel that nuclear weapons, through their deterrent value, have kept the peace, prevented global war, and contained unjust regimes.

On the other hand, there is the total pacifist view, one formerly held at Cambridge by Stott himself and often espoused today in Britain and the United States by Mennonites. To them, the fact that Jesus did not himself use force means that Christians today should renounce it altogether. In this view not only are nuclear weapons wrong, but so is the whole concept of armed defense. They advocate "transarmament" which involves the use of discussion with invading armies. To them, "nonviolence [is] a part of conversion."

Stott, however, takes a line between these two views. He has shifted his position in recent years, rejecting the pacifist option in the 1950s. He has been careful to stick to the idea of outlining the moral principles while leaving the details in more expert hands in order to avoid the problems of those mentioned earlier who got bogged down in macroeconomic detail over the world hunger issue.

He would, he told me, like to believe in the just war doctrine long espoused by the Christian church. However, as he has written, "our evangelical concern is with Scripture, rather than tradition." The nuclear pacifist position is compatible, he feels, with both.

The just war theory states that resistance to evil must be both proportionate to the amount of suffering caused and discriminate in its effects—which in practice means that armed defense can lawfully destroy military targets, but not civilian, since innocent civilians are not part of the conflict. A nuclear war, however, according to Stott, is by its nature both disproportionate and indiscriminate; since millions of civilians would be killed or injured, "a nuclear war could never be a just war."

This view, he feels, has two biblical bases—first, that the shedding of innocent blood is forbidden in the Old Testament, and second, that the state, whose powers are laid down in Romans 13, is in the light of Romans 12 entitled "to promote good and to restrain and punish evil" but with "the minimum necessary force." Both these doctrines are, to him, incompatible with what would occur in the event of a nuclear war.

Although he is a nuclear pacifist, he is emphatically not a unilateralist. As he has written, he finds himself therefore in a "moral dilemma . . . Morality leads me to declare the use [of nuclear weapons] evil; Christian realism to warn that unilateralism might make nuclear war more likely. Therefore, the urgent search for balanced, multilateral, and verifiable disarmament . . . is more prudent than unilateralism." He concedes that his view of nuclear armaments—"immoral to use, prudent to keep"—is "a paradoxical position," and certainly both Jerram Barrs and Mennonites such as Alan Kreider have gently accused him of being inconsistent. But perhaps the most important thing is that in the debate the proponents of all three positions agree that the supreme arbiter is Scripture, "God's Word written," as Stott has described it, to whose authority they must all submit as evangelical Christians.

John Stott has written on many more issues than can be considered in this chapter. But in all of them he has sought resolutely to base himself on Scripture—to try to discern what God is saying to us through his Word. This is why Stott has such a high view of preaching; what could be more important than the proclamation of the revealed truth of God? This is also why he has the ear of both sides in many disputes—they are confident that he will base his view on the Bible, and that even though they may differ as to what the Bible is actually saying, everyone nonetheless believes in its authority.

The force of this is vital today, perhaps all the more so in our present climate. Os Guinness, a writer close to both Francis Schaeffer and John Stott, has shown clearly in his book *The Gravedigger File* that present-day Western Evangelicals have been infiltrated to an alarming extent by existential thought. It is subjective experience rather than objective, scriptural truth that is the base of too much of today's Christian faith and practice. Perhaps one of the reasons that John Stott has been so well received in the growing churches of the Third World is that they, like he, are determined to resist this trend.

Others also feel that perhaps John Stott's career has been too sheltered and that he has been over-inclined to address the more intellectual questions and audiences in society. There is some measure of truth in this; as noted earlier, All Souls, where he has been centered all his adult life, is not exactly a typical parish, and he has been heavily involved both in student work and with thinking people generally. Many also feel that his approach has been based on theory and not hard-bitten experience.

Two things can be said. First (and this applies equally to Francis Schaeffer and the work of L'Abri), intellectuals need the gospel too. God calls individuals to different ministries. One he sends to the slums of Calcutta, another to a central London church with many students, professional people, and other intellectuals. The main point is that all obey God as he has called them.

Second, we live in an age where many Christians have thrown their God-given minds out of the window. Too many today live in pietistic evangelical ghettos, neglecting their duty to be Christian salt and light in the world in which God placed them. Such Christianity is mindless and irresponsible. John Stott, who wrote *Your Mind Matters*, has fought for a Christianity that is both firmly based on Scripture and which cares for the world around us. He believes, as his book on Timothy, *Guard the Gospel*, clearly shows, that as Evangelicals there is a sense in which we must be profoundly conservative. We are faithfully to keep the treasure committed to us by God in Scripture.

Another important aspect of John Stott's thought is that he believes that a Christian may be fully Christ-centered and radical at the same time. Many Evangelicals in the United States, especially younger ones, have reacted against the dead, formal, civic religion of their evangelical parents, where to be a born-again believer was a normal part of being a patriotic American. This pseudo-Christianity was lacking in genuine love for the poor and oppressed, unthinkingly backed the status quo, and thus discredited evangelical belief in the eyes of many of the children raised under its protective sponsorship.

Unfortunately, a large number of the "new Evangelicals," in their desire to rediscover biblical teaching on social justice, peace, and other issues, went too far in their rejection of the tradition from which they had come. They rightly laid stress on Christ's teaching of the kingdom, and the fact that it had profound economic, social, and even political implications. The incarnation was re-emphasized—Christ as man on earth, the friend of the poor and oppressed. This often led to a failure to realize the primacy of Calvary. The older generation, with its constant desire to win "decisions," had emphasized the fact that to be born again means taking a very personal step of repentance. In a vital sense, Christianity is a personal and private faith, resting as it does on the individual's relationship with God the Father through Christ the Son. But the traditionalists had made an in-group of Christianity, utterly neglecting the fact that such a personal step as conversion has momentous public consequences. Christians are not just people who have good personal morals; they are members of God's new society, the salt of the earth, redeemed humans who share their Savior's love and concern not just for the souls of those around them, but their bodies too. The radicals, in rejecting the extreme from which they had come, embraced the other extreme and reduced the centrality that Calvary should have in the Christian's life.

John Stott's writings may be said to show that he is a Calvary-centered radical. His book *Basic Christianity* makes this central fact clear—that it is through Christ on the cross we are saved. But equally, his works such as *Christian Counter-Culture* on the Sermon on the Mount and *God's New Society* on Ephesians demonstrate the life-changing consequences of a true conversion. Christianity is both personal and corporate; we are individually born, but into an international, multi-ethnic family where there are both rich and poor, young and old, clever and obtuse. Christians have a duty to evangelize, but they also have an obligation to ensure that God's standards prevail on

God's earth, in fighting poverty as strongly as pornography, and in standing for social justice as well as for school prayers.

Above all, for Christians to know these things, the Scripture must be central in their lives so that Christ can be the head. They need to have the Word of God faithfully proclaimed to them in all its richness, and for this to happen they must hear it preached biblically in their churches. This has been at the very heart of John Stott's life and message. It is why he has been so involved in the Third World with social and peace issues, and why he has now set up the London Institute to help Christians think through secular issues in a scriptural way. His actions have stemmed from his deepest convictions about Jesus Christ and about God's Word proclaimed to God's people—convictions which we need to urgently heed today.

MARTYN LLOYD-JONES

1899–1981

Martyn Lloyd-Jones

M artyn Lloyd-Jones, the great expository preacher and pastor, was born on December 20, 1899, the second son of Henry and Magdalen Lloyd-Jones. Although his life began in Cardiff, it was in the beautiful countryside of Wales that his roots really lay: in the hills, farms, and villages of Cardiganshire, little touched by outside English influence. Most of his life was spent in England, especially in London, but he always regarded himself as, first and foremost, a Welshman.

In 1905 he moved with his family—his parents and brothers Vincent and Harold—to Llangeitho, the small town where the great Daniel Rowlands preached in the eighteenth century. There Henry Lloyd-Jones ran the general store. With his culture and love of learning, he would have gone to the university had he lived in our day. But higher education in those days took more money than Henry had.

However, he was able to raise his three sons in a lively, stimulating atmosphere, filled with talk and debate. He himself was a keen liberal, but, unlike his son Martyn who supported the fiery Welsh radical David Lloyd George, he followed the more moderate H. H.

Asquith. He also advocated the "new theology," which mixed social action with nonconformist churchmanship. His wife, Magdalen, came from a successful farming and horse-breeding family in nearby Llwyneadfor, none of whom were Christians.

Martyn's early childhood was happy. At first he was more interested in playing football with the boys than in schoolwork. As his home was also a store, he met all kinds of people, and later in life maintained that small country communities like Llangeitho produced more "characters" than the big, anonymous cities of today. He particularly enjoyed watching the local blacksmith, who, it was said, held the record for long-distance spitting! He had great fun visiting his grandfather's big farm and riding the ponies—a pleasure he never lost. In 1908 he had a special treat—a trip to London and back in one of the earlier makes of car. On the way home, the car had a puncture in Oxford and so they had to buy a new tire from a small bicycle shop owned by Mr. Morris, later Lord Nuffield, founder of Morris cars and inventor of the Mini (a small but popular British car).

But the happy days sadly came to an end. Early in 1909 a fire destroyed the family store and Martyn survived only by escaping from an upstairs window. His grandfather hinted to him that the accident meant hard times ahead for the family, and little ten-year-old Martyn from then on became more serious and studious. In 1911 he won the second scholarship to the county intermediate school in the nearby town of Tregaron. Because of the distance, Martyn could no longer live at home; he joined his older brother Harold as a weekly boarder in the town from Monday to Friday. He became desperately homesick and always regarded his three years in Tregaron as miserably unhappy.

At the school itself, however, his talents blossomed, and thanks to the fine teaching, he began to realize for the first time that he had an above average ability. The history teacher, S. M. Powell, was his favorite, and throughout his later ministry Dr. Lloyd-Jones was to urge Christians again and again to know their history, especially that of the church. He was convinced that it not only explained the present and showed what mistakes to avoid, but also revealed the great divine interventions—the Reformation, for example, and the lives of the Puritans and the eighteenth-century revival, all of which could teach Christians so much. In 1913 he visited the Summer Association of Calvinistic Methodists, held that year in Llangeitho. Many people were later to call him the last of the great Calvinistic Methodist preachers, combining Calvin's love of truth and sound doctrine with the fire and enthusiasm of the eighteenth-century Methodist revival.

In 1914 Henry Lloyd-Jones became bankrupt. For awhile it looked as if the family would emigrate to Canada, but in God's providence they moved instead to London, where Henry set up a new business. The early days were extremely discouraging, and young Martyn almost had to leave school and become a bank clerk in order to help out financially. But, fortunately, trade at No. 7 Regency Street picked up sufficiently for him to go on to the famous St. Marylebone Grammar School, where his brilliance soon became evident, and he prepared himself for the medical career upon which he had already decided.

The family decided not to attend nearby Westminster Chapel (of which he was later to become minister for over thirty years). They went instead to that great meeting place of exiles, the Welsh Chapel on Charing Cross Road. On their first Sunday they sat in the row in front of the family of the eminent Harley Street eye surgeon, Tom Phillips. Bethan Phillips, the daughter, remembers noticing the three Lloyd-Jones brothers, little realizing at the time how one of them would change her life.

The minister of the Welsh Chapel, Rev. Peter Hughes-Griffiths, was a strong character and individualist, and like Martyn, he had a passion for politics. Martyn would often come home late, having spent the evening in the gallery of the House of Commons, watching his hero and the other great orators debate. But the grand hopes of the liberals faded, instilling in him a lifelong distrust of the power of Parliament to change the world. It was the gospel, he was later to argue, that was the only hope for a fallen humanity.

The Bart's man

In any case, nothing deflected him from his desire to study medicine. "I was never an adolescent," he used to say, and at the age of only sixteen he entered the medical school of St. Bartholemew's Hospital (commonly known as Bart's) near the center of the old city of London. Bart's was undoubtedly one of the best of the famous London teaching hospitals—and all its students knew it. It was said that you could always tell a Bart's man, but you couldn't tell him much. Martyn's teacher was the leading physician of the day, Sir Thomas (later Lord) Horder, the royal physician, whom his admiring pupil later described as "the most acute thinker that I ever knew."

Above all, Horder was a "thorough diagnostician"; he taught his pupils to collect the facts and then reason through them until they had reached the correct diagnosis. They were always to work from first principles, never to jump to conclusions. Through Horder they were ingrained with the Socratic method—asking the right questions and precise, logical thinking were essential to the effective practice of clinical medicine. Young Lloyd-Jones became a star pupil, and Horder rewarded him with his own copy of Jevon's book, the *Principles of Science: A Treatise on Logical and Scientific Method.*

If preaching is "logic on fire," Martyn Lloyd-Jones undoubtedly inherited the "fire," in human terms, from his Welsh background. The Welsh are a very emotional race, and he was no exception. But mere emotion often lacks depth, a failing of many of the Welsh preachers of his day. What was to give his preaching such power was its "logic," the way in which, in evangelistic sermons for example, he would examine the facts of the plight of man, reject the false remedies one by one, then show the true biblical diagnosis, and the only cure—Jesus Christ. He would maintain to the end that his rigorous medical training under Horder was God's preparation for his later preaching ministry.

His time at Bart's also helped him as a pastor. He often discovered that people who came to him with what they thought were spiritual problems were physically ill or just over-tired. When ministers visited or telephoned him about difficulties in their churches, he would refrain from giving them direct advice, asking questions about their situation instead. Many soon found that he had guided them to a solution to their problem by making them think it through logically. Such help proved even better than advice because it taught ministers to think for themselves and learn how to deal with future difficulties on their own.

Martyn Lloyd-Jones kept up his medical interest throughout his life. He continued to read the scholarly journals; indeed, he often knew more about the latest treatment of an illness than practicing doctors or even specialists. (He acted as an unofficial medical advisor to his family and close friends till his late seventies.) But it was as a physician for the spiritually sick that he was to become best known. It was with good reason that he was universally nicknamed "The Doctor."

The call to Wales

In 1921 he obtained his M.B.B.S. with distinction, and his M.D. and M.R.C.P. not long after. (In later life he consistently refused all honorary degrees and other distinctions because he considered his London doctorate honor enough.) The same year he was, as the result of an especially brilliant piece of diagnosis, appointed Horder's junior house physician, and two years later, aged only twenty-three, became his chief clinical assistant. In 1924 he received a major scholarship to study bacterial endocarditis (though in fact he never became a heart specialist).

But despite his meteoric progress in the medical world, his mind was already turning to other things. He had been struck by the ungodliness and moral emptiness of many of Horder's aristocratic patients, and this in turn had made him painfully aware of his own sinfulness. The sad death of his father and the tragic early death of his older brother Harold gave him an acute sense of life's transience, and made him realize that he was spiritually dead to God. He knew he had been trying to escape God and needed to turn to him for forgiveness.

His changing attitude can be seen in the three talks he delivered to the Literary and Debating Society of the Welsh Chapel. In 1921 he spoke on "Modern Education," followed in 1924 by an address on "Signs of the Times," an attack on contemporary fashions. (One of the most fashionably dressed people in the church was the girl he most admired—fellow medical student Bethan Phillips, for whom his ardor was, at that time, unreturned.) But by 1925 his subject was "The Tragedy of Modern Wales," a sermon on his country's loss of true spirituality. The only answer to Wales's problems, he now felt, was the real Christian gospel, not the social gospel preached from the pulpits. Such views were highly controversial, and the public uproar against him, when his talk became more widely known, was immense. But it convinced him more than ever that he was called to Wales to preach the truth.

His first sermon was in Pontypridd in April, 1925. Once again, he preached a message distinctly different from those normally heard in Welsh pulpits of the time. Social action was all very well, he proclaimed, but what Wales really needed was a "great spiritual awakening." However, after much deep thinking, he decided that for the time being he should continue with his medical career. He still felt unworthy to be called to the ministry and struggled with himself throughout that year. By 1926 his turmoil was over. As he said, it was "God's hand that laid hold of me, and drew me out, and separated me to do this work." He was called to be minister of the Bethlehem Forward Movement Mission Church in Sandfields, Aberavon and accepted their offer.

Many years later, in his book *Preaching and Preachers*, he argued that men should never enter the ministry as a profession, but should only do so if they felt they had no other choice and were being compelled to enter it by God. Ministers certainly ought to have the natural talents necessary for a preaching career—a gift for clear public speaking, a good mind (though not necessarily an academic one), and a fine character. But they should also be men filled with the Spirit, with a concern for the spiritually lost, and with a thorough knowledge of Scripture. Such men did not call themselves, but were recognized by the church as called by God. Preachers, he used to feel, were born and not made.

He never had any formal theological training. To him, a minister was not a Bible scholar skilled in expert knowledge of New Testament Greek—though ministers ought to have learned it—but primarily a preacher and pastor with a divine commission. To be a preacher was to possess a gift from God and too much academic learning could even be harmful. So when, fifty years after becoming a minister himself, he and a group of friends set up the London Theological Seminary, they took immense pains to emphasize the essentially practical nature of the course. There were to be no degrees awarded. All students were to be men recognized by their local churches to have the gift of preaching, and all the lecturers were to be pastors of churches skilled in particular areas—church history, Greek, etc.

He always maintained that his medical training under Horder had been, in human terms, as crucial a part of his training for the pastorate as anything else. Many have felt over the years that it was his diagnostic approach, both in his sermons and as a pastor, that made him the great preacher and Christian leader that he became—skills that no amount of seminary training could ever have given him. In an age where book learning is often rated above practical experience, where a business will often employ a fine arts graduate rather than a man who left school at sixteen and worked in industry, we need to remember Lloyd-Jones's view.

Another equally important event happened in 1926. Bethan Phillips, whom he had loved from afar for over nine years, now finally returned his affection. He proposed to her (for the second time) in June, and she accepted. The wedding took place on January 8, 1927 and attracted far more attention than either of them had imagined. By now the fact that he was abandoning a most promising career in Harley Street to go off to South Wales to preach was becoming widely known. The fact that the beautiful daughter of an eminent

surgeon was marrying such a man amazed people even more. But
it was a real love match—and one that was to be totally happy for
the rest of their lives. The couple complemented each other and
were able to strengthen each other in the difficult task that now lay
ahead.

Early days in Sandfields

The young pair were off to Wales almost immediately. The Doctor
had been strongly influenced by his father's radical views and felt
called to preach among working-class people. The Forward Movement Mission Church in Sandfields, Aberavon, South Wales was
located in an extremely poor area, centered near the rather rough
Port Talbot docks and the great steel mills then privately owned. The
town was best known for the fact that its member of Parliament was
Ramsay Macdonald, then leader of the Labor Party.

The church itself had been noted for its social activities, but was
not very successful. Dr. Lloyd-Jones scrapped all these on arrival—
the sports club, the drama group, the temperance league. Unlike
many today, he felt passionately that the "business of preaching is
not to entertain, but to lead people to salvation, to teach them how
to find God." He was convinced that only preaching would get
people into church, not activities or attractions designed to try to
win their interest.

He also believed, unlike many middle-class ministers then and
since, that working-class people were just as capable of listening to
preaching as anyone else. His style reflected his medical training.
He would argue not only that Christianity was reasonable, but that
nothing else was. The gospel was open to all; the "most respectable
sinner," he preached, had "no more claim on it than the worst."
The offer of salvation was open to the "very worst man in Aberavon"—and the town had many contenders for that position.

He refused to model himself on any of the famous local preachers—
he was "one-of-a-kind" from the start. He was neither emotionalist
nor liberal theologically. He adopted a "medical approach," with the

hearers as his patients. The mind, he felt, must be struck first; a Welshman could easily be moved, but to change him, and the way in which he thought, was a much greater challenge. So the Doctor's message was that Christianity was "very relevant and urgently important." He never used jokes, anecdotes, or personal stories; he felt too aware of the glory and grandeur of God to do so and also that such things diluted the seriousness of his message. Instead, he based himself firmly and solely on the Bible. The gospel was truth not "based on experience," as were many false faiths, but "on great external facts."

Such preaching was to form the basis of his style for the rest of his ministry and was to be his hallmark. It was biblical—or expository—yet also clearly relevant to the modern age. It was reasonable, appealing to the minds of the listeners, yet the effect it produced in them also engaged their emotions. He would refer to current events, yet show that it was the biblical text from which he was preaching that had the true, and only, answer. It was no coincidence that his first sermon in Aberavon in November, 1926 was on the text: "I determined not to know anything among you save Jesus Christ and him crucified," the words which now appear on his gravestone in Wales.

The ministry grows

The whole church in Aberavon would meet regularly on Wednesdays to discuss practical living, while the men's "Brotherhood Meeting" gathered for a more theological Bible class on Saturdays. The Doctor took the view that working-class men were just as capable of logical, biblical debate as those who were highly educated. Indeed he often felt that his people had a finer grasp of the great doctrinal truths than many professors of theology. His method of leading them was the same Socratic diagnostic, the approach he had learned under Horder, and which he was later to use both at the Friday night discussions at Westminster Chapel, and, above all, in his thirty-eight years as chairman of the Westminster Ministers' Fraternal.

He felt that the best way for people to learn something was by working the issue out for themselves. So he would ask them to find reference to the issue in Scripture (no other sources allowed), see what the passage said about it, how it fitted into the context of other passages, and then go on to work out what the Bible's teaching on the subject must therefore be. He would make people pursue the logic of their conclusions and, if necessary, point out to them where they had gone wrong. He was always in control of the discussion, and his own wide knowledge of Scripture enabled him to keep it on the right track. As with the ministers who came to him for advice, ordinary Christians learned through his diagnostic approach how to think through for themselves what Scripture taught. Many who knew him, throughout his ministry, would say that when crises arose in their own lives, they were able to survive them because they had learned from him how to deal with them biblically.

. . . and widens

Soon his distinctive preaching not only marked him in a Wales dominated by liberal theology, but also bore remarkable fruit in his own church. Where social activities had failed, the proclamation of the gospel in the Spirit's power worked. The Doctor was convinced that it was the action of God which saved, rather than human effort, though it was through the words of Christ-centered preaching that people heard it. He felt deeply that sinners needed not to be entertained but to be humbled and convicted. The result of this radical approach was that many were converted, including many nominal Christians in his own congregation, the church secretary among them.

As a secular journalist wrote at the time, there was "no drama except the great drama of salvation . . . Public emotion leaves him cold, yet his passion for human salvation sets his people on fire." There were seventy converts in 1929, 128 in 1930, often from among the deprived and unemployed—the very categories which the church in the West is so singularly failing to reach today—and without any of the gimmicks usually thought necessary to win them. The corporate life of the church changed and made a massive impact on the locality. Faithful, regular, expository preaching of the gospel and the day-to-day witness of ordinary Christians whose lives had been transformed brought about a remarkable growth. One of the converts, "Staffordshire Bill," had been a notorious drunk, yet he died a radiant Christian. Such things had a far greater effect on the local people than any amount of publicity could ever have hoped to achieve.

Dr. Lloyd-Jones also found himself called upon medically. He was far better qualified than most of the local doctors and solved many cases which had baffled them completely. Initially he was resented by them, but when they saw that he had no intention of setting up in competition with them, a close relationship soon grew, and his part-time medical practice became a help in spreading the gospel, the only final cure.

Canada

Inevitably his fame spread far, first of all in Wales, where the meeting places were packed with people flocking to hear his message. He always spoke in a language which everyone could understand and with a logic that convicted them.

Then in 1932, he was asked to preach in Canada. His first sermon was in Toronto, at the church of Dr. Richard Roberts, a Calvinistic Methodist who had become a liberal. But the most prominent minister in the city was Rev. T. T. Shields. He had much in common with the Doctor—both were keen Calvinists and amillenialists. But Dr. Lloyd-Jones soon disagreed with Shields because he strongly disliked the Canadian's polemical approach, always disagreeing with others. This, he felt, was far too negative.

"You can make mincemeat out of the liberals," he told Shields, "but still be in trouble in your own soul." Rather than adopt an antagonistic, drastically invasive approach, the Doctor preferred that of the healer. "Preach the gospel to people positively," he suggested, "and win them." Dr. Lloyd-Jones never believed in being aggressive and always stressed the positive aspect of the truth. He never hesitated to enter enemy territory—he held strong views on many subjects—but he would do so in a Christian spirit, not one of worldly spite. It is important to remember this, because there have been those who have, after his death, given him a negative image, stressing more what they felt he was *against* rather than, as he would have preferred, emphasizing what he was *for*. For most of his life he believed in reasoning with people whose opinions on various issues differed from his own, whether in debate with fellow Evangelicals or in explaining the truth of God to those who did not know it. Even in his evangelistic sermons, he would not so much denounce error, as logically demonstrate its futility. As will be seen, for the majority of his ministry he worked with fellow Evangelicals of all backgrounds, seeking to persuade them both by discussion and example to his own point of view.

After Toronto he went on to a conference organized by the Chautauqua Institute near Buffalo, New York. This gathering was no longer remotely Evangelical and invited speakers such as Eleanor Roosevelt and the humanist Sir Julian Huxley. But the Doctor felt that God had guided him there, and the unknown preacher from Wales was such a success that the small meeting place allotted to him had to be changed to the largest auditorium of all, where he was heard by an audience of over 6,000. As he said, Paul did not hector Peter in Jerusalem, but won him.

Beginnings with student work

In 1935 he began his lifelong involvement with InterVarsity Fellowship (IVF, now the UCCF), which had been set up in 1927 by Christians from all denominations in order to unify student Christian unions in different universities and medical schools. He was asked by its general secretary, Douglas Johnson (himself a former medical man) to speak at its annual conference, as his "Pauline" preaching manner had impressed them. The Doctor was hesitant at first, as he was unhappy about the rather English, hearty, anti-intellectual style then characteristic of IVF. But he finally agreed and soon made such an impact that in 1939 he was chosen as its president.

In those days, truly evangelical students were in a minority, often frightened by the larger, respectable, but extremely liberal Student Christian Movement. As a result, they had retreated into a shell, emphasizing experience and "muscular Christianity," with a doctrinally feeble kind of evangelism. The Doctor, with his robust Welsh background and his emphasis on the mind, totally rejected this approach. But instead of denouncing it from the outside, he joined it and completely transformed it from within. He breathed a new air of confidence into the IVF that led to its becoming the main Christian group in every university.

He did so by giving it the solid doctrinal base in Scripture that it had lacked. He taught students not only how to think, but to be unafraid to do so in public. He removed the rather other-worldly ghetto atmosphere by telling students how to relate their Christian faith to the subjects they studied. Although a medical graduate himself, he enabled arts and literature students to feel that what they were studying was perfectly appropriate so long as their faith did not suffer as a result.

The idea that Christians should only be doctors, ministers, missionaries, or school teachers was to him ridiculous. He strongly disliked the influence in England of the public school ethos—that of the sports-mad, unthinking individual who repressed his emotions beneath his stiff upper lip, distrusted the intellect, and cultivated the tradition of the gentleman amateur. This was partly because the Doctor himself had been miserable living away from home, and because he had a Welshman's innate suspicion of the English ruling classes who had suppressed the Welsh and their language for so long.

But it was also a matter of emphasis. To him, the rather pietistic climate of English Evangelicalism was a result of the malign influence of the public school tradition and therefore did great harm. The Welsh, by contrast, were able to express true emotion; at the same time they loved doctrine and revered the mind. By introducing the Welsh outlook into English Christianity, the Doctor made a major contribution to Evangelicalism as a whole.

He therefore encouraged Christians who were entering the mainstream professions, such as industry and law, just as much as those who were going into the traditional callings such as medicine or paid, full-time Christian work. At the same time, he enthusiastically supported overseas missions, and served for many years on the candidates board of the China Inland Mission (now the OMF) and spoke at several missionary conferences. He was also a strong supporter of the Christian Medical Fellowship, frequently lecturing at their meetings and always interested in their problems and ready to give advice.

Decisions

Revival and the need for it remained Dr. Lloyd-Jones's lifelong passion. The secular press called him the greatest preacher since the Welsh revival of 1904 (in which his wife's grandfather, Evan Phillips, had played a leading part). But, as he told the 7,000 who came to hear him at the Daniel Rowlands Centenary meeting in 1935, Wales had forgotten the truths upon which revivals were based. Nor, as he observed to a packed Albert Hall the same year, could revival be artificially induced. Evangelism had become too obsessed with "results," and decisionism was no substitute for the chief need: the simple, bold preaching of the truth in all its breadth. The Doctor always preached the gospel on Sunday evenings, and a regular flow of conversions took place. But he never made a special appeal or altar call. Those who wished to see him could visit him in his vestry after the service. If the Word was faithfully proclaimed, God could be trusted to work in the sinner's heart.

His own preaching had become highly successful, and this has been attributed, in human terms, to three reasons. First, he preached to everybody, regardless of age, class, or sex; he never preached to special categories. Second, the language he used was the sort that everyone could understand, regardless of educational background. Third, and most important, his clarity, seriousness, and authority compelled people to listen and take notice of what he said; it was "logic on fire."

In 1937 he went again to the United States and preached in Philadelphia. Sitting in the congregation was Campbell Morgan, once again minister of Westminster Chapel. Deeply impressed, he felt that he must ask the Doctor to join him at the Chapel. For the time being, Dr. Lloyd-Jones declined, deciding to remain in Aberavon, but by the end of the year he felt that God was calling him to leave the church there, and he did so in 1938, to his own and his congregation's sorrow. Then the most remarkable series of coincidences took place, demonstrating clearly to him what God wanted him to do.

Earlier in 1938 he had been called to be minister of St. Marylebone Presbyterian Church in London. He had refused because there was also the possibility of his being chosen to be the principal of the Calvinistic Methodist College in Bala in North Wales. While he was waiting for the college's decision, he was persuaded by Campbell Morgan to fill in the time by coming temporarily to help at Westminster Chapel. In September, 1938 he preached his first sermon there, on the importance of doctrine in the Christian life.

In December the Chapel asked him to stay on permanently, but he refused, as he was still uncertain as to his future. Then in 1939 the college rejected him (his main supporter missed the train and failed to appear at the selection meeting). They had disliked his strong and uncompromising stand on the gospel and his attacks on liberal theology.

There was now no hesitation in his mind; he accepted Westminster Chapel's call, and was to remain there for the next twenty-nine years until his retirement in 1968. As a preacher, he was different from Campbell Morgan, whose joint minister he now became. Theologically, Morgan was an Arminian, and his style was largely exegetical, whereas the Doctor's approach to preaching was expository, and he believed staunchly in the sovereign power of God in salvation. (However, although he was very much of a Calvinist, he disliked labels and would say that he only supported Calvin in that Calvin agreed with what he felt was clearly taught in Scripture.) But in spite of these differences, a warm relationship existed between the two men, and they were able to work happily together. Both were Evangelicals who loved the gospel, and that was what mattered.

Some have felt that he made a mistake in leaving Wales. But this is probably a faulty view. It could be truthfully said, as with his influence on the IVF, that he brought Wales to England, to the widescale benefit of English Evangelicalism. He was able to exercise considerably more influence in England than he could ever have done had he remained in Wales. This was all the more true because Westminster Chapel, being in London, was at the center of the British Empire. As will be seen, people came not just from all over Britain, but also from all over the world to London. Many of them attended Westminster Chapel.

It is very difficult to imagine thousands of such people going regularly over a period of many months, or even years, all the way to Wales on Sundays, however fine the preacher was. It would have been physically impossible. As it was, the Doctor was able to exercise an enormous influence over an exceptionally large number of people in a key place at a crucial time. In addition, he frequently went back to Wales, either on holiday or to preach, and retained an informed and intimate interest in the spiritual health of his native land. His influence in Wales was undiminished despite his having left it for London.

The start of international student work

In 1939 the Doctor's presidency of IVF led him to take part in what later turned out to be one of the most influential Christian gatherings of this century: the International Conference at Cambridge that was ultimately to lead to the setting up of the International Fellowship of Evangelical Students—the IFES. This organization was to be an umbrella to all the national movements such as IVF and IVCF and is now one of the biggest international student organizations in the world.

Many of those closest to the Doctor feel that his role in establishing IFES, and especially its doctrinal foundation, was undoubtedly one of his greatest achievements. When asked the question, "What did the Doctor stand for?" they would unhesitatingly answer, "the Christ-centered, international vision of IFES."

The 1939 conference, held under the shadow of approaching war, was attended by 800 students and staff from thirty-three different nations (including countries soon to be fighting each other, such as Britain and Germany) and represented committed Evangelicals from many denominations, state churches, and Free churches alike. In sharp contrast to the events around them, the delegates were united. The Doctor preached on "The One Essential"—the need to have Christ both as Savior and Lord.

Dr. Lloyd-Jones felt an especially deep commitment to this particular movement among the students of all nations. As a Welshman he had a strong empathy with those Christians from colonial nations, such as Indians and Africans. He very much supported the firm doctrinal stand taken by many of the Christian unions, especially by the Norwegians, under the influence of their great leader, O. Hallesby.

The outbreak of war in September, 1939 prevented their plans from being put into immediate action. But the vision of a united, international, uncompromisingly evangelical body that arose out of the Cambridge conference was not forgotten, nor were the words spoken by the Doctor.

"The Chapel"

Martyn Lloyd-Jones remained joint minister of Westminster Chapel until Campbell Morgan's retirement in 1943 and then stayed on as sole minister for a quarter of a century until 1968. Unlike many provincial preachers who lose their reputation on coming to London, his dramatically increased. By 1947 the Chapel averaged a congregation of 1,500 in the morning service and 2,000 every Sunday night. What drew them was the quality and power of his preaching. To him, preaching was "theology coming through a man who is on fire," filled with the power of the Holy Spirit and called by God to proclaim it.

For him, Scripture showed that preaching was "God's own method." The task of the preacher was not to pass on his own ideas but to make known the message of God, based on God's Word, the Bible. The preacher was Christ's ambassador, and it was this responsibility that gave him his authority. All preaching had to be based on Scripture. As all the Bible fitted together into a single whole, all preaching "must be expository," based firmly on a biblical text, and never taken out of context. Ministers, he felt, should always know and draw from the whole of Scripture and read it at least once a year.

So he would preach through a book, verse by verse, showing clearly what it taught, how it fitted in with what the Bible taught elsewhere, why it was important, and how it applied to the problems of the day. As Chua Wee-hian, a former Westminster Chapel regular and now general secretary of the IFES, has said that the Doctor, unlike so many preachers, always gave one the *whole* message. Graham Harrison, a close colleague and fellow Welshman, has written of the "power of argument and logical progression as he unfolded his message in such a way that the simplest could follow him and the deepest could but marvel at his profundity." The Doctor felt that everyone was a sinner, whether intellectual or not, and all could be convicted by the Holy Spirit.

To him, the idea that because of the influence of the media, people could not follow logical argument, was simply not true. Furthermore, he believed that it was wrong to tailor one's preaching of the gospel to one's audience—which was why he preached in a language that could be understood by all. All were sinners in need of the same message. The minister did not need to know the details of individual struggles in his congregation when preaching; it was sin itself that was the problem, not specific sins.

Harrison has written that he always pointed to the glory of God, the living God who intervened in human affairs. He would confront his listeners with this—and it was not often a "comfortable experience" for those in the pew. When he proclaimed the gospel of salvation, it was with the firm and sure belief that it was the only solution. He "reasoned with men as he preached," making them think hard as he argued in "big, bold, logical steps that were so compelling in their presentation of the truth." He was always diagnostic; as John Stott has said, he "combined the analytical prowess of a scientifically-trained mind with the passion of a Welshman," which is another way of saying that his preaching was "logic on fire."

His style was pastoral on Sunday mornings and evangelistic in the evenings. He had a ministry that was prophetic in its breadth and authoritative in its presentation. In his somber Geneva gown he would amaze visiting Americans by his seriousness and lack of gimmicks. He never made jokes in the pulpit (although privately he had a well-developed sense of humor) and one of his first acts on becoming sole minister was to scrap the choir. Yet when his long prayer began, everyone felt the whole atmosphere change. As one American visitor, Eric Fife, later wrote, the Doctor was simply the "greatest preacher this century."

To Martyn Lloyd-Jones, preachers were born and not made. Thus it could be said that the main secret of his success was that it was from God, in whose sovereignty he believed very deeply. In human terms, however, his preaching possessed a unique degree of authority. This lay not just in its presentation, but because he was able, in what he said, and the serious way in which he said it, to convey such a sense of the majesty of God that people sat up and listened. He himself often said that he could forgive a poor sermon if the preacher gave him a sense of the presence of God.

He really believed in what he preached and in its urgent importance. He was relevant and up-to-date, but never trendy. He disliked the fashion of preaching from topics, preferring to stick to systematic, biblical exposition instead, but he was aware of and was able to refer to all the important current trends, not in order to display his learning (he always disliked preachers who did so) but in order to show the shallowness of contemporary thought so that his listeners' need for the gospel would become plainer to them.

The extent of his reading, both spiritual and secular, was enormous. His daughter Elizabeth often remembers her father, fully clothed (including waistcoat, socks, and hat), sitting on the beach, reading what seemed to be a library of books. Ministers, he felt, should be fully aware of what was going on around them, without being influenced by the spirit of the age. What was most important was that they should know and believe their Bibles from cover to cover.

He was opposed to putting pressure, emotional or otherwise, on his hearers. This was why he never made "altar calls" at the end of his evangelistic sermons. To him, it was wrong to push people into such a decision. Conviction, brought about not by human manipulation (he had a special dislike for certain kinds of emotive music), but by the power of the Holy Spirit came first to the mind and will, not to the emotions. As he said, in preaching, a minister was "to present the truth, and, clearly, this is something first and foremost for the mind."

On the other hand, although he always used reason and logic in his sermons, he felt that no one could ever be *reasoned* into the kingdom. First all had to be humble and then realize they were sinners in urgent need of salvation. He never attempted to make the gospel attractive, but many were converted through his preaching of it week after week. Nor did he ever "go for decisions"; rather he urged people to repent and turn to Christ as their only hope. In human terms he did none of the things thought so necessary to win people today. There was no excitement, no rock music, no trendy language—only the preaching of the Word by a serious man in a somber Geneva gown. Yet, above all, he believed in the power of the Holy Spirit. To him, freedom in the Spirit when preaching was the key. It could be described as the secret of his success.

The congregation

All these different factors—logic and emotion, relevance and Bible-centeredness, reason and urgency—drew to him one of the most varied congregations that London has probably ever seen, a cross section not only of ability and social class, but also of national origin. The fact that people from such a wide background came to hear him, Sunday after Sunday, year after year, shows that his preaching was of the kind that could be understood by everybody.

Many of the congregation were from abroad. Christian Chinese in London would come en masse every Sunday morning. Many former international students went on from fellowship at Westminster Chapel to hold key positions in their own countries and elsewhere. These include an African head of state and Gottfried Osei-Mensah, now general secretary of the Commission for World Evangelization. What these students especially valued was the fact that the Doctor, unlike many of his contemporaries, treated them on a level of complete equality with everyone else. As a patriotic Welshman (who always spoke in Welsh to his wife and daughters at home), he fully understood and shared the feelings of those who felt dominated by Anglo-Saxon culture. They, in return, had a deep reverence and affection for him.

He rejected the paternalist approach so often shown by whites to those of different skin colors, and while this utter lack of racial consciousness was evident in his pioneering work in IFES, it was also a mark of his internationally effective ministry in Westminster Chapel, and in the success he had in other countries when preaching there. (His family, in their travels, have often met Christians in other countries who recalled the Doctor's exact words many years after the visit.) His appeal to a diversity of Christians is especially interesting, as, consistent with his policy of treating everyone the same, he made no special effort to attract them to the Chapel. As with each of the wide variety of groups that came, they attended because he had a message that they wanted to hear.

In the rest of the congregation there were civil servants and indigents, professors and lunatics, students and laborers, young and old. He was available in his vestry to see anyone who needed to speak to him after the service. As Ray Gaydon, a former East End "rocker," (who under the Doctor's ministry became first a school-teacher, then a minister himself) has said, the Doctor could be a "lion in the pulpit and a lamb in the vestry." In this pastoral side of his work, Dr. Lloyd-Jones found his medical training to be especially useful; when talking to people who thought they were suffering from spiritual ills, he was often able to diagnose physical causes. He was also the only preacher in London who had more men than women in his congregation.

For many years he held discussions on practical Christian living in the church hall every Friday night, when he would use the Socratic method, which he had employed so effectively in Aberavon. But in 1953 so many people came that he decided to move into the main church building and to preach instead. He began with a series on Christian doctrine.

Increasingly he felt that doctrine should arise out of an exposition of a whole book, and that if he preached on one from start to finish, his congregation would learn all that was important to know. So he began his famous series on Romans to parallel the series on Ephesians on which he was preaching on Sunday mornings. Both these series became books after his retirement and have reached a new congregation of hundreds of thousands all over the world who could never have hoped to have heard them at Westminster Chapel.

He was able to sustain a sermon, or indeed whole group of sermons, on just one verse. He could do so because he always stuck to the main point and refrained from using Scripture as a springboard for pet theories of his own. Many of his wiser followers today, knowing their tendency to digress, have preferred instead to preach on longer passages or chapters.

The student world at home

A large proportion of the Chapel's congregation were students and recent graduates. (Among them were the past and present general secretaries of the UCCF, Oliver Barclay and Robin Wells, both of whom enjoyed a close relationship with the Doctor.) While he would never tailor a sermon especially for students, he had a lasting impact on the thinking and general spiritual outlook of generations of them over the years.

First, as Oliver Barclay has observed, he taught them to "value and love doctrine," by making it powerful and alive. Next he showed them, especially the theological students, how to stand fearlessly on biblical truth. By ridding them of their inferiority complexes, he gave them a boldness in the face of attack that was not worldly but firmly rooted in Scripture. Last, he taught them to bring everything under scriptural authority and to "see human knowledge in its place under the revelation of God." All his hearers (not just students) were encouraged to reason from a scriptural base.

Dr. Lloyd-Jones also applied these principles to the student world at large. He served for many years as the chairman of IVF (now called UCCF) advisory committee on doctrine and policy. He was a regular conference speaker, molding the movement's philosophy and action. Many of the students who attended such conferences went on to hold important positions in British evangelical life or to lead secular careers where they were able to put into practice the biblical principles which they had learned from him. Often it was not so much a particular talk that helped, but the fact that they could now reason scripturally for themselves.

The Doctor also conducted several university missions, but never felt at home with these. He preferred instead to preach the gospel Sunday by Sunday in the Chapel, and although he never made special concessions for them, he knew that many students were converted as a result of the sermons they heard preached there. He did enjoy the pastoral side of student conferences, however, when young people would gather around him to listen to his advice.

The student world abroad: the vision of IFES

When war ended in 1945, those who had met in Cambridge in 1939 were able to get together again and start the International Fellowship of Evangelical Students—the IFES. C. Stacey Woods, its general secretary for the first twenty-five years (and also general director of IVCF USA for many years) wrote:

No history of the IFES would be complete without some account of its first chairman, Dr. Martyn Lloyd-Jones . . . He did more to

lay a solid biblical foundation . . . than anyone else . . . his influence and leadership in the growing young international movement was great. From his busy life, not only was he always available as an occasional speaker to students, but always for counsel to the general secretary. He freely gave several days each year to the executive committee and longer periods to the general committee which student delegates attended every three to four years.
He also attended several of the IFES conferences.

He had, Woods recalled, "great skill as a chairman, patience so long as the speaker dealt with the matter in hand, but insistent that time was not wasted with irrelevant gabble. He loved keen debate, liked to be challenged, but woe betide the opponent who entered into the lists of debate with him unprepared but full of self-confidence . . . In spite of that keen, incisive mind, our chairman was a leader in committee, not director or dictator."

One of the main features of his chairmanship, which he held from 1947 to 1959, was the way that he would insist that on the evening prior to the executive meeting, all the members would get together, not to discuss business, but to pray and to talk over important theological issues in order to set the right spiritual tenor for the next day. As Stacey Woods wrote, "decisions and questions on the following day seemed clearer, answers more obvious, as a result of the stimulus and enlightened conversation of the previous evening" under the Doctor's guidance.

Dr. Lloyd-Jones was asked by the IFES to draw up their basis of faith and action. The executive committee thanked him for the "able, patient, and very clear manner" in which he did so—another example of his logical mind at work. He made the aims of IFES plain from the start. First, they were to foster "Christian fellowship and helpful association between existing" national evangelical unions (NEUs); second, that "there was a great missionary evangelistic work to be done in the many countries where there are as yet no NEUs and in other countries where NEUs are weak and need help." Then came the statement which for those days was quite revolutionary and shows the extent of his vision for the future of Evangelicalism.

"The task of IFES is to initiate and to help establish national evangelical unions that are to be autonomous, and, once they are established, withdraw from any direct action except at the request of the said national committee when some aid or cooperation in some new activity were asked."

This was still the age in which Western missionaries dominated Christian activities in Third World countries, many of which were still under colonial rule. But the Doctor had powerful memories of how the English had oppressed his people in the recent past, his own father's generation included. He had a strong sense of how the African and Asian Christians felt. He therefore insisted that national Christians in each country should take over the leadership of their national movements as soon as possible.

This has been a firm IFES rule ever since and is one of the features that makes it unique among the major Christian organizations in the world today. It is now largely led by Christians from the Third World. Thanks to the Doctor's deeply-held beliefs, the IFES was thus distinctive from the beginning and has been highly successful in the developing world in a post-colonial era, where European and American-dominated missionary movements have often failed.

One of the other distinguishing features of the IFES is that it represented a coming together of conservative Evangelicals from many different denominational backgrounds. Some, like the Scandinavian Lutherans and British Anglicans, were from state churches. Others, such as the Doctor himself, from Free Church backgrounds. But what separated them was not nearly as important as what bound them together—a common love for the Lord Jesus Christ springing from their shared new birth in him, and a desire that the spiritually lost would hear his gospel, the only hope of salvation. While denominational differences were never minimized, they were subordinated to the greater purpose of true, biblical unity among all Evangelicals despite disagreements on lesser matters.

One of the reasons for this unity between Evangelicals from different denominations was the solid doctrinal stand of IFES itself. This position was in no small way due to Dr. Lloyd-Jones and was why he remained totally loyal to it and all it represented for the rest of his life. The basis of faith, which he wrote, and a separate statement on the clear doctrinal distinctives of IFES are, along with his address to the IVF in 1952 (published as *Maintaining the Evangelical Faith Today*), the best guides to his personal doctrinal position.

He was, he told the IVF, "by nature a pacific person," but one who felt obliged to be controversial because of the growing challenge of the ecumenical movement, especially that of the World Council of Churches. Evangelicals were called to defend their position more than ever before, not out of party spirit (he always opposed such a mentality), but because the Bible gave them no alternative. Christians had to be quite clear on who Christ was and why he had come. In stating strong biblical convictions they were sometimes called intolerant; but so were men like Martin Luther.

God demanded faith in himself and obedience, and such a stand made compromise impossible. Biblical unity, as plainly shown in Acts and in the Epistles, was always on the basis of "doctrine and fellowship," centered on Christ. Evangelicals should therefore separate themselves from those who "preach another gospel." But they should only split on matters "absolutely essential" to the truth, not on issues such as baptism or the millenium. They should also watch carefully what men did *not* say, as all real Christians were bound to preach certain things sooner or later. The evangelical faith was not new, but historical, one on which all Evangelicals ought to be abundantly clear themselves.

The IFES statement added a paragraph on the evangelical view of the true church. The last fifteen years of the Doctor's life were to be taken up with this issue, and it was one which caused immense controversy among fellow evangelical believers. His views on the subject went back considerably beyond 1966, however, and they appear strongly in the IFES statement. As will be seen, it was not so much his views that were later to change, but the method of putting them into practice, and their relative importance in relation to other issues. The memorandum read:

The church of Christ consists of all those who in all ages have been or are in vital relationship with our Lord Jesus Christ as a result of the 'new birth.' The New Testament itself recognizes only two aspects of the church: (1) the whole company of believers in heaven and on earth; and (2) the local manifestation which is the gathering in fellowship of all who are in Christ and, in the midst of whom, according to his promises, Christ is present, who is the only Lord and head of the church.

This meant that the church consisted of all true evangelical Christians regardless of denomination—the only two categories recognized being individual believers and local churches consisting of those same individual believers in that particular area. The unity that mattered was the unity of the gospel, which brought together those whose lives the Holy Spirit had changed on their hearing it, and who now wished to proclaim it in his strength to others. Such unity knew no human barriers. IFES was therefore composed of state and Free Church Christians alike, but who came together as Evangelicals first and last.

However, the position held by those in denominations that contained non-Evangelicals, such as the Lutheran and Anglican churches, soon became, by implication, quite untenable. If, as the IFES paper made clear, the true church was the fellowship of all those who were born again, what then were the Anglicans, Lutherans, and others doing in denominations with people who denied the very tenets of the faith?

The immense strength of the Doctor's position at this time was that although he made his views abundantly clear, he did so in a very positive way. This was the principle he had enunciated to T. T. Shields in Canada many years before. "Preach the gospel to people positively and win them"—the physician's, not the surgeon's, approach. So throughout his chairmanship of IFES he worked with those of his fellow Evangelicals whose gospel he shared but whose decision to remain within doctrinally-mixed denominations he felt was clearly inconsistent with their evangelical faith. True unity mattered more. Further, by being positive rather than negative, he was able to exercise a far wider and deeper influence than would have been possible had he adopted a more negative, antagonistic attitude. As it was, he stayed in fellowship and active partnership with them and was able to steer IFES firmly onto the doctrinal path in which he felt it ought to go.

Another of his beliefs that made a major impression on IFES during his long chairmanship of it was his resolute conviction that it was essential to trust totally in the power of the Holy Spirit. The role of IFES, he taught them, was to be both faithful and prophetic in their own generation. God was sovereign, and it was only by trusting on his Spirit and his Word, the Bible, that the IFES would bear fruit.

He therefore rejected all five- and ten-year plans and all the long-term planning goals that were put forward, especially those by certain Western nations, and one in particular. If the IFES was walking in the Spirit, and remained true to Scripture, he argued that God could spring surprises on them for which they must be ready. But how could they if they had committed themselves to a plan that bound them for years ahead? (It was the same principle that always made him reluctant to give sermon titles out for the week ahead, in case the Spirit led him to preach on something else from the text.)

In 1959 he retired as chairman and became president until 1967 when he was named vice-president, a post he held for the rest of his life. In 1959 the executive committee, "conscious of its privilege of association with Dr. Lloyd-Jones during the last twelve years," and of the "leadership, counsel, and inspiration he had given to IFES" unanimously passed a motion stating that it wished to "express its thanks and appreciation to him and to his wife for the generous giving of themselves to this work," and to him for "his leadership not only in the committee as chairman but more particularly for his spiritual leadership and direction in the work as a whole."

Not only was he to be president, but he was asked by the executive committee to find time to "be with us and address us at each general committee meeting and whenever possible to be present at future meetings of the executive committee. We would also assure him," the committee continued, "that we feel the need of his continued leadership and counsel in the work and therefore in no sense do we regard him as having retired from IFES." This was proved to be true; he never lost his deep love for and enormous interest in all that IFES did and stood for, right up until his death.

In 1971 he attended and spoke at the twenty-fifth anniversary meeting (and general committee) of IFES and retained close personal links with many of the staff, including Stacey Woods and Chua Wee-hian, Woods's successor as general secretary. His establishment of it on firm doctrinal grounds kept it true to the faith in stormy theological times. If he never lost his strong affection for IFES, neither did the many member movements across the world ever lose their love and respect for him.

IFES—a model of the positive unity of Evangelicals across the denominational barriers on the basis of the gospel of salvation in Jesus Christ—was what the Doctor stood for. It was a biblical emphasis that brought people together on the one essential and sought, within the evangelical family, to lead people of differing viewpoints to a scriptural outlook. This was done not by hectoring or denouncing them, but by showing them the way, both by example and reasoned debate among brothers and sisters in the Lord. It was this attitude that accounted for the immense and beneficial influence for the truth that the Doctor was able to have, and which had such an effect internationally. Under God he had a vision of what could be done to reach the lost across the nations in his generation. IFES will serve as a fitting memorial to all that he fought for and believed in.

The "Fraternal"

Dr. Lloyd-Jones was also involved in groups at home in Britain. The first, and the one for which he would most want to be remembered (even more, he said, than for being minister of Westminster Chapel) was the Westminster Ministers' Fraternal which he chaired for forty years. As his closest collaborator and right-hand man in this work for thirty-eight of those years—John Caiger—has said, the Doctor was the pastor's pastor. Dr. Lloyd-Jones himself described his membership of the fraternal as "one of the greatest privileges of my life."

It began in 1941, originally just as a study group, at the request of Douglas Johnson of IVF. But by 1943 it had become a much wider body of ministers who met monthly on Tuesdays in Westminster Chapel for lunch. By 1954 it had expanded to meeting all day on one Monday a month, averaging 200 ministers a meeting in the 1950s and climbing to 400 in the 1960s. It was essentially a pastors' fellowship, and for its first twenty-five years, was open to Evangelicals of all denominations, doctrinally mixed and pure alike. Any minister could air an urgent question, always in the strictest confidence. The Doctor, with his incisive, diagnostic mind, would help them sort out their problems and clarify unclear matters of doctrine.

He regarded these men very much as his flock, and several of them became like the sons he never had. Many of their families were also to grow close to him, especially after his retirement from Westminster Chapel in 1968 when he was free to go and preach in their churches. (In one family he was the only visiting minister for whom the little girl never short-sheeted the bed! With two daughters and then six grandchildren of his own, the Doctor was always natural and at ease with children and they with him.) His influence on the ministers of the fraternal was enormous, and he shaped the doctrinal thinking of many of them, and through them, their congregations.

The Puritan Conference

He was also involved at an early stage with what has been called the Puritan Conference (since 1966, the Westminster Conference). It enabled him to emphasize his conviction of two things: the importance and relevance of history to present day Evangelicals and that of Reformed, Puritan thought in particular. He would deliver the final paper, based on solid historical research, every year. He felt that Christians should never forget their Protestant doctrinal foundations, especially the Puritan era, in which the theological implications of the Reformation had been fully worked out.

He was convinced that what was important about the Puritans was the way they combined sound doctrine with a sense of the reality of life. To them, truth was not just something to be grasped with the head, but experienced in everyday life—"experimentally" as they described it. This combination, truth on fire, naturally attracted the Doctor, whose own aim was to produce such a synthesis.

But his main reason for supporting the Puritans (as with his great love of the eighteenth century revival) was not because he felt they were right in and of themselves, but because he considered their teaching to be true to Scripture. It was the Bible and what *it* taught that really mattered. Even if someone could prove that Calvin or the Puritans had taken a particular line on an issue, his reply would be: But what did Scripture teach? What made the Puritans so important was the way in which they made the eternal truths of Scripture come alive in their own generation, as he tried to make those same, unchanging truths live in his own.

His great strength was that he made Puritan, Reformed doctrine relevant to the twentieth century and in such straightforward, contemporary language that everyone listening to it could understand. (He always despaired of those of his followers who, helped by the Puritans to see the application of Scripture to everyday life, insisted on preaching these insights to their congregations in the seventeenth century language in which the Puritans had written. It was not the language that mattered, he knew, but the message.)

Many young ministers and others were influenced by the renaissance of Puritan theology fostered by Martyn Lloyd-Jones. As his son-in-law has written, he "established a tough theological position in the face of the rise of situational ethics and the general repudiation of authority by the clerical establishment in the fifties and sixties." To start with, the conference was open to Evangelicals of all denominations, and one of the Doctor's chief early assistants was the young Anglican theologian, J. I. Packer, who had been a contemporary of his elder daughter at Oxford.

Connected with the revival of Puritan theology was the founding of the Banner of Truth publishing house by his personal assistant and subsequent lifelong associate, Iain Murray. The Banner's aim was to republish many of the great Reformed texts along with other solid doctrinal material. Dr. Lloyd-Jones warmly supported the enter prise from the beginning and submitted many of his own books to be published, notably his series on Romans and Ephesians. The Banner's publications influenced a whole generation of ministers and theologians. As Dick France, the Anglican New Testament scholar, has commented on his own contemporaries, "We were all Banner men." Through the Banner, the Doctor's books were to reach Evangelicals around the world, in Nigeria, the United States, and many other nations.

The Welsh movement

Dr. Lloyd-Jones was also involved in a remarkable moving of the Spirit that took place among many young students in Wales in the late 1940s. He had maintained keen interest in his native country and became very active in doing all possible as a spiritual advisor and encourager to these men. Eventually an interdenominational body, the evangelical movement of Wales came into being and always had an especially warm place in his affection. Many in it saw him as a spiritual father figure, retaining their closeness and loyalty to him in his doctrinal thinking. One of the young Welshmen, J. Glyn Owen, later became his successor as minister at Westminster Chapel (before moving on to Knox Presbyterian Church in Toronto, Canada).

It was no coincidence that Martyn Lloyd-Jones's funeral service in 1981 was held in Wales by Hywel Jones, Graham Harrison, Omri Jenkins, Elwyn Davies, and Vernon Higham—all deeply involved in the evangelical movement of Wales. Though they had not been converted through him, they had all received from him their solid doctrinal foundation. They felt, one has recalled, that life and doctrine went together, and in its simultaneous emphasis on both knowing the truth and experiencing it, the movement adhered to the kind of doctrine that was especially close to the Doctor's heart.

1966: crossing the Rubicon

By 1966 his thinking on the doctrine of the church, while essentially unaltered, underwent a change of emphasis. As seen earlier, he had long been of the view that true Evangelicals could not really remain loyal to their evangelical position and at the same time continue in the same denomination with those who openly denied the basic tenets of the faith. The standing of such Evangelicals was, to him, utterly illogical. But for forty out of what turned out to be the total fifty-five years of his ministry, he had adopted a positive approach to such people, hoping to win them by argument and example and by keeping in close fellowship with them in groups such as the IFES, IVF, and so on. Many of his closest friends were in doctrinally-mixed organizations, including his own brother-in-law, Ieuan Phillips, who was for a year moderator of a mixed denomination.

But in 1966 the Doctor decided that such was the menace to true evangelical faith posed by movements such as the World Council of Churches that Evangelicals could not in good conscience remain in denominations affiliated to the WCC. He therefore chose to use the opportunity of a talk he had been asked to give on October 18, 1966, to the National Evangelical Assembly in Westminster Central Hall. It has been called his "rubicon" and created a storm that has continued in evangelical circles in England ever since.

The Evangelical Alliance who organized the meeting knew that he was bound to be controversial, a witness has recalled, so they asked the chairman, the leading evangelical Anglican, John Stott, to say a few words. They had no idea how explosive the Doctor intended to be. He made it clear from the start of his speech that Evangelicals should face up to the issues raised by the biblical doctrine of the church. Too often, it seemed to the Doctor, they appeared "more concerned to maintain the integrity of their denominations than anyone else." The growing power and influence of the ecumenical movement made the matter more crucial than ever before.

There were two urgent issues. First, were Evangelicals really prepared to be no more than a wing of their own denominations? Second, what exactly was the true Christian church? Evangelicals, he stated, "rightly put doctrine before fellowship." The church was made up of the saints, and for true Christians to insist on staying in different denominations was, in effect, to be guilty of the sin of schism. The need for the "ancient witness" as shown by the Protestant Reformers had never been stronger. Only by standing together could Evangelicals expect the Holy Spirit to send them revival.

There would be difficulties to face for those who pulled out of their doctrinally-mixed denominations and joined their fellow Evangelicals outside. But Christians, the faithful remnant, need never fear, as the Bible clearly showed. Evangelical Christians should "rise to the occasion and listen to the call of God." If they had one objective only, namely the glory of God, they would be "led by the Spirit to the true answer," which was to leave the liberal denominations in which many of them still remained.

John Stott, whose views were presented earlier, became seriously alarmed that many young Evangelicals in mixed denominations, such as the Church of England, would suddenly pull out that night, on the spur of the moment. So, in his own description of the event, he thanked the Doctor for his talk and added, "with much nervousness and diffidence," that Dr. Lloyd-Jones's view of the remnant had "both history and Scripture against him." The intensity of his emotion created an electric atmosphere in the hall for which Stott later apologized to the Doctor. Unfortunately neither this, nor the kindness he showed to Mrs. Lloyd-Jones during her husband's illness two years later became publicly known.

As John Stott has written, both he and the Doctor "continued to have a warm personal relationship." But the general debate caused much dissension. Many who had long been close to him, such as J. I. Packer, felt that by making the church issue the most important one, the Doctor had significantly diminished his influence on the whole of English Evangelicalism, becoming instead the leader of one particular group within it.

Certainly, the Doctor separated himself from much evangelical activity, and was, in turn, ignored by many of the younger Anglican Evangelicals. (Older ones, such as Dick Lucas, continued to regard him affectionately as a father figure.) But he maintained that it was he who was following the Word of God and that misunderstanding and misrepresentation was what the faithful remnant had always had to suffer. While some Anglican Evangelicals missed him deeply there were others, such as Herbert Carson, who had already left the Church of England and became his assistant at the Chapel and supported his views. He gave special care to those who suffered as a result of their decision to follow him, as was shown by the generous support he gave to Vernon Higham in Cardiff who had come out of the Presbyterian church of Wales. (This particular case shows that it was not only the Anglican church he urged people to leave, as is often supposed, but *all* denominations that belonged to the WCC.)

He also always emphasized the positive side of his position, and many felt that he was done a severe disservice by the harsh, unforgiving, unloving, and negative attitudes shown by some of his followers. As a leading Third World Christian who worked particularly closely with him for many years has said, the "Lloyd-Jonesites," did him harm by attributing their own hard prejudices to him. This was most unfair; not only did he frequently not believe what they claimed he did, but when they proclaimed his opinions, they did so without any of the love and the concern for the glory of God that was at the center of everything that he preached.

It seemed to Lloyd-Jones that he was asking his fellow Evangelicals to pull out in order to come *into* the church made up of true believers. When he and a few close associates drew up a private memorandum stating their position, they made it very clear that they recognized that "all conservative Evangelicals do not see eye to eye with us over the issues" and that it was perfectly possible to be a true Christian while remaining in a doctrinally-mixed denomination. The Doctor would never accuse someone who disagreed with him on this issue of ceasing to be an Evangelical—even though he would vigorously assert that that particular Evangelical's position on the church question was quite mistaken.

He kept several Anglicans as close personal friends. One of them, Professor Philip Edgcumbe Hughes, the theologian, was, he told his family, completely at one with his way of theological thinking. Another very dear friend was John Gwynne Thomas, Herbert Carson's successor as vicar of St. Paul's in Cambridge. As John Stott has written, the Doctor "always distinguished between principles and personalities."

Dr. Lloyd-Jones knew that his grouping would not stay pure forever, but he felt that each man had to do what was right in his own generation. He strongly opposed factionism, in-fighting and empire building among his followers. When he removed Westminster Chapel from the newly formed United Reformed church, he insisted against some opposition that they join their brethren in the Fellowship of Independent Evangelical Churches (FIEC), instead of trying to form a group of their own. Though he held his beliefs passionately, it was always in a spirit of humble obedience to God and not out of any concern for human glory.

The strength of his beliefs can be seen in the address he gave to over 3,000 people in 1967 in Westminster Chapel. This was to commemorate the 450th anniversary of Luther's nailing-up of the Ninety-five Theses, the event which marked the start of the Reformation. He had become extremely worried, he told them, by the trend of the ecumenical movement towards reunion with Rome. He often enjoyed reading the writings of individual Catholic authors, including charismatic priests. But for the Roman Catholic church herself, there could be "no compromise" between her and Evangelicals.

He was concerned about many of the statements made that year at the evangelical Anglican conference at Keele. It was, he felt, "impossible" for an Evangelical "to be yoked together with others in the church who deny the very elements of Christian faith." Evangelicals who remained in mixed denominations were, he said, "virtually saying that though you think you are right, they may also be right" in their doctrine and interpretation of Scripture. "That," he asserted, "is a denial of the Evangelical, the only true faith." The idea put forward by Stott, Packer, and other evangelical Anglicans (whose views are examined in the relevant chapters of this volume) that Evangelicals could, by staying in mixed denominations, reform them and make them truly Evangelical again, was to him, "midsummer madness."

As he said in the private memorandum quoted earlier, there was "no hope whatsoever" of such internal reforms taking place or being successful. For him, there was only one option for Evangelicals and that was to heed Revelation 18:4: "Come out of her my people!" He urged them to "come into fellowship with all like-minded Christian people," to join, in the private memorandum's words, "together on an uncompromising gospel basis" with those whose "first loyalty" was to the "conservative evangelical faith, rather than to any inherited traditional position."

Many heeded the call and took their churches into groups such as the FIEC. Not many Anglicans followed him however. The Ministers' Fraternal and the Puritan Conference were also reformed to accept only those who took his position—though the reason for this was to prevent endless internal bickering on the subject and not to impose any kind of dictatorial uniformity.

His vision of a united evangelical church, with the gospel of Jesus Christ at its center, was a great and glorious one. To him, the division of Evangelicals into different groups was tragic. While he recognized that Evangelicals would continue to disagree on less important issues such as baptism, types of church government, the gifts of the Spirit, and so on, he felt that they should all come together on the gospel that bound them together under Christ's headship.

The trouble was that although his vision was a positive one, Evangelicals in the mixed denominations received a negative impression of it. To him, it was a move towards biblical unity; to them it was a mandate to leave groups to which they had formed a strong personal attachment and to abandon what they felt was an evangelical voice and influence for good in their particular denomination. Because of these different ways of looking at the same problem (the coexistence of Evangelicals with those who disclaimed many of the bases of biblical faith), much misunderstanding arose between the Doctor and those who chose to stay within. He could not understand their failure to see the biblical logic of his appeal; they could not fathom how he, who had worked so closely with his fellow Evangelicals in the mixed denominations for over forty years, was now seemingly going back on all he had stood for.

Many Evangelicals in the Free Church mixed denominations did heed his call; former Baptist Union or English Presbyterian churches pulled out and joined the Fellowship of Independent Evangelical Churches. Some of those closest to him in the last years of his life were those whom he helped through the terrible transition period between withdrawing from one denomination and finding renewed fellowship and support in another.

However one large group failed to heed his call—the Anglicans. Very few responded. Some Anglican Evangelicals such as John Stott and Jim Packer had deeply-held theological reasons for remaining within. Others had more pragmatic grounds—people in England would be more likely to speak to the local vicar on the doorstep or visit the parish church than talk to the nearby Baptist minister.

As Don Carson, the Canadian theologian at Trinity Evangelical Divinity School in Illinois, has pointed out, it is possible that the Doctor's strong Welshness prevented him from seeing the powerful appeal the idea of the English national church had for many English Anglican Evangelicals. In Wales, especially the rural Wales in which the Doctor had spent so much of his childhood, the Anglican vicar was an alien creature. The Doctor's own father had taken part in the national struggle of Welshmen against the legal imposition that compelled them to pay tithes to the Church of England's offshoot, the rather misnamed Church of Wales. (Ironically, Martyn Lloyd-Jones's cousin by marriage was the late Glyn Simon, archbishop of Wales for the investiture of Prince Charles—a fact about which some of us in the family used to tease him.) The idea of a state church, so natural to the English, was thus quite foreign to him. For the Doctor, as indeed for many Welshmen or Free Church Englishmen, the church was built on doctrine alone, and tradition or national affection were irrelevant.

As years went by Martyn Lloyd-Jones acquired an unfortunate, negative image in the eyes of many. He was seen as the man who was "against the Anglicans." Younger Anglican Evangelicals often did not know who he was. He preached to the Christian Union at Oxford during my time as a student there. While those students from Free Church backgrounds all knew who he was, those with

Anglican backgrounds had either only dimly heard of him, or as in one case, thought he was a famous preacher of the nineteenth century! Some of this group came up to me after his sermon and said, "Christopher, your grandfather wasn't at all bad"—probably the one and only time that Martyn Lloyd-Jones was known for being the grandfather of Christopher Catherwood.

Many of those closest to him felt that the tragedy of the split was that Evangelicalism in Britain was divided over what was essentially an ecclesiastical issue at the very time when evangelical unity became vitally important in the face of the attack on Scripture and of the infiltration of neo-orthodox views into the evangelical movement at large. One who sympathized greatly with the Doctor at this time was Francis Schaeffer who had known him since the 1940s and invited him to Switzerland to conduct the marriage of his eldest daughter. (During the Lloyd-Jones's visit to L'Abri in 1957, the Doctor found in Schaeffer a kindred spirit—someone who, like himself, thoroughly enjoyed a good, meaty, theological discussion into the early hours of the morning.)

As will be seen later, Schaeffer had come out of a mixed denomination in the 1930s. When the prevailing view of these member churches had become anti-gospel, Schaeffer and others split off to form the Bible Presbyterian church, a wholly evangelical group of the sort that the Doctor advocated after 1966. The purity of the visible church decreed that those who truly believed the Bible could not stay in the same denomination as those who denied the very basis of the faith.

At the same time, Schaeffer noted, those who pulled out often developed a very bitter, harsh attitude towards those of their fellow Evangelicals who remained within the mixed group. He regretted this, for while he could not support their position, he felt it was not for him to dictate to them what the Holy Spirit alone should do. If those who stayed out became bitter, however, he noted that those who stayed in often had to draw the line beyond which they would not compromise ever wider and wider if they wanted to continue as members of the mixed denomination.

So though the purity of the visible church did indeed decree that

Evangelicals not unite with those who did not proclaim the gospel, the love that all true Christians should show one another and the unity of the visible church equally decreed that all Evangelicals should continue to love one another in the Lord and enjoy fellowship together. What united them was the gospel, and as long as this unity remained, it would be wrong for Evangelicals to refuse to have fellowship with one another. It was no help to the cause of the gospel if all outsiders saw Evangelicals as a group of people endlessly bickering with one another in public. If, however, (Schaeffer felt) an Evangelical was asked to share a platform with a non-Evangelical on a spiritual issue—someone with whom gospel unity did not exist—then the Evangelical should refuse.

What mattered above all else was the defense of the gospel itself. While many Evangelicals deeply sympathized with the Doctor's position, they felt that to make an ecclesiastical issue the priority—however compelling the motive might be—was a mistake. What mattered more was to defend the gospel against attacks from outside. The doctrine of Scripture, vital to the whole evangelical position, was under assault. Some Evangelicals, they noted, were ceasing to hold fast to the stand that Evangelicalism had taken ever since the Reformation and which the Bible itself took. If those defending the evangelical faith also refused to have fellowship with the erring Evangelicals who most needed guidance in the unrelated issue of their denominational membership, then the defense of Scripture and the struggle to maintain evangelical unity would be all the more difficult.

Martyn Lloyd-Jones did however recognize (unlike a minority of his followers) that many of those who stayed "within" were still conservative Evangelicals—as he made clear in the memorandum quoted earlier in this chapter. He continued active in the IFES. He spoke at the twenty-fifth anniversary conference in Mittersill in 1971 and served as a vice-president until his death, maintaining a keen interest in all it did. This was despite the fact that it contained many Evangelicals from mixed denominations such as Anglicans and Lutherans. So while many of them had cause to regret the fact that the Doctor was not with them side by side in the theological struggles of the late 60s and the 70s because of his separatist stand, they knew that he had not abandoned the wholly positive attitude to evangelical unity for which he had fought so passionately for over forty years.

New horizons

Despite his loss of influence in some quarters, his reputation grew in others, particularly through his books, which, as seen earlier, now started to reach people across the world. Their simplicity and directness (they were mainly editions of his sermons), while often a hard task for the literary editors, appealed to the widest range of readers, not just to the more academic. The Doctor (and later his widow) received countless letters from ordinary Christians in out-of-the-way places in Britain, the United States, and further afield, all thanking him for the way in which his books had, under God, transformed their lives.

The second reason for his increased influence was that a change of emphasis in his thinking brought him a new audience. In his sermons on Ephesians he had stressed the need for Christians to know the sealing or "baptism" of the Holy Spirit in their own experience. He had himself, after the war, been responsible for the revival in Reformed—Calvinist—theology, especially in systematic form. He never ceased to stress the need for sound doctrine, and passionately believed in the sovereignty of God in salvation to the end. But he became increasingly anxious lest this growth in Reformed theology turn into an "arid doctrinaire hardness" separated from life and experience.

He felt that although Christians received the Spirit on conversion, they did not wholly have it in its fullness and needed a greater measure following, and quite distinct from, conversion. He never taught that any particular gift came with baptism of the Spirit—he never believed that the gift of tongues were a compulsory or an automatic part of baptism of the Spirit—but preached, especially toward the end of his life, that what was needed above all else was a revival and a mighty outpouring of the Spirit of God: a "baptism of fire."

At the same time he refused to be labelled either as a "compromising charismatic or a cold-eyed Calvinist," as one Pentecostal minister wrote of him. He told a group of ministers involved in the renewal movement that "subjective experience should not precede objective truth." While he opposed quenching the Spirit, he "insisted that everything must be decided by Scripture." Although the miraculous still existed, as he told the Christian Medical Fellowship, "phenomena must not determine belief." The Bible "teaches us to take our doctrine from it alone." While Christians should never deny the present-day existence of tongues and of healing, there were abroad "false Christs and false prophets," who, with "great signs and wonders" would deceive God's own children.

He felt that Christians should neither be frightened by the supernatural, nor "become uncritically credulous," believing that simply because something unusual had happened, the person involved was from God. Christians needed to be filled with the Spirit and at the same time remember that "our doctrine must in every respect be determined by the Bible."

The Doctor always gave encouragement to those involved in the renewal movement. Many of the early meetings of the Fountain Trust took place in Westminster Chapel, and leading charismatic Anglicans such as Michael Harper have paid warm tribute to the help and encouragement he gave them over the years. (He also gave valuable advice to Terry Virgo, a senior figure in the house church movement who holds the same Reformed, Calvinist views on doctrine as the Doctor did.)

At the same time, Dr. Lloyd-Jones never believed that baptism of the Spirit could be induced or produced (either instantly or gradually) by human means—it was something sent by God in his sovereign power and grace. He would never make the experience a test of church membership or a condition of church office. His deacons at the Chapel held a multitude of views on the subject, and he would have been horrified if people thought that in his view of the Holy

Spirit he supported an interpretation of Scripture that effectively divided Christians into first and second-class believers, depending on whether or not they had received a particular gift.

In every area of life the Doctor believed passionately in balance. Where some of his fellow Calvinists were doctrinally correct but lacked zeal and power, he emphasized the importance of experiencing the truth, as well as knowing it—the need to feel with the heart as well as to assent with the head. Where some of those who shared his views on the baptism of the Spirit went off into emotional excess, downplaying doctrine, preaching, and the mind, he reemphasized the importance of sound teaching, of faith being objectively based not on feelings but on what Jesus Christ accomplished on the Cross, and of the importance and centrality of preaching to true worship. It was, as always, "logic on fire," that special combination that made him the man he was.

After the Chapel

In 1968 he became seriously ill. He decided that this was a sign from God, telling him to move on to a wider ministry. The regular pastorate and preaching ministry at Westminster Chapel had become increasingly exhausting, and so he took the illness as an opportunity to retire. After recuperating from surgery, he spent a time at Westminster Theological Seminary in Philadelphia. There he delivered a major lecture series, now published as the book *Preaching and Preachers.* (Many quotations on his view of preaching in this chapter are drawn from this book.) Although he had now left the full-time ministry, he hoped to inculcate into the new generation of ministers his own high view of preaching and its crucial importance in the life of the church.

His main ministry was now writing, especially the series of books on Romans and on Ephesians. He had had some volumes published before, such as his expository sermons on the Sermon on the Mount. But he felt that the Romans and Ephesians series contained the major Christian doctrines and had them published not in chronological order but in what he decided was the importance of the subject matter.

He would go to the country house of his elder daughter Elizabeth and her family in Cambridgeshire where, away from all the pressures and distractions of London, he could get on with correcting the sermons for book form. Often he would leave the spoken repetitions in, as he believed that effective teaching techniques were more important than flawless literary style.

He always maintained that hardbacks were superior to paperbacks—if one bought a hardback it meant that one took the book seriously as something to be treasured, read, and reread often over many years. Yet, ironically, his most widely-acclaimed and helpful book was a paperback—*Spiritual Depression: Its Causes and Cure.* (Many of his shorter works and two of his major works originally published in hardback—*Preaching and Preachers* and *The Sermon on the Mount*—appeared subsequently in paperback. The Romans and Ephesians series were all hardbacks.)

The spiritual physician

Spiritual Depression is important to an understanding of the man; it not only demonstrates his spiritual insight, but also reveals two other important sides of his life. He was very much the pastor as well as the preacher, and as seen earlier, he was greatly helped in his pastoral work by his medical training. Often, using the Socratic method in which he had been trained by Horder, he could deduce what was wrong with someone, diagnosing whether a problem was spiritual or in fact physical or emotional.

In his sermon on Psalm 42 he stated that while "temperament, psychology, and makeup do not make the slightest difference in the matter of salvation," they do "make a very great difference in actual experience in the Christian life." Not all people, Christians included, responded in the same way, and there were some who were by temperament "particularly prone to spiritual depression." As a doctor he knew that "you cannot isolate the spiritual from the physical, for we are body, mind, and spirit."

Often, he discovered, physical causes such as overtiredness or stress had spiritual effects. The ultimate causes, however, of spiritual depression were the Devil and human unbelief. Too many Christians were miserable because they had failed to grasp the glorious doctrine of justification by faith and thus were unable to enjoy the knowledge that they were saved.

To Dr. Lloyd-Jones, the Christian life involved the mind, the heart, and the will, as shown by Paul in Romans 6. People who thought that once they were converted, they would find total happiness had forgotten Satan. Truth was found in obedience (the will), coming from the heart (the emotions), guided by sound doctrine (the mind). The Doctor felt that the Bible demonstrated the "balance of the Christian life" revealed in the "balanced finality" of Jesus Christ. The "heart," he taught, was "always to be influenced through the understanding—the mind, then the heart, then the will."

Depression came from imbalance. Indeed the "very existence of the New Testament Epistles shows us that unhappiness is a condition which does afflict Christian people." Christians were permanently engaged in the "fight of faith" and constantly passing through trials, and the Doctor felt that those who claimed to be Christians without ever having had any spiritual difficulties were probably not true Christians at all. To the countless people who had suffered spiritual torments these words were very comforting because they reflected their own experience. There was a balance to them that was missing in the teaching of those who believed that Christians were always supposed to be joyous or victorious.

As Dr. Lloyd-Jones said in a sermon on 1 Corinthians 15, "Christianity is common sense—and much more—but it includes common sense." There was no limit to God's forgiving power. Individual sins were not the problem. Rather it was the whole relationship with God, and for this Christ's death was enough. Christians had within them the "Spirit of power" and "of love" to help them through all their trials. To him, this was a "superb bit of psychology."

Christians, he preached in a sermon on 1 Timothy 1, should not be dominated by their feelings, but by what they know with their minds to be true. Faith was always a positive action, of reliance in an all powerful Lord Jesus. The "great antidote to spiritual depression" was a knowledge of biblical doctrine, not "having the feelings worked up in meetings, but knowing the principles of the faith"—the "biblical way."

The pastors' pastor

Martyn Lloyd-Jones was not just a pastor, but the pastors' pastor. When he retired from full-time ministry in 1968, he used the freedom that this gave him to travel and preach, especially in the smaller congregations where he could help struggling ministers or those just finding their feet. (Peter Lewis, a minister himself and a friend of the family, has written that the Doctor was a great encourager of those whose preaching careers had recently begun.) News of his visit would invariably fill the little chapel in which he preached and draw local Christians' attention to its existence.

Many of the ministers for whom he spoke were also part of the Westminster Fraternal which, as seen earlier, was reconstituted in 1966 in accord with his views on the separated church. In this way he was the counselor of a whole movement and the leader of a powerful sector of Evangelicalism after 1966. In thirty-eight years as chairman (if one includes the period 1943-66), he missed a meeting only if severely ill. To him it was a binding commitment, especially after his retirement from Westminster Chapel. As he told his close associate (and successor as chairman) John Caiger, he sometimes felt "a lunatic" for taking on so much, but he refused to be deflected from the task.

The proceedings of the meetings were kept confidential in order to encourage free speech, and the Doctor would guide the discussion in a careful, judicious manner, without speaking much himself. He would then summarize the proceedings, adding his own considered views. (In later days he felt freer to talk, passing on his many reminiscences to the delight of the assembled ministers.)

He would combine in himself, as one of those closest to him has recalled, views over which others would often split, such as the importance of doctrine versus the need for freedom in the Spirit. He was both orthodox and contemporary; while despising "topicality" for its own sake he would urge the ministers to live in the twentieth century. As a leader he was acutely aware of where people were and would never leap too far ahead of them nor demand that they act impulsively, but he encouraged them to think through issues before acting.

He felt different things needed emphasis at different times, and he always opposed controversy for its own sake (including the issue of church separation). While theology was important, what mattered more, he would tell ministers, was "life" experience, practical and personal knowledge of, and obedience to, God. Church rules had their place, but they should never imprison. (He was often asked to preach at Baptist churches who would have been obliged to reject him had he applied for church membership because he had never been immersed. He would never insist on any one method of baptism, and he offered Communion to all who truly trusted and believed in the Lord Jesus Christ as their Savior, regardless of the denomination from which they came.)

He never ceased to press home the need for revival, and as a close Welsh colleague has said, when many ministers were distracted, "he kept us to the main things." He gave them the sense of perspective they needed to get on with what really mattered—the proclamation of "empowered truth" that would change the lives of those who heard it.

He made pastors' welfare a priority, spending hours either in person or on the telephone with those who needed his help. As a result, they would take from him advice that they might have rejected from anyone else. His diagnostic mind and wealth of experience, along with his prodigious knowledge of church history (by which he set much store), all appealed to ministers who took their problems to him. He was thoroughly versed in the difficulties and heresies of the past and how they had been resolved or exposed.

The state of the nation

His diagnostic mind excellently affected the major addresses that he was asked to give after his retirement. He would often give the closing address to conferences such as those of the British Evangelical Council. One of these, "The State of the Nation," is also evangelistic and demonstrates the careful, reasoned logic through which he would carry his hearers, showing the symptoms, diagnosing the disease, and then prescribing the only cure. It was preached fifty years after he gained his medical degree with distinction from Bart's, yet reveals that he was still as much the star pupil of Lord Horder in the seventies as he had been in 1921. His words were heard that evening by an audience of over 2,000.

He began by quoting the book *Surviving the Future* by the eminent humanist historian and philosopher, Arnold Toynbee. "The morality gap is now greater than ever before." He then read from *Facing Reality* by the Australian Nobel prizewinner for medicine, Sir John Eccles. "In this tragic hour," Sir John had said, mankind must regain hope or all would be lost. (Significantly, both these books were newly published, and the Doctor had learned about them in the course of his regular reading of the literary pages of the quality newspapers.)

These statements were, the Doctor argued, a perfect description of humanist despair in the face of man's predicament. History showed that this was not the first time in which Britain had felt herself to be in such a state of moral decline—public sentiment had been the same during the Restoration and Regency eras. But it was now more serious. There was not just disobedience, but a very denial of all moral principle and law itself. In the eighteenth century people had been disobedient, but there was now a poison in the system.

This was seen not just in outward symptoms such as pornography and violence but in a cynical, lawless attitude of mind. How should the church respond? The state of the church had often determined that of the nation, and she alone had the truth. What was necessary was to examine the causes of today's decline; having identified the symptoms, a diagnosis must be reached.

The decline, he felt, had begun in a reaction against Victorianism with its smugness and respectability that sharply contrasted with true Christianity. The novelists and aristocrats of Edwardian England had started a moral decline that was speeded up by the breakdown of conventional morality caused by the First World War. The popular press, including television, had trivialized the important issues, en tertaining the people rather than informing them. Church leaders had failed to take a moral stand, and the double standards of many politicians only made people cynical.

The "real trouble," however, was "theological." The church had dethroned the Bible and elevated philosophy and science. Darwin and Freud had reduced humanity to a helpless mechanism. So-called "scientific thinking" had removed the necessity for the supernatural, as well as for any kind of moral restraint. Darwinism had become a religion and science arrogant. But dehumanized man was reacting against all this. Opposition to nuclear technology, a sense of futility, and a distrust of reason were all setting in. Young people were growing cynical or following the revolutionary teaching of Marcuse.

But the modern world was ignoring the only cure to what it sensed was wrong with itself. Man, the Bible taught, could not save himself; the Christian gospel was the only cure. Individual Christians in key places could accomplish much, but the church as a body, he felt, should never become either a protest movement or part of the establishment. It existed to proclaim the Good News of Jesus Christ and the salvation he offered.

The more convinced Christians there were, the greater the influence they could have. Romans 1 made it clear that there could be no morality without godliness—as the Old Testament prophet voiced it, "Where there is no vision, the people perish." Many top scientists were coming to believe in the soul. Schrodinger, a leading physicist, had stated that the most important issue now was: "Who are we?"

The Bible had the answer. Man had been made in God's image, but had lost sight of his identity because of sin. Christians, the Doctor felt, "must proclaim the biblical doctrine of God's judgment upon evil and sin." Modern man had forgotten this, and Christians should declare that Christ had come to save the lost. The church's task was "to call men to repentance, and then to offer the glorious gospel of salvation." It had always been said that people would not listen to this kind of preaching, yet a few fishermen had turned the world upside-down. "The supreme need of this hour," he proclaimed, was "a spiritual revival and nothing else."

Family life

In his last years, the Doctor used to divide his time between his two daughters. He and Mrs. Lloyd-Jones lived for much of the year in London on the ground floor of the house of their younger daughter Ann and her three children, Elizabeth (born in 1968), Rhiannon (1970), and Adam (1971). He and his wife would, however, spend long holidays in Balsham with their elder daughter Elizabeth, her husband Frederick, and their three children, Christopher (born in 1955)—the author of this book, Bethan (1958), and Jonathan (1961).

At Balsham he would spend time on his books, sitting in his favorite chairs (he had one in each room), undisturbed by telephone calls except from the few friends who knew the number. He would discuss the issues that had arisen in sermons or ideas he had discovered in the books which he had just bought or borrowed from his favorite library. He loved discussion and would egg his three eldest grandchildren on, then fight back if they disagreed with him. To all his grandchildren he was "Dadcu" (Welsh for grandfather), and they would debate with him in a way that nobody else ever dared.

For relaxation, he played croquet (he partnered me, against his wife and daughter, who usually won), the word game Lexicon (in which his granddaughter Bethan also often took part), and billiards, which he played with his middle grandson Jonathan. He thoroughly enjoyed the company of all his family. He was perfectly matched with his wife and close to all his descendants with whom he discussed everything. It was typical of him that he showed a real interest in the lives of all his grandchildren. He was as ready to discuss school, TV programs, and wrestling with the younger three,

Elizabeth, Rhiannon, and Adam, as he was to talk about Lloyd-George, poetry, and American politics with the older ones. If he saw a book that he thought one of his family would enjoy, he would either hand them a review of it, or, more often, buy it for them as a present.

He was also very close to his brother Vincent and his family. The two of them would get together to discuss the present (his brother had become Sir Vincent Lloyd-Jones, a judge of the high court) and the past—their childhood days in Wales and the characters they had known. They shared a love of literature and opera and enjoyed cracking puns. The Doctor often visited his relations in Wales, many of whom were still farming and very proud of their cousin who had done so well. He was also very close to his wife's family, the Phillipses; he in his turn was proud to have a link with the great Evan Phillips of the 1904 revival.

Books

Books were another great love—one which he inculcated into all his family. His theological knowledge was enormous. He not only knew the Puritans better than anyone else and the classics of the eighteenth century revival, but was well-read in secular history, poetry, politics, and philosophy. He also kept his medical reading fully up-to-date. Once, when I developed a reaction to a series of eye operations, the doctors thought it was post-operative nerves, but Dr. Lloyd-Jones recognized the symptoms from a recent article in a medical journal. He consulted his reference books, and using the old Harley Street doctors' network, achieved access to my medical charts. I had indeed been prescribed a drug that caused the reaction from which I suffered; the Doctor's love of reading and his continued diagnostic ability had saved the situation.

In spite of his love for books, he felt they never should be a drug. They should be read for profit and for enjoyment but should never dominate life. A minister should never spend so much time reading that he fails to adequately prepare himself spiritually for preaching.

Above all, there should be a balance between sound doctrine and life—the cognitive world of books and the active, outer world of experience.

This was why, as Peter Lewis, the young minister from Nottingham has pointed out, the Doctor so loved the eighteenth century. Lewis has written that the Doctor "feared a ministry which was 'all doctrine' as much as he feared a ministry which was 'all experience,' and always sought to encourage the marriage of both truth and unction, doctrine and experience, in the lives and ministries of those he influenced. That was why he placed Jonathan Edwards in a category of his own among the Reformed 'greats' and that is why he so repeatedly urged a study of the eighteenth-century revival and its men."

Vitality

The primacy of "truth" and "fire" led him to the conclusion that what really mattered about an individual Christian or a church was whether real life was present. He could forgive much about a person or a group if he felt that he or they were alive in Jesus Christ and showed it. He utterly rejected the increasing narrowness and sectarian spirit of many of his self-professed followers, as amply demonstrated in his address in 1968 to the British Evangelical Council (and printed as "What Is the Church?").

A Christian is a changed man, he is a new man, he is a man who is born anew. Christ is in him. The Spirit is in him. Christians, in other words, are unique people because they share a common life. Peter says that as members of churches we are living stones.

The unity that is characteristic of the church, then, is an organic unity, it is a vital unity. Look at the obvious illustration. What is a body? Is it a mere collection of fingers and hands and arms and forearms stuck together anyhow? Of course not. It is organic. It is one.

This is the church: not an institution, not a mere gathering of people as such. These people are special because they have all undergone the experience of regeneration, sharing the same life.

This has got to come first because it is the only way to avoid a dead orthodoxy. You and I are living in this evil hour in the history of the Christian church very largely because of what became of our grandfathers. They held onto their orthodoxy, but many of them had lost the life. The only way you can safeguard yourself from a dead orthodoxy is to put life even before orthodoxy. All appeals for unity in the New Testament are based on life.

This is what makes schism such a terrible sin. It is not merely that you disagree with others, it is that you are dividing Christ, you are dividing a body. And so the apostle brings out his mighty powers of ridicule in 1 Corinthians 12. He says, 'What would you think of a hand that said to a foot, I have no need of you? You would say that is lunacy!' It is only in terms of this doctrine that he is able to show the character of the sin of schism. For brethren who are agreed about the essential of the gospel, and who are sharing the same life, to be divided by history, tradition, or any consideration, is the sin of schism, and it is a terrible sin.

This was what gave the Doctor so much of his power—his zeal for spiritual life. This was also why he was so involved in organizations such as the IFES—they were filled with Christians who were alive, united across the denominational barriers in the service of the living Lord Jesus Christ. To him anything that stifled life was to be opposed. While he had reservations about much charismatic thought and practice, he always encouraged Anglican charismatics such as Michael Harper or Pentecostal house-church leaders such as Terry Virgo because he felt that their churches had a life that should be nurtured.

Denominationalism, he thought, stunted true growth, and if, in the very last years of his life, he negated much that he had stood for earlier by his attacks on Anglican fellow-Evangelicals, it was in part because, in staying within a denomination that contained so much spiritual deadness, they had failed to come out to join those of their brothers and sisters in Christ for whom life, rather than status within a mixed denomination, was everything. (The chapter on Jim Packer will show the case for those Evangelicals who believe that fighting for life within a mixed denomination is possible.)

Last days

In 1979 illness forced him to cancel his engagements. Early in 1980 he was preaching again, and he preached his last sermon in Barcombe at a thriving new Baptist church whose minister, Ray Gaydon, later became closely involved in the work of distributing tapes of the Doctor's series at Westminster. But in June he became too ill to continue any longer, and his great preaching ministry ended, fifteen years after most men retire.

He still gave advice to friends and others who sought it and worked gently on his books, but by December, 1980, his eighty-first birthday, he was forced to give these up too. He had firmly resisted all attempts to persuade him to write his memoirs, but now he decided (to the great delight of his family) to dictate his early memories to his close associate and publisher, Iain Murray.

He now had to spend much of his time at the Charing Cross hospital where, with his still up-to-date medical knowledge, he insisted on a specific type of modern treatment. It amazed many that a man in his 80s should be given such a course of chemotherapy. But the doctor in him felt that he should use it, and he also had the sure conviction that God meant him to have the extra months. He was fortunate in having a Christian surgeon, Grant Williams, who not only understood the Doctor's spiritual motives, but also welcomed the willing cooperation from a fellow medical man.

In February, 1981 Dr. Lloyd-Jones told his family that his earthly task was done. He ended the treatment and cancelled his newspapers from February 28th. "Don't pray for healing," he asked the family, "don't try to hold me back from the glory." He died peacefully in his sleep on March 1, 1981, appropriately both a Sunday and St. David's Day, the national day of Wales.

Over 1,200 attended the funeral service in Newcastle Emlyn, in the church where his grandfather-in-law, Evan Phillips, had preached during the 1904 revival. The memorial service a month later in London drew a congregation of over 3,500 and more in the halls around the back. They were people who had come great distances to thank God for the life and ministry of this extraordinary man. It was not a sad occasion but a joyous one as the thousands present and still more throughout the world knew that a great saint had gone to his rich reward.

God's Welshman

Martyn Lloyd-Jones was a rare combination. He was a great intellect with a fiery emotion, and it was these two strengths in him that gave his life and ministry its special power and impact. He cannot really be understood, in human terms, apart from his Welshness. His background was Calvinistic Methodism, and, in a sense, that is what he was himself. He had the solid doctrinal base of Calvin, together with the passion of the Methodists of the great eighteenth-century revival.

He had such a wide-ranging impact because he could appeal to both brilliant minds and simple ones alike. His preaching never had any of the gimmicks so often thought necessary to grip people's attention. While he had an effective voice, it was never the sound of it, but what it proclaimed that held the congregation. He had converts Sunday after Sunday without the use of choirs or altar calls. What drew the crowds was that his message was both reasonable—"logic," and urgent—"on fire." It was cogent, structured, yet filled with power, so that he himself would often get carried away. His content was thoughtful but not arid or emotional. To the Doctor, the proclamation of God's truth in Scripture was power enough to move the hearts of those that heard it.

Peter Lewis has described this well. "Some preachers," he has written, "make their hearers everything and the truth nothing. Others make their hearers nothing and the truth everything. Dr. Lloyd-Jones eschewed both extremes of error in the pulpit. He preached to bring the truth to men and to bring men to the truth.

His sermons were therefore Christ-centered and people-oriented. He never presented Christian truth before his hearers (much less out of their reach) with a 'take it or leave it' attitude, but he began where men and women were, that he might take them where they ought to be. You could call it incarnational preaching!"

If he was a Calvinistic Methodist, he was also a Puritan. He brought the art of systematic, expository preaching back to the forefront. As he stated in *Preaching and Preachers*, all true preaching ought to be expository, based on the Word of God. With this emphasis he reintroduced Reformed thinking and a solid doctrinal base to Evangelicalism. The Westminster ("Puritan") Conference and the Banner of Truth were all sustained by him. Reformed thought had been neglected since Spurgeon's death, and the Doctor brought it to life again with a new zeal and relevance.

But the Puritans were more than just Reformed. They believed passionately in the "experimental" side of Christian life, that truth should be experienced as well as known. With this the Doctor fully agreed. As Peter Lewis has put it, he preached "the relevance of timeless truth and the vital importance of right thinking for right living. For him the 'victorious life' was not based upon experience (assumed or real) but upon a right understanding and possession of Christian truth and a true grasp of one's new status as a child of God. Christian doctrine . . . was inseparable from Christian life and was the foundation of all our peace and joy." The Doctor showed a whole generation of young Evangelicals the "power of Spirit-anointed expository and doctrinal preaching."

Truth and life together—"eloquent reason," as the Doctor described his preaching—these were the twin facets of his personality and message that made him the man he was under God. The emotional side of him came from his Welshness. The power of his intellect, although present from birth, was refined by his medical training at Bart's; his clear, logical, analytical way of thinking was instilled into him under that great diagnostician, Lord Horder, and never left him.

But it was his ability to make complex doctrine simple and understandable to the ordinary Christian that accounted for the breadth of his appeal. As his friend, Philip Edgcumbe Hughes has said, one of the most outstanding features of Martyn Lloyd-Jones was the sheer quality of his mind. Yet this same characteristic was also of exceptional help in his pastoral ministry—in the Chapel, in IFES, and as the pastors' pastor. He could, by using the Socratic method taught him at Bart's, preach a brilliant sermon on the spiritual health of a Christian or a nation. He would then use the same means to help a young Christian, a minister, or an IFES staff worker in acute spiritual distress. Almost uniquely, what made him so great in the pulpit made him equally capable outside it.

He was a man filled with a great vision—that of a united body of Christ proclaiming the message of Jesus Christ to a fallen world. If his dream of a united evangelical church did not turn out quite as he had hoped in his own country, that same vision was outstandingly successful in the organization which he helped to establish and nurtured through its early days—the International Fellowship of Evangelical Students (IFES).

If he could be said to have monuments, the first would be his books, which are the edited transcripts of his sermons (or lectures such as "Preaching and Preachers"). Many feel the first of these is the IFES which was the embodiment of all that he stood for and believed in. His mind made it possible to see the issues that really mattered and to set out the priorities that would establish the infant movement on a sound, secure base.

The IFES was a positive, Christ-centered unity of the kind that Martyn Lloyd-Jones fought for all his life. The ideals of IFES were created by him, and long after he is forgotten they will continue to be held by *all* evangelical Christians who love and wish to serve their Lord as he did. Above all, the greatest monument will be the many thousands of Christians whose lives he changed, either directly or through the IFES and his books.

Martyn Lloyd-Jones was buried in his beloved Wales, in the cemetery of the Phillips family in Newcastle Emlyn, but not far from Llywncadfor, the farm from which his mother's family came. The words on his gravestone symbolize the one thing in his life for which he wished to be remembered, the motivation for his entire career. They are from Paul's first epistle to the Corinthians: "For I determined not to know anything among you save Jesus Christ and him crucified."

FRANCIS SCHAEFFER

1912–1984

Francis Schaeffer

Francis August Schaeffer IV, pastor to modern youth and Christian interpreter of the twentieth century, was born on January 30, 1912, in Germantown, Pennsylvania, the son of a caretaker and laborer of German ancestry and his wife Bessie, whose family originally came from England. In Susan Schaeffer Macaulay's words, the Schaeffers were "very much a working-class family." Theirs was a home with no books and little culture; a big treat was a day trip to nearby Atlantic City, New Jersey. Young Francis helped his father with carpentry, and, as an eleven-year-old at Roosevelt Junior High School, he chose to take both woodworking and technical drawing to please his parents.

At Germantown High School he began to feel dissatisfied with life. Each Saturday he went hiking in the countryside. To reach it, he said, "I used to save a couple of miles by tramping through the city dump. I have never forgotten it—a place of junk, fire, stench. It has helped me tremendously to think back on that place, because even as a boy I realized I saw there almost everything people spend their money for." His poverty of upbringing gave him a rawness of outlook that enabled him to see life clearly; it also gave him an open, searching mind, an ability to learn about the wider world without the particular preconceptions that often go with a privileged background.

At seventeen he started working part time on a fish wagon. There he found himself introduced to another world through having to teach English to an exiled White Russian count. The book that the count chose to learn from was Greek philosophy. Francis had studied a little philosophy in high school, but this text aroused his curiosity in a powerful way. His family was not Christian, and the only church he knew, a very liberal one, had given him no answers to questions he was starting to raise. Soon he began to read the classics, Ovid in particular. But, aware that American culture was based on Christian thought, he decided also to study the Bible.

He would read passages of Ovid and then of Scripture, starting in the book of Genesis. He discovered that the Bible provided answers to questions he was asking, and over a six-month period he became a Christian. On August 19, 1930, he wandered into an evangelical church, where he heard evangelist Anthony Zeoli. He realized that there were other Christians who believed as he did, and by September 3, 1930, he wrote in his diary that "all truth is from the Bible."

Student days

That same year he graduated from high school and went to Drexel Institute in Philadelphia to study engineering. Already he was faced with a dilemma. He wanted to please his parents by becoming an engineer, but at the same time he felt a strong call from God to enter the ministry. He worked part time in a factory, then on a grocery delivery route. By December, 1930 he decided that his true vocation was to be a minister. His father, who had hoped that his son would be a fellow craftsman, was hostile at first, but eventually both parents accepted his decision.

In September, 1931 Francis Schaeffer enrolled at Hampden-Sydney College in Virginia. Life was hard there for a northerner, and even worse for ministerial students, who were bullied especially by the heavy drinkers. Nonetheless, young Schaeffer got good grades, won over the bullies, and gained valuable experience through helping out at a nearby Sunday school for blacks. He became president of the Student Christian Association and in 1935 graduated magna cum laude.

That summer he was married to Edith Seville, whom he had known for four years. She was the daughter of former missionaries to China, who had now returned to the United States. As one of the Schaeffer daughters has said, the freshness of insight of Francis's working-class background, merged with the culture and refinement of Edith's, combined to give their marriage the unique power and effectiveness in God's plan that was, twenty years later, to make the work of L'Abri possible. During the early years of their married life in the United States, the Schaeffers had three children: Priscilla, born on June 18, 1937; Susan, on May 28, 1941; and Debby, on May 3, 1945, just as the war in Europe was ending.

"Come out of her, my people . . ."

Francis Schaeffer went on to become a graduate student at Westminster Theological Seminary in Philadelphia, which was then still under the leadership of a renowned evangelical scholar and apologist, Dr. J. Gresham Machen. Not long after the young couple's arrival in Philadelphia, however, the dispute over scriptural authority within the Northern Presbyterian Church came to a head. It led to Machen's leaving the Northern Presbyterian Church, along with others, and forming a new denomination of their own. Schaeffer followed Machen's lead, although later he came to regret the harshness that ensued from that split. Describing his feelings on that issue, he later wrote:

> To be really Bible-believing Christians we need to practice simultaneously, at each step of the way, two biblical principles. One principle is that of the purity of the visible church: Scripture commands that we must do more than just talk about the purity of the visible church—we must actually practice it, even when it is costly. The second principle is that of an observable love among all true Christians.

Those who stayed in the doctrinally-mixed denominations, he felt, developed a cooperative latitudinarianism: always redefining the bottom line of what they were prepared to put up with before being obliged to resign. Those who left, by contrast, often manifested a harshness of spirit and bitterness toward those who had refused to join them. Neither way of behaving was truly biblical.

Because of this, Schaeffer always had immense sympathy with Evangelicals like Dr. Martyn Lloyd-Jones in England, who felt that separation from doctrinally-mixed denominations was a crucial issue. But he himself was never to feel that it was *the* issue—the doctrine of Scripture was more important—the watershed, as he called it. Christians, he said, should in their doctrine of the church be imitators of the character of God. The holiness of God dictates that true Christians depart from those in the professing church who have ceased to believe in and teach the truth. But simultaneously they must also practice the love of God, which in reality meant that they continue to show love for other evangelical Christians who had, even if mistakenly, chosen to remain in the mixed denominations.

That kind of response to a thorny problem was of considerable help to Schaeffer's later ministry. Those who did not agree with his denominational separation continued to listen to him when he spoke out on urgent doctrinal and contemporary issues. Those who made the narrower church issue the key test of orthodoxy could never have found such an audience. By placing a positive emphasis on truth, as well as on the biblical revelation of the character of God, Francis Schaeffer not only was clarifying his own priorities, but was also establishing a firm base for the greatness under God that his later ministry showed. He felt that his life was like being on an escalator, with God taking him on up to ever wider responsibilities. His duty was to ride along and let God provide the momentum.

Early ministry

A further denominational split took place among those who had broken away from the large Presbyterian church, and Schaeffer then attended Faith Theological Seminary in Wilmington, Delaware, newly formed under the leadership of Dr. Allan A. MacRae. In 1938 Schaeffer became the first minister to be ordained in the new Bible Presbyterian denomination, at Covenant Presbyterian Church in Grove City, Pennsylvania, a church that had seceded from its former denominational ties. In 1941 he moved to another Bible Presbyterian church in Chester, Pennsylvania, which also had left its previous denomination. Many of his congregation were working-class people—shipyard workers, truck drivers, shop assistants, farm laborers. Because of his own background, he found he was able to reach them, something not always possible for other recent seminary graduates.

To him, both intellectuals and workers were asking the same basic questions. The only difference was that more highly-educated people asked them in a more articulate way. He always tried to make sure that his preaching was understandable to all members of his congregation. He took care not to be too intellectual, but at the same time never to be condescending. He sensed that better-educated people sometimes looked down on those less educated, underestimating their ability to understand complex issues.

Later Schaeffer said that just as Hudson Taylor learned Chinese in order to work with Chinese people, so he attempted to state truth in a way that was clear to anyone listening. Because not everyone who came to L'Abri was an intellectual, the training he received as a pastor, coupled with his ability to shift gears in personal conversation, proved of immense value.

Edith Schaeffer likewise gained experiences that would be useful in future years. In 1942 their church organized a summer camp for people of all ages in the Blue Ridge Mountains. When over a hundred people turned up, but not the cook, Mrs. Schaeffer found herself single-handedly in charge of all the food.

The call to Europe

The following year, in 1943, the Schaeffers were called to the Bible Presbyterian church in St. Louis, Missouri. There they set up, in a small way, the work of Children for Christ as part of the outreach ministry of their church. As a result, Francis Schaeffer developed an interest in international youth ministries, particularly in Europe, which by 1947 was slowly recovering from the effects of war. The denominational board gave him a special leave of absence to go and discover for himself what was happening.

He first traveled around France—to Paris, Bordeaux, Nimes, Marseilles, and Aix-en-Provence; in July, 1947 he arrived in Geneva, Switzerland, where he sensed firsthand the great heritage of the Reformed faith. After visiting pastors in Lausanne, he stayed at the famous Emmaus Bible Institute, where both he and the director, de Benoit, found themselves in agreement on the Evangelicals' "need of separation" from the growing ecumenical movement.

His conviction of standing fully for biblical truth was reinforced in Schaeffer's mind when he reached Oslo, Norway, in order to attend the Young People's Congress of the World Council of Churches. The Presbyterian groups there struck him as being in a "most unhappy" state, and after hearing the eminent theologian Reinhold Niebuhr, he wrote home to his family, "The whole conference makes me desperately lonely for some Christian contact."

On Sunday, when he worshiped in a local Baptist church, he "understood them better in Norwegian than the World Council people . . . in English." He told his family he prayed "for the filling of the Holy Spirit" as he had "never prayed before." Liberalism was not changing, he decided, so much as putting on a new face. Clearly the truth of God was never worth compromising; that view was further strengthened in his mind after meeting the great Norwegian evangelical leader, O. Hallesby.

Schaeffer went on to visit several more European countries, finishing with Britain, where he had a warm meeting on September 30 with Dr. Martyn Lloyd-Jones, who fully shared his concern over the World Council of Churches. He returned to the United States in October to continue his ministry. But a sense of God's calling him to Europe grew stronger in his mind. By Christmas he was asked to go there again by his denomination's international board to help set up events for the International Council of Christian Churches' gathering in Amsterdam in August, 1948.

Nomadic life

He felt a "dense fog ahead" when he and the family set out for Europe in February, 1948; Mrs. Schaeffer later commented, "Our nomadic life had started." After staying in the Netherlands, where Francis Schaeffer was to meet his lifelong friend and collaborator Hans Rookmaaker, they traveled to Lausanne, Switzerland. There they rented a small pension, at nearby La Rosiaz.

Schaeffer used the pension as a base for going around Europe, preaching on the dangers of liberalism, including the teachings of Karl Barth. He believed that Barth had introduced existentialist thought into theology, just as Sartre and others had introduced it into philosophy. The old, rationalistic, liberal theology had become bankrupt. What Barth brought in was a new idea, neo-orthodoxy. On the one hand, Barth claimed that the Bible contained mistakes, on the other that it nonetheless contained religious truth. To Schaeffer, such a thesis was "pure existential methodology using theological terms," and he described it as such to all his audiences. Meanwhile he and Edith did what they could to help strengthen struggling European churches and to establish Children for Christ.

In 1949 the three children became ill in the little two-bedroom apartment the family was renting in La Rosiaz, so it was suggested that they move to a healthier part of Switzerland. After trips to the Netherlands and France, they visited the Swiss village of Champery for a summer break—and liked it so much that they decided to move there. It also had the advantage of being a cheaper place to live. Although they intended to stay only a short while, they ended up living there for the next several years. They set up a Children for Christ work in that area, and a parallel but independent work among English girls in nearby finishing schools. On August 3, 1952, the

Schaeffers had a son, Francis August Schaeffer V (known as Franky). His birth was a special joy, since Edith had suffered a miscarriage the year before.

It was during those years that Schaeffer began to write articles, one of which proved to be the germ of *The God Who Is There*. He spoke out strongly against the Bible Presbyterian Church's joining the Reformed Ecumenical Synod and continued to lecture on the dangers of the neo-orthodox, Barthian view of the Bible. In his articles he stressed the need for a balanced Christian approach: adhering faithfully to the truth as well as being loving in seeking solutions to differences.

As his resolute biblical stance became more widely known, Schaeffer was asked to speak all over Europe. In addition to attending the ICCC Conference in Geneva in 1950, he lectured in Scandinavia, France, and Germany. He attended the Assumption of Mary proclamation in Rome, which provoked him to write an article, "The Bible Is Our Authority," in which he argued that Christians should both *act* in the light of that truth and *fight* for it.

The hayloft experience and the origin of L'Abri

In 1951 the family moved to Chalet Bijou, still in Champery. In its hayloft, Francis Schaeffer was to have a major spiritual crisis without which, he maintained, he would never have been able to start the work of L'Abri. He had felt a "strong burden to stand for the historical Christian position, and for the purity of the visible church." Now he was suddenly struck with "the problem of reality"—the fact that so many orthodox Christians exhibited so few of the fruits that "the Bible so clearly says should be the result of Christianity."

He realized that his own faith was now less real to him than at his conversion. "I had to go back and rethink my whole position . . . I told Edith that for the sake of honesty I had to go all the way back to my agnosticism and think through the whole matter." He paced around in the mountains and in the hayloft of their chalet.

I walked, prayed, and thought through what the Scriptures taught, as well as reviewing my own reasons for becoming a Christian . . . I saw again that there were totally sufficient reasons to know that the infinite-personal God does exist, and that Christianity is true. In going further I saw something else that made a profound difference in my life.

I searched through what the Bible said concerning reality as a Christian. Gradually I saw that the problem was that, with all the teaching I had received, . . . I had heard little of what the Bible says about the meaning of the finished work of Christ for our present lives . . . That was the real basis of L'Abri.

As Schaeffer said in a lecture, "True Christianity is a balanced whole. [It is] not only intellectual, it is not only our cultural responsibility. Christianity is being born again on the basis of the finished work of Christ, his substitutionary death in space-time history." As he put it in *True Spirituality*, the book that he later felt should have come first, the only way to be converted is by "accepting Christ as Savior. No matter how complicated, educated, or sophisticated we may be, or how simple, we must all come the same way . . . the most intellectual person must become a Christian in exactly the same way as the simplest person."

There is, he wrote, "no way to begin the Christian life except through the door of spiritual life." Further, Christian life is no mechanical, intellectual exercise. It is, as he had seen again in the hayloft, above all a personal relationship in obedience to God, a "moment by moment communion, personal communion, with God himself . . . letting Christ's truth flow through me through the agency of the Holy Spirit."

Christianity is a system, but its life is no passive acceptance such as that practiced in Eastern religions. It is an active life, lived in the "power of the crucified, risen and glorified Christ, through the agency of the Holy Spirit, by faith." And that transformative power also applies to Christians corporately: "There is to be moment by moment supernatural reality for the group as well as for the individual."

L'Abri has often been misconceived by Christians as a place purely for intellectuals. Schaeffer himself has been thought of primarily as a philosopher. It is true that he dealt with problems raised by twentieth-century thinking, yet he was equally emphatic in stressing what the Puritans described as the "experimental" (experiential) side of Christian life.

Edith Schaeffer has said of her husband that he was "really . . . a very emotional person." That part of his character became evident to many who went to L'Abri over the years; he took immense care with each one. As his son-in-law Ranald put it, Schaeffer had compassion for the "little people." Truth mattered to him, and he would occasionally get very sorrowful at the sight of so many who did not know truth through Jesus Christ. In later life, in his campaign against abortion, the thought of the loss of so many human fetuses would sometimes reduce him to tears. He was always a family man and each year looked forward to their annual reunion.

The vision of L'Abri that was developing in his mind at that time was not of an academic forum for discussing abstract ideas but of a place where he could help the needy whom God sent to him, including confused young people with the intellectual doubts that churches often seemed unable to resolve.

The work begins

Schaeffer has described the beginnings of L'Abri in *Reclaiming the World*. The "essence of L'Abri," the French word for a shelter, was "a desire . . . in my mind," and in Edith's, "to demonstrate that God exists. That is really the heart of the whole thing. It was that specific historic situation that we found ourselves in . . . We moved ahead one step at a time . . . it was not our calling abstractly, but [rather arose on] the basis of my wrestling with the truth of God."

Between 1951 and 1954 Francis Schaeffer had continued to travel all over Europe. During a furlough in the United States, he spoke 346 times in 515 days. Returning to Europe in September, 1954, he decided to turn their chalet into a shelter for men and women who were searching for help. *L'Abri was born.*

They would live by prayer, and operate on four principles: They would not ask for contributions but would rather make their needs known to God alone. They would not recruit staff but would rely on God to send them the right people. Plans would be made day to day and not far ahead, in order to allow for God's sovereign guidance to them. They would not publicize themselves but would trust the Lord to send them people truly seeking and in need.

The Schaeffers were taking an immense risk. "We were really on a limb." By venturing out alone, they were abandoning all security. "But," Schaeffer said, "I had enough leading so that I was sure that we, and I as the father of a family, would have been disobedient not to step forward." In setting up L'Abri on those principles, they were not claiming that this was a "higher way." It was "our calling . . . someone else can feel called in a completely different way."

Many young people had already come, among them several girls from nearby finishing schools. One of them was Deirdre Ducker, now an artist and designer in Britain. She had heard Schaeffer speak at a local English church, and, with other girls, had responded to an invitation to attend regular Thursday night Bible studies. Several of them were converted, and when L'Abri was formally set up, Deirdre kept in touch.

By 1954 visitors were already turning up from as far away as Asia and Central America. As Francis Schaeffer recalled, he and his family "never sought to be far-reaching in our work . . . We simply did the job that was given us . . . Gradually it grew. There was no great propaganda. It has grown constantly from one person telling another."

The crisis

In 1955, after only a few months, it seemed that their vision might be shattered. In February the local cantonal government told them that their foreigners' residence permits were to be cancelled; they were to leave the country. In January, Edith had read in Isaiah that "the Lord's house shall be established in the tops of the mountains." It was a perfect description of L'Abri. Her husband determined not to launch a campaign, but to pray instead. "Do we believe our God is the God of Daniel?" The family felt certain that somehow God planned for them to stay in Switzerland.

The local United States consulate proved hopeless, but the consul in Berne, the capital, had been at school with Francis Schaeffer and arranged for the American ambassador to raise the issue with the *Chef du Bureau des Étrangers* in Vaud. He told them that if they could find a house in his canton, they would be permitted to stay there, in Vaud. So Edith Schaeffer began hunting for a place, losing a vital day in the process through having to nurse a sick Czech emigré. She discovered various chalets in the Villars area, but they were all too expensive.

The Schaeffers deliberately kept to their principle of not publicizing their plight. But they had established a "praying family" of close friends who would pray for the work on a regular basis. Those friends prayed them through "those rough days in 1955."

Their prayers were answered. A remarkable series of coincidences occurred that showed beyond doubt the sovereign hand of God in the final establishment of the Schaeffers' lifelong work at L'Abri. Edith Schaeffer met a real estate agent in the street who took her to the nearby village of Huemoz, where there was a place to buy: Chalet les Melezes. The deadline for their possible expulsion was getting closer, and matters were becoming urgent. Then three letters arrived, all containing unsolicited money.

An American couple sent $1,000, but 8,000 francs was still needed. Almost immediately 8,011 francs arrived unsolicited in the mail. The local committee for religion and education, who had to make the final decision for the Vaud permit, had their decision speeded up by a man who bumped into Francis Schaeffer seemingly by chance.

By April only the decision of the Swiss federal government was still to come. Edith Schaeffer had to make several telephone calls and discovered a telephone in a pension owned by two elderly women. She told them of her family's plight, and they promised to contact their brother who was not only Switzerland's national defense minister, but was also the current president of the country. She then happened to meet a retired pastor who also offered to help by informing his nephew, the head of the *Bureau des Étrangers* in Berne.

By June every permit had been granted, and with young people already on the doorstep and the necessary money coming in, the Schaeffers were able to start. On June 4 Francis and Edith resigned officially from their mission board in the United States, and the real work of L'Abri finally began.

Scenes from L'Abri

There was one rule for discussion at L'Abri: it was to be based on ideas, not on organizations. Francis Schaeffer expanded this principle in *True Spirituality*. The "real battle," he wrote, " . . . is in the world of ideas, rather than in anything outward. All heresy, for example, begins in the world of ideas. That is why, when new workers come to L'Abri, we always stress to them that we are interested in ideas rather than in personalities or organizations." That rule had exceptions, however. If a student (to use the L'Abri term) had a particular problem in relation to the teaching of an individual or organization, then the workers could discuss it with that student, using names.

Schaeffer's Sunday preaching was also about ideas, "flaming ideas, brought to men as God has revealed them to us in Scripture. It is not a contentless experience internally received, but it is contentful ideas internally acted upon that make the difference." L'Abri was not just about ideas, however, but about changed lives. Christ, not the intellect, was the "integration point."

Although many young people coming to L'Abri had psychological problems, Christ's message saved them and gave them "substantial healing of the whole person." As Schaeffer commented, "Find me the faithful pastor in the old village, and I will find you a man dealing with psychological problems on the basis of the teaching of the Word of God, even if he has never heard the word *psychology* or does not know what it means."

Few leading Christians have stressed the importance of the mind more than Francis Schaeffer. But he has always made clear its true function under the totality of the lordship of Jesus Christ.

L'Abri expands

The work at L'Abri expanded at an ever increasing rate. By the first month, students were coming from England, the Netherlands, Germany, Canada, Greece, Portugal, and the United States, as well as from Lausanne University, near which Schaeffer held discussions in a café. There were existentialists, liberal Protestants, Roman Catholics, Jews, humanists. Those converted at L'Abri would tell their friends, and then they would come and become Christians too.

In April, 1956 two American opera singers studying in Italy turned up. One of them, Jane Stuart Smith, was converted after a conversation that took place because she narrowly missed a bus. A discussion group in Milan followed not long later, and Jane was to start a long association with L'Abri. In July, Hans Rookmaaker came, with the result that he was made L'Abri representative in the Netherlands, and many Dutch students found their way to Huemoz.

The message of L'Abri

Francis Schaeffer always took seekers coming to L'Abri right back to the basics. Edith Schaeffer recorded four of the questions he asked one interested student. First, did she believe that God existed—God as clearly revealed in the Bible, who was infinite and yet could be known personally? Second, did she recognize that she was a sinner in the light of his standards? Did she believe that Jesus Christ truly came in space, time, and history? Did she bow to him, and accept what he, Christ, did for her individually by taking her deserved punishment on the Cross?

In talking to students, Schaeffer always tried to see what lay behind each question. As Os Guinness, later a close colleague, observed, Schaeffer intuitively went for the whole picture. He saw the "gap between the clouds" that helped him delve to the heart of the issue. He and his wife emphatically insisted that they were not simple-answer-givers.

We cannot apply mechanical rules . . . we can lay down some general principles, but there can be no automatic application. If we are truly personal, as created by God, then each individual will differ from everyone else. Therefore each one must be dealt with as an individual, not as a case, a statistic or a machine.

With the immense success that L'Abri started to enjoy, onlookers in the evangelical world often felt that Schaeffer must have developed some formulaic pattern. But Schaeffer himself was quite mystified by talk of "Schaeffer's apologetics." There is, he wrote, "no set formula that meets everyone's needs, and if applied only as a mechanical formula, I doubt if it really meets anyone's needs." Had he been in prison with Paul in Philippi, he would not have spoken with the jailer on the problem of epistemology. But if dealing with someone who had honest problems in that area, it was another matter. He would "keep talking in the way they needed."

The facts of reality necessitated the answers that only Christians could provide. Scripture's "emphasis is that there are good and sufficient reasons to know that Christianity is true, so much so that we are disobedient and guilty if we do not believe it." Christianity is founded on historic facts, not the speculations of human thought. As a result, it appeals to an individual no matter what his or her level of education.

But the great task which God had given L'Abri was to reach people for whom traditional concepts were meaningless. Schaeffer has described the three types of students who came. First were what he classified as twentieth-century people, mainly of university age, devastated by the humanistic relativism of modern thinking, who believed that truth and sin were nonexistent. Most of those arriving in L'Abri in the fifties and sixties were in that category. Then there were young people from Christian backgrounds, who had been turned against biblical faith, either because their churches or youth groups had demanded that they believe without answering their legitimate questions, or because they had been antagonized by seeing little or no Christian love in their church or group. A third category consisted of older Christian workers who realized they were no longer able to cope with questions raised by modern youth; many of them were in L'Abri on sabbatical leave.

Schaeffer understood an important truth about the first category that many churches either failed or refused to acknowledge.

What we must realize is that these people do not realize that they are lost evangelically. How could they? They do not believe that there is right or wrong, they do not believe there is a God, they do not believe there is an absolute, there is no reason for them to see themselves as sinners. Few people believe in guilt anymore . . . How much meaning does our talking about accepting Christ as Savior have for such a person?

[Their] lostness is answered by the existence of a Creator. So Christianity does not begin with "Accept Christ as Savior," but with "In the beginning God created the heavens and the earth." [As will be seen later, Schaeffer fought resolutely for the truth of Genesis 1-11.] That is the answer to the twentieth century and its lostness. At this point we are then ready to explain the second lostness (the original cause of all lostness) and the answer in the death of Christ.

Faith, he explained to the confused of the fifties and sixties, was not the leap in the dark that existentialist philosophers were teaching them it was. There were good reasons to believe the Bible's picture of the human condition. Further, whereas in all human religions, such as Hinduism and Buddhism (in which many of these young people believed) man had to do everything—in Christianity God did it all: "We can do nothing for our salvation because Christ did everything."

What he told students was a total contradiction to rationalism, although, ironically, that was exactly what many Evangelicals who did not fully understand his purpose at L'Abri accused him of preaching. The rationalist was a person who started with himself and worked outward. Christians, however, believed in God revealing his truth to humanity, the "very opposite of rationalism." Schaeffer carefully distinguished between rationalism, which was wrong, and rational thought, which was thoroughly biblical, based as it was on antitheses, like good and evil.

To him, his work was "all pastoral." He saw himself primarily as an evangelist, dealing with the specific problems raised by those whom God had sent him, and whose problems were mainly intellectual. He denied that he was an academic philosopher, while at the same time insisting that his philosophy was accurate. Many Evangelicals had, he argued, a Platonic view of spirituality; their faith applied only to spiritual matters.

One of his greatest achievements was to show that such a view was false. The Bible clearly taught that "Christianity is the truth of all reality." God in Scripture decisively answered all the major problems in a way that "no other system does." If Christianity really was absolutely true, what Schaeffer called "true truth," then it logically followed that there was no area of life that it did not touch, no area whose problems it did not answer.

Life was not a series of watertight compartments. That principle applied equally to evangelism and to apologetics. Christians, especially those espousing teaching that placed experience above content and doctrine, were as guilty as the existentialists of living in "upper storey" belief without using God's gift of reason.

Consequently, when young people flocked to L'Abri, he found that "my talking about metaphysics, morals, and epistemology to certain individuals" was

part of my evangelism just as much as when I get to the moment to show them that they are morally guilty and tell them that Christ died for them on the Cross . . . It is not that suddenly, for some strange reason out of nowhere, if you accept Christ as Savior you are in. Christianity . . . has got to be the whole person coming to know this is truth, acting upon it, living it out in life, and worshiping God . . . Thus apologetics, as I see it, should not be separated in any way from evangelism. In fact I wonder if apologetics that does not lead people to Christ as Savior, and then on to their living under the lordship of Christ in the whole of life really is Christian apologetics . . . Our primary calling is to the truth as it is rooted in God, his acts, and revelation.

Schaeffer was aware, however, that in dealing with intellectual or cognitive issues there was a danger that in opposing Christians whose faith was based on experience—"Christian existentialism"—both he and L'Abri could slide into the other extreme. His hayloft experience had been crucial in that regard.

One day he and Edith took one of their usual hikes up into the mountains. It was pouring rain. Then, as they were having tea, he took out a pencil and scribbled on his napkin:

If the basis of your Christian faith is *only* the experiential then that base is not strong enough, and when the winds of adversity come, your faith will blow away. But if you turn Christianity into pure intellectualism, then when the winds of adversity come, it will also blow away. However, the *base* must be the content and not the experiential. Then Christianity involves the whole person, but the base is the cognitive.

In other words, the mind comes first, and then the will and the heart.

Daily life at Huemoz

The work at L'Abri was far from being solely matters of discussion. Two other factors played a vital part in the overall pattern of evangelism. One was the beauty of the surrounding country. The spectacular views of the mountains from wherever one looked made the students realize that there must be something, or Someone, beyond the despairing existentialist philosophies they had brought with them to Huemoz. But the key in all the discussions was love, not just as a concept, but as an emotion. Love showed that Christianity was not just a set of correct propositions, but something true in experience as well. That was why Schaeffer insisted on dealing with each person as an individual. "Love," he said, "means meeting people where they are."

There was more to it than that, however. L'Abri's success had no human explanation. With his Reformed theology, Schaeffer was very much aware of the sovereignty of God and the power of the Holy Spirit being at the heart of all salvation. But, he felt, "in some poor way, it's been this interrelationship between the intellectual presentation of the truth and simultaneously showing love" to the lost.

Os Guinness summarized it like this: "Truth mattered and people mattered; those were the two secrets of L'Abri." Joe Martin, a former L'Abri worker, felt that the pastoral touch, the sense of love for the individual that Schaeffer always had, made the difference.

Deirdre Ducker, who with her husband Richard acted as houseparents for the newly-acquired chalet of Beau Site, observed that Schaeffer used three methods in dealing with those who came. First were the sermons, which were usually kept as simple as possible, so that even children could understand. He would take his text and go through it logically in an expository way, building up the total picture so that the essential truth in each passage would be revealed. Every sermon was an entity in itself, unlike his second method, the lectures, which were delivered in series. These would be more complex in language, and frequently formed the material for his later books. Then there were the one-to-one conversations with seeking people, where his incisive mind and immense compassion would be seen side by side. He would listen carefully to the questions, and then, as he worked out where that person's own position was, would pose probing questions in reply. He would lovingly lead that individual to see the logic of his or her own position and convince them of its error. In human terms, Deirdre felt, "they . . . convicted themselves."

Students soon decided that he had "thought about practically every angle to life . . . as each fad came along he was aware of what it was." He read as widely as possible from books and magazines and, as Joe Martin recalled, always picked the brains of knowledgeable visitors, such as when some pupils of the German philosopher Martin Heidegger visited L'Abri.

Learning at L'Abri

Schaeffer also learned and taught through discussion and seminars. As the work grew, the long-term students would be added to in large numbers every weekend. Many short-stay visitors would arrive in the bus on Friday night. The Saturday evening meal was outside, the tables carefully set by Mrs. Schaeffer. Vivaldi's "Four Seasons" played in the background. During the meal, students and workers discussed issues and ideas. Then Francis Schaeffer appeared and all adjourned to the livingroom for hot drinks around the fireplace.

Everyone was invited to take part in the discussion. "No questions were disallowed." As Schaeffer briefed the workers, "We must never be shocked." He would "put the question into the broad Christian framework," and thereby draw further questions. No clichés and, as said earlier, no mention of personalities or organizations were allowed. "What," he would ask, "are the issues?"

Students of many different nationalities and a wide variety of backgrounds were present. An ex-worker recalls, "A lot of individuals found their questions answered in an individual way." Schaeffer learned from students' comments how young people were thinking; it enabled him always to be contemporary. But he would never let changing currents of thought alter his message, which remained resolutely the same. "Unless our feet are anchored in truth," he said, "it's very easy to go along with what is chic."

Many of the students were rebels against society. He sympathized with their rejection of artificial, "plastic" Christianity, which was more middle-class than Christ-like. He also realized that many of them, in being rebellious, were being totally conformist, rebelling because it was the trendy thing for their age-group to do. "Christians were the real rebels." "The only way to reach our young people," he wrote in 1970, was "no longer to call on them to maintain the status quo, but to teach them to be revolutionary, as Jesus was revolutionary equally against both Sadducees and Pharisees."

Christianity changed the whole person, unlike the dead-end message of the hippies. It was a "revolution based on truth," on a personal saving relationship with the risen Jesus Christ, a living faith that was "true to what is really there." The fashionable Eastern cults, with their view of reality as illusion, gave no hope. As a result, Schaeffer, by sticking unashamedly to the conservative faith of the Bible, was able to reach people who were the most anti-conservative in their own societies.

Many students who came to L'Abri and were converted there wished to consider those issues in greater depth. As a result the Schaeffers used some financial gifts to establish a place where such study could be carried out. It was named Farel House, after the Swiss Protestant Reformer.

It was, as Deirdre Ducker, one of its first residents, said, "jolly hard work." As well as their own private studies, students would listen to talks given by Schaeffer himself. He lectured on the book of Romans, on Hinduism, on the vital tasks faced by Christians in today's world. He told students to be "aggressive, fighting for our Christianity . . . because it is so urgent."

The start of the tapes

Many of the workers felt that the content of Schaeffer's lectures was so important that each talk ought to be preserved for others to hear and benefit from, and a tape recorder was sent over from the United States. Schaeffer himself disliked the idea; he felt that recording the seminars would spoil their spontaneity. So the recorder sat in the office for months.

Eventually, in order to preserve an especially good conversation Schaeffer was having with a group of American college students, one of the workers, with Edith Schaeffer's agreement, hid a microphone in a plant while tea was being served and thus recorded the talk. The next morning all the students wanted copies, and the tape ministry of L'Abri had accidentally begun. Schaeffer's Farel House lectures were then taped as a matter of course, assisted initially by Richard Ducker, who drilled a hole in the ceiling through which to slip the microphone.

Francis Schaeffer, as senior tutor, chose the tapes best suited to the needs of each student, many of whom also prepared talks which were then discussed by Schaeffer himself along with the others. In no time, the tapes were being sent abroad, and several of the series— "True Spirituality," "The God Who Is There," and "Escape from Reason"—ended up as books.

The books

Francis Schaeffer never intended any of his lectures to be published. As with the tapes, the books appeared at the request of others. He had gone on a major speaking tour of universities in Europe and the United States, lecturing on the place of historic Christianity in the twentieth century. As a result of the questions put to him, the material became gradually modified. Then he gave a series of talks to students at Wheaton College in Illinois. Those addresses were so well received that the college asked if they could be turned into a booklet. Schaeffer consented on the condition that only the students would have it.

When he read the booklet, however, he saw that it contained the germ of a longer work that he had a responsibility to bring out. He therefore carefully reworked the material, which appeared as *The God Who Is There*. Not long afterward, Oliver Barclay of the British IVF asked if talks he had given in Swanick to British students could also be published, and so *Escape from Reason* appeared.

Those books, the contents of which will be discussed later, became famous for the new terminology they introduced into the vocabulary of many Christians: the line of despair, "upper storey" thought, and so on. Those terms derived in part from diagrams that Schaeffer used to convey his basic points. Grace, the spiritual—and nature, the created—had over the years become separated, especially since the time of Aquinas. Thought was now divided by a horizontal line:

GRACE—God the Creator, heavenly things, the soul, etc.

NATURE—the created, earth and earthly things, man's body

By the time of the Renaissance, and especially by the eighteenth-century Enlightenment, secularism had gone so deep that rationalism had taken over.

God and the spiritual ceased to play any part in thought; many people ceased to believe in God altogether. This universe—the observable—became all that there is. Man noticed the particulars of life and from them derived theories about what was universally true. The universe, instead of being seen as God's creation, was now seen as a closed, mechanistic system. Man was a machine. Then came the nineteenth century and Hegel, who completely altered the way in which Western man thought. Instead of antithesis—all that is *A* is not *non-A*—came synthesis. Absolute truth, based on God's revelation, had gone. Only relativism remained.

As a result, the thought processes of subsequent generations were totally different. They took awhile to work themselves through into different areas of life, but could be represented diagrammatically like this:

FAITH

RATIONALITY

Above the line was the "upper storey"; below it was the "lower storey." Rationally it seemed that "man as man is dead," indeed had never really been alive. Above was a nonrational experience that provided the only hope of being able to prove to oneself who one really was. In secular thought, this philosophy was existentialism. In the theological field, it was Barthian neo-orthodoxy.

Schaeffer expounded his thoughts and criticisms of the way that modern thinking had developed in more detail in the books that followed and in conversations he had with people at L'Abri. Many young people found in the books the answers for which they were seeking. Through the books, many casualties of twentieth-century thought found a place where people would care for them, understand their struggles, and tell them what they yearned to know.

Portrait of a shelter

The books changed L'Abri. More people than ever now came to Huemoz. The hippie era was at its peak. The group of chalets that made up the community were filled with students demanding what Os Guinness called tough answers to their passionate questions. The atmosphere at that time has been described by Michael Diamond, a former Farel House student and now an Anglican vicar in Cambridge, and his wife Sylvia.

The Diamonds arrived in May, 1969 as houseparents of Chalet Bethany. There was an "open door policy," and the chalets were swiftly crammed to capacity with twenty-four overnighters and thirty guests at meals in that one chalet alone. Some students had to sleep in camp beds in the corridors; on weekends people filled even the balconies (Swiss authorities later clamped down on overcrowding).

Breakfast was always eaten in the assigned chalet, and students were farmed out to different chalets for other meals. Everyone had to help with chores, and city types soon had to discover the art of life "from scratch," gardening and peeling potatoes. Mealtimes often spun out for several hours, especially at the Schaeffers', where lunch could last until 4:30 or later. Those discussions fostered a family atmosphere in each chalet; houseparents could pick up on and discuss whatever students were learning that day.

Still L'Abri's fame spread. Some came from as far as Japan. A large number of Malays appeared, from Muslim backgrounds. For them, conversion meant they had to make the colossal sacrifice of never returning home; conversion to Christianity of Malay Malaysians (as opposed to those of Chinese origin) was forbidden. Schaeffer intervened on their behalf with the Swiss authorities and took immense care in following them up.

But the largest number was American "college kids," many of whom were on the notorious "drugs trail" to India. Drugs were banned at L'Abri, but some of the visitors caused a few problems in Huemoz, which, until L'Abri's foundation, had been a little farming village. Despite the slightly anti-bourgeois feeling of many of the students, the Schaeffers managed to preserve good neighborly relations with the solidly respectable local Swiss.

In summer, under Edith's influence, most meals were eaten outdoors. A former helper vividly remembers the atmosphere she created, with her love of music and her insistence that table settings should be regarded as works of art.

Os Guinness has said that "Mrs. Schaeffer is the secret of Schaeffer." It was not just their Christian witness of a happy marriage. As noted earlier, much of the evangelism at L'Abri resulted from the visible love shown to seekers. Further, the corporate life of helpers and workers reflected a "community modeling the truth." It was, Sylvia Diamond noted, one rooted in reality as well as in the powerful witness of "real experiences of answered prayer."

Deirdre Ducker has expanded on those dynamics: Prayer was seen as "absolutely essential," the "mainstay of the whole work." Francis Schaeffer instilled in everyone "such a biblical emphasis on the Holy Spirit," especially in his sermons. The undergirding prayer of the community was organized mainly by Mrs. Schaeffer. As he took people off for evangelistic treks in the mountains, she arranged for prayer for God's blessing down in the chalets. There were two prayers at meals and, if a crisis occurred, everything stopped for prayer. Day-to-day life at L'Abri was a "visible walk with the Lord."

The Schaeffers had established their work to prove that God was no illusion, but really existed. They stuck firmly to their foundation principle that they would have no publicity and no appeals for funds. Edith's father helped distribute her family prayer letters, which described the work to concerned friends, many of whom contributed faithfully. Many elderly people, who had probably never heard the word *existentialist*, kept the work going. But financial crises continued, and it became apparent to all that prayer alone was the answer.

One Christmas, Deirdre Ducker remembers, the situation was particularly desperate. No less than $3,000 was needed that month. That same year the son of a wealthy Swiss Armenian family had been spared in an accident and had invited everyone at L'Abri to join him and his family for Christmas. After an excellent meal, the young man handed the Schaeffers a donation of exactly $3,000. No one outside L'Abri had known of the urgent financial need. It is not surprising that so many young people were converted. As one ex-L'Abri worker said, it is a shame that those who know only the books of Francis Schaeffer did not see the prayerful atmosphere of dependence on God that made everything possible.

Three memories of L'Abri

Three accounts from guests of L'Abri bring out the different sides of Schaeffer's character. The first is from the fifties, by a young European from an orthodox but narrow Christian home. Francis Schaeffer gave him a challenge that his own church did not provide. Finding Schaeffer "gracious and patient," he was soon converted. Schaeffer tried to talk to students at their own level, that young man said, and possessed an ability not just to communicate with them but to learn from them as well.

Even in those years, Americans were regarded as having a high standard of living, and the fact that the Schaeffers refused to own a car and have the latest gadgets made an enormous impact on young Europeans. Schaeffer's burden for souls, his innate seriousness that made it so precious when he laughed, his commitment to prayer, and the informal, relaxed atmosphere at L'Abri struck them as immensely refreshing.

Schaeffer was, this European recalled, marvelous during the chats around the fireside. Everybody would sit on the floor, and he would take on anyone. He was big-hearted, making each student feel important. The climax of an individual's visit could be a trek up the mountain, "walks with a purpose" that were "real business sessions on a one-to-one basis."

The number of people there could increase dramatically from thirty to 130 in a flash, but Edith Schaeffer would cope. Countless conversions took place. Occasionally the Schaeffers would tire and slip down to the apartment of a Swiss-English couple, Jacques and Frances Beney. (According to one ex-worker, it was some time before L'Abri developed a methodical system of days off.)

By the late sixties, things were even more hectic, and that was when Sylvester Jacobs came (his story has been published as a book, *Born Black*). He had been to Bible college in the United States, where blacks were still treated badly even by professing Evangelicals. He had come to England with an Operation Mobilization team, and at the orientation conference heard Francis Schaeffer speak on the "phenomenon of our post-Christian West." Jacobs felt lost from the "first sentence." It all seemed so intellectual until Schaeffer mentioned he had taught Sunday school for black kids while a student in the South at Hampden-Sydney. "We were able," he said, "to talk to one another as human beings"; he spoke of their "common humanity," which bowled Sylvester Jacobs over. When the lecture finished, crowds gathered around Schaeffer, but instead of speaking to them he went up to Jacobs, invited him to L'Abri, and asked him about himself. It was as if Schaeffer knew "how to read the spaces between people's words," Jacobs said.

Not long afterward, Sylvester Jacobs and the rest of the OM team set off for Trieste, Italy. En route, they stopped at L'Abri. It was the middle of the night, yet despite the time they were welcomed by Edith Schaeffer (who vividly recalled the event sixteen years later). "I couldn't figure this place out," Sylvester Jacobs wrote. "It didn't seem like an intellectual community; more like a real homey home." Some time later, back in England, he heard a Schaeffer tape. The talk was not "preaching at people," but "explaining it to people," despite all its quotations from philosophers. Jacobs decided to go back, this time for a proper visit.

He stayed at Chalet les Sapins. Again his initial impression was that L'Abri was indeed a "brainy place." But, unlike his experiences at Bible college, he found the white people friendly and natural; they genuinely embodied the "common humanity" to which Francis Schaeffer had referred. And humanity in all its possible variations seemed to be there as well.

Sylvester Jacobs's love of photography had in the past been frowned upon by Christian acquaintances. Here he was told, by Os Guinness, to stop being a "hair-shirt Christian." Os amazed him by saying that not only was it perfectly permissible for him to own a camera, but he should also develop his ideas on how best to use it. More important, he discovered that if "I, a black, matter to these people, could it be because I matter to God?" In his talks with Hans Rookmaaker, and with others there, he found he could trust them. When Martin Luther King was assassinated, the "whites dripped sympathy that spring morning."

Udo, who was married to Schaeffer's youngest daughter, told him he could make decisions that counted, just as whites did. So L'Abri helped Sylvester Jacobs to accept himself. They "didn't quote memory verses; they gave me biblical ideas to work with." He met his future wife Janet there. At Bible college mixed dating had been forbidden. At L'Abri the biblical teaching that there were no barriers of color, race, or class was fully practiced. With initial help from Hans Rookmaaker, Sylvester Jacobs was able to go on to be the well-known photographer he is today.

Another person changed by L'Abri, this time in the early 1970s, was popular poet and rock journalist Steve Turner. The hippie era lingered on. Students discussed drugs, violence, and Eastern mysticism. Rock music played a crucial role in everyone's life, and all the basic values were deeply questioned. "What is truth?" was the burning issue, if indeed such a thing as truth could be said to exist. (It was for people such as these that Schaeffer coined his expression, "true truth.")

Most of the young people were Americans, taking time off from study, and over seventy percent were non-Christians. For the first six weeks of Steve Turner's visit, Francis Schaeffer was away; he became, to those who had never met him, a somewhat "mythical figure." In his absence everyone concentrated on listening to his tapes. When he finally arrived, all the students crowded in to hear him, especially at his informal seminars, where, as always, anything could be asked in a relaxed atmosphere. He possessed an "ability to see what was behind a question," and impressed the motley bunch of rebels sitting around him by the way he "discussed relevant issues in a relevant way."

Schaeffer had a unique openness to what mattered to young people, and an understanding of the subtleties of contemporary life. Unlike many churches, who dismissed rock music wholesale, he had listened, for example, to many Beatles' records, and was able to distinguish between what was important or valuable and what was not. It was, for him, "not a simple case of acceptance or rejection." Evangelicals could have differing levels of response to the great events around them.

Because so many Evangelicals were simplistic in their approach, many young Christians like Steve wanted to know how to react to the culture in which they lived. L'Abri was "not there to tell people what to say, but to provide a structure in which they could do their own thinking." Schaeffer would lay the biblical foundation for them, upon which they could then develop their response to whichever part of the modern world God had called them to enter.

Further, Francis Schaeffer showed that the historic evangelical faith had an integrity of its own. One did not have to abandon one's intellect on becoming a Christian. He was a "man thrown up by the needs of that time." The old answers that society had traditionally given, and to some extent those of Christians too, were no longer relevant to the questions being asked by young people. On the one hand, Schaeffer was able to explain to bewildered older Christians, who cared enough to listen, what was going on. On the other hand, he showed the youth of that confused generation that Christianity had the answer to the root questions they were posing.

Family life

Other events took place in the Schaeffer family's life. Each of the daughters married a man fully committed to the work of L'Abri. Priscilla married John Sandri in 1957. Susan married Ranald Macaulay, soon to help found English L'Abri and later to become influential among younger British evangelical leaders. Debby married a German, Udo Middelman, who, along with the Sandris, stayed in Switzerland to help with the work there.

L'Abri comes to England

In 1958 the work the Schaeffers had begun in Switzerland came to England. A young Jewish woman converted at L'Abri sent Deirdre Ducker money so that the Schaeffers could be there for a while. They met a wide cross-section of people, including a group of Cambridge students. One of them had heard of the Schaeffers through a converted cousin and came to the tea to see what this couple were like. Francis Schaeffer spoke on "The Supernatural Is Right Here," which hit those listening as "brand new stuff."

Several of those students went to Swiss L'Abri as a result and got Francis Schaeffer back to lecture in England in 1959. Michael Diamond, who first heard him in 1961, was impressed with how he dealt with major theological issues of the day. Schaeffer, he felt, displayed "terrific insight" into Barthian thought, and after exposing its existentialism showed conclusively that one could be both a theologian and hold to the conservative view of Scripture that the liberals had rejected. "We were," said Michael Diamond, "given a background to be able to cope with the 'Honest to God' debate."

Schaeffer's influence in Britain grew; until his books were published it was probably greater in England than in the United States. Ranald and Susan Macaulay set up English L'Abri first in Ealing in London, and then in 1971 in an old manor house in Greatham in Hampshire. A major turning point was when Francis Schaeffer was asked to speak at British IVF student conferences. He was able, as Robert Horn (now editor of the *Evangelical Times*) explained, to give an "overarching view of Truth." On one occasion his lecture "took the place by storm." He showed how certain trends were slowly permeating different aspects of life and how those events fitted into an overall pattern. He proclaimed an "integrated view," a "sense of wholeness," but with a strong practical emphasis on "reclaiming the world for God."

This, as Professor Mark Noll of Wheaton College has pointed out, was a thoroughly Reformed, Augustinian view, both in its desire to put the whole culture under Christ's lordship and in its "realism about the state of the natural person and the need for redemption." To be Christian was to be fully human; such an emphasis was important in counterbalancing the prevailing pietism of English evangelical life.

Travels abroad

Schaeffer's fame spread. In 1971 he met Congressman Jack Kemp and his wife Joanne, who later set up a Schaeffer study group in Washington, D.C. In 1972 Schaeffer embarked on a world speaking tour to Hawaii, Hong Kong, Singapore, Malaya, and India. Two years afterward, Schaeffer was asked to address the International Congress on World Evangelism in Lausanne, a conference that changed the face of international Evangelicalism. He had come to believe, as his book *The Church Before the Watching World* makes clear, that the "real chasm" in the outward church was not between the denominations, but between Bible-believing Christians and everyone else. He expanded that theme at Lausanne in order to remind delegates of the basics. The "crucial area of discussion for Evangelicalism in the next several years will be Scripture. At stake is whether Evangelicalism will remain evangelical." There was

no use in Evangelicalism seeming to get larger and larger if at the same time appreciable parts of Evangelicalism are getting soft at the central core, namely the Scriptures. [While it was wrong to be simplistic, there was a danger of compromising the truth, of] not holding to the Bible as being without error in all that it affirms.

That clearly included a literal interpretation of Genesis 1-11. Jesus himself believed in it as a "historical statement," as did Paul. Christians, Schaeffer reminded the Lausanne delegates, should not panic in the face of science and must reject the notion that "scientific truth will always be more true" than biblical statements on such matters. The Bible's teaching about history and the cosmos was as true and inerrant as its teaching about anything else. (Schaeffer elaborated these ideas in *Genesis in Space and Time*.) Scripture, and "holding to a strong view of it or not holding to it was the watershed of the evangelical world." Otherwise an "existential methodology" would prevail, in which spiritual truths were divorced from the real world, and Christianity was a mere irrational experience like any other.

The inerrancy issue is dealt with more fully in the chapter on James Packer, but it must be said here that in making Scripture the essential test, Schaeffer was surely right. His emphasis on that in recent years lost him some of the support he once had, from those who have ceased to take a stand on inerrancy. But unlike those who lost influence in insisting on making ecclesiastical purity the dividing line, Schaeffer was able to retain influence over a wide spectrum of Evangelicalism, including those who, although not agreeing with him on whether Evangelicals should pull out of mixed denominations, still warmly supported him on the more important issue of Scripture. Indeed some of the people who most appreciated him at Lausanne were those who had split on the church issue, but who found they could unite as Evangelicals together in defense of Scripture.

New beginnings

By 1974 the era of intellectual debate that reached its peak in the late sixties (and inspired so many young people to travel to Huemoz) had come to an end. Many wondered what the continuing purpose of L'Abri should be; some of the staff even suggested closing it. One of them commented, "Swiss L'Abri went to seed." Others, while feeling that such a view was too strong, nonetheless agreed that Huemoz had, for the time being, lost its sense of direction. (That did not seem to be the case with English L'Abri or with the new work in the Netherlands.)

Schaeffer completely disagreed. L'Abri, he argued, had been set up to help people and to show that God existed. In the sixties those in need had been students with particular intellectual problems. The fact that things had changed, that apathy was widespread, did not in any way alter L'Abri's basic purpose: guiding the lost to the God who was there. The problems were now different.

For a time in the seventies, L'Abri became a place on the spiritual tourist map of Europe, a spot on American college kids' itinerary. One day some Germans came, found a "hippie," took a few pictures of him, and left. Several of the original staff resigned (amicably). But an era had ended, and in some ways that was helpful. Some restructuring took place. Chalets were made more self-contained, so that a better sense of belonging was able to develop in each of them. With fewer people, more of a family atmosphere prevailed.

By the early eighties, Swiss L'Abri found its feet again. Students continued to come in, many from Australia. Although the debate might not have been so passionate, it was sincere and conducted with the seriousness that marked the "new realism" of the eighties.

L'Abri was different in other respects too. First, Schaeffer himself was there less often. He had begun to travel abroad on speaking tours. But the end of the sixties era was, arguably, for him the equivalent of the illness that Martyn Lloyd-Jones suffered in 1968. Dr. Lloyd-Jones took his illness as a sign from God that He wanted him to go on to do different things. Now Schaeffer too had to look for something else. Some critics alleged that he had gone "over the hill"; he had nothing new to say. But he was in fact about to begin a phase of his career that would bring him a far wider audience than he had ever had by the fireside at Huemoz.

Second, the work of the different L'Abris had, because of his absences, become independent of him. His youngest daughter Debby and her husband Udo turned the new family chalet just up the valley in Chesieres into a mini-L'Abri in the old style. English L'Abri, in an old Hampshire manor house, prospered under the leadership of Ranald and Susan Macaulay. Under the dynamic team that Ranald assembled there, it began to play an increasingly important role in British evangelical life.

Origin of the films

As changes in the intellectual climate became marked in the mid-seventies, new methods of spreading his ideas seemed to Schaeffer to be the best way forward. A different format was needed.

In August, 1974 Franky Schaeffer approached his father with the idea of putting his thoughts into a major film series on Western culture. Schaeffer considered it and during a walk with Edith, formed the basic outline. A title, "How Shall We Then Live?" came to him while reading the book of Ezekiel. To him, this was confirmation that God wanted the series made. It would be a way to "blow the watchman's trumpet" in an age that had lost its way. The films' aim was to be a "study guide . . . for Christians to get a better understanding of the basics, for non-Christians to get a better understanding of what humanism is all about, in contrast to what biblical teaching gives as a base to understanding the universe and life." It was not intended to be directly evangelistic (something that not all Christians watching it later fully understood). The project lasted two years, and involved much research, filming in many places, and a lot of effort by many people. Naturally this proved a very expensive process, and it became necessary to appeal for money.

That change in procedure upset some of the former L'Abri workers. One of them wrote to Schaeffer,

Where did all the commercialism come from? What happened to you? . . . You used to say that numbers weren't important but that God would bring his own people to hear without advertising. You and Mrs. Schaeffer gave up years of your family life to demonstrate it. You used to deplore religious commercialism, castigate appeals for money, and denounce a preacher star-system. What happened to you?

Schaeffer's reply was that "nothing has happened to us or to L'Abri." In establishing the no-appeal principle, they had never claimed it was a *better* or spiritually superior system, but something that God had called them to in that particular situation. The series was a different situation, with different needs. Further, the film series was not really a part of L'Abri, but was made by a separate company, Gospel Films. "Each person," Schaeffer wrote, "in each Christian work must follow the Lord's own leading for them" and stands before God in relation to that alone. The books, tapes, and now the films all represented changes from the small beginnings in Chalet les Melezes. The ex-worker replied that it was not the idea that Schaeffer had "ceased to be spiritual" that concerned people—everyone knew he was spiritually unaffected by it all—but that he had been sucked into a commercialist, thrusting world, with ballyhoo personal appearances, etc. It was a "stone of stumbling" to many of the old L'Abri folk, the writer charged. He had acted with "the best will in the world," but had made a mistake in doing so.

Schaeffer was aware of the dangers and was taking steps to avoid them. God would judge whether he had been right. But

with the world on fire, when one has an opportunity to speak, one has a responsibility, and when so much of Evangelicalism has on one side the devaluation of Scripture . . . and on the other side such trashy material, and then suddenly one can speak where it counts (or at least one hopes it can count), where to say *no* and where to say *yes* is not always easy.

But he tried. Evangelicals had a voice as never before, and it was his responsibility to use it. The films reached more than could ever have been possible at L'Abri. Yet if he felt God calling him to return to the fireside at Chesieres, to go back to the old work of helping small numbers of people as in the early days, he would do so without hesitation.

The film, as the accompanying book explained, in no way made "a pretense of being a complete chronological history of Western culture," but rather analyzed key moments in history that have formed our present culture. There was a flow to history and culture that was "rooted and has its wellspring in the thoughts of people." Each person's presuppositions stem from the way he or she thinks.

The film aimed to show the effect of that process on a larger scale, starting with ancient Rome, then the Middle Ages, and next the Renaissance and Reformation. The Renaissance saw man as autonomous from God. The Reformation, which witnessed the "removing of the humanistic distortions that had entered the church," restored God and the Bible as the real answer to human problems.

The Enlightenment followed, with a silent God who never acted. Science had begun with a Christian basis: uniformity in an *open* universe created by a God who acted. But the heirs of the Enlightenment created a closed, mechanistic universe, without God, and with Darwinian evolution as a substitute. Philosophers began the slide down what Schaeffer called the "line of despair." All was relative. God, the original ultimate reference point, had been abolished. Rationality led only to despair in a universe that had become deterministic, was based on an impersonal beginning, and had evolved by chance. So there was an *escape from reason* into existentialism, a philosophy that separated reason from meaning and reduced religion and belief to a nonrational part of life, which Schaeffer called the "upper storey."

From this flowed liberalism and Barthianism in theology, which stipulated that Christianity was true even if many of its founding historical events had never happened. In secular philosophy, mysticism, and the whole drugs/hippie phenomenon, one saw the consequence of that existential outlook. In the seventies, with the failure of the counterculture, people simply escaped into what Schaeffer called "personal peace and affluence." Each person just gets on with his or her own life, enjoys his or her own pleasures, and ceases to care about anyone else—as long as his or her own security is not threatened. That view is a form of materialism. Its danger is that it prevents people from realizing the threat posed to their basic freedoms by the growing power of secular humanism.

Humanism, a godless system that was replacing laws based on Christian moral absolutes with "sociological law," had terrible consequences in areas such as abortion and euthanasia, both of which were becoming acceptable and being legalized. Through the media and government, secular humanism was taking over society, abolishing the Christian consensus on which post-Reformation society was based. With that consensus gone, there was severe danger of a takeover of society by an authoritarian system—whether of the Right or the Left.

Schaeffer was not one to see endless conspiracies. The real worry to him was that a humanist minority—in the media, educational system, and so on—had altered what was "thinkable" by the average member of society, so that what was unthinkable a generation or so back was now regarded as acceptable. Humanists, he said, whether clear or "hazy" in spreading their views, had been able to exercise influence out of proportion to their numbers—which is why he felt so deeply that Christians too should be active in public affairs.

The films soon became a topic of conversation among the many Christians who saw them in Britain, the United States, and further afield. In general they made a favorable impression. Some people, however, although sympathetic to Schaeffer's views and aims, wondered whether film was the best medium for expressing his important message. Much of his appeal, they thought, had been the man himself, especially his obvious love for people who came into contact with him at L'Abri and elsewhere. One ex-L'Abri worker said, "Schaeffer's special qualities can't be put on film," and thus the series was depersonalized. Further, it gave ammunition especially to those who were suspicious of any kind of Christian involvement with the arts.

The fact that Schaeffer wore his usual Swiss mountain clothing on screen enabled his opponents to ridicule him and dismiss him as a would-be Christian guru. They maintained that he was saying that *all* Christians had to be aware of the latest developments in art and philosophy, that those who were not were second-class. That was, of course, both untrue and unfair, but the films made openings for critics in a way that the books had not. Another problem was that the mass publicity and enthusiasm of many Christians who watched the films led to an image of Schaeffer as *the* great expert, even though he never saw himself as anything like that.

As Professor Mark Noll of Wheaton College wrote: "Francis Schaeffer has been one of our most effective evangelists and apologists. The American tendency to transform leaders of one field into another, however, has not served Dr. Schaeffer well." Although Schaeffer did not encourage such tendencies—far from it, in fact—the films, and the need of some Evangelicals to have a figure whom they could put up against the non-Christian world, caused something like a transformation of the Schaefferean image in the eyes of some.

Part of the explanation for that is the inferiority complex suffered by some Evangelicals today. Instead of basing their defense of faith on the study of God's Word, and resting secure in the confidence that comes from relying on the Holy Spirit, they have turned to big names in order to show non-Christians that Christians, too, can be intellectuals or rock stars. They depend on making the gospel credible to nonbelievers not through its message, the person and work of Jesus Christ, but through authoritative individuals within the church.

As an ex-L'Abri student said, Francis Schaeffer taught him how to think and argue for himself, but the new generation sometimes uses Schaeffer in order not to have to think through major issues for themselves at all. Tragically, that is the opposite of what Schaeffer taught.

Another problem arising from the films concerns the nature of film itself, a restriction that applies not just to Schaeffer but to anything that appears on TV or in the movies. Films can portray only what can be *shown*, whereas books can both discuss complex ideas and illustrate them if necessary with pictures, as was done in the books that accompanied each of the films. The books also have footnotes, which give greater detail than is possible in a short film segment. Yet it was inevitable that some academics, seeing the episode in the series that covered their own area of expertise, found what they saw to be simplistic. It was not so much the fault of the films or of Schaeffer, but of the nature of the medium in which the ideas were being expressed.

Schaeffer has been defended on two grounds. The first is that we are plagued today with overspecialization—what Os Guinness calls the "footnote mentality." Schaeffer's panoramic view of issues gave a picture that would otherwise be lost. He saw the forest, whereas specialists tend to notice only the twigs. Above all, he showed how today's developments fit into a pattern that can be seen by ordinary persons.

Professor Wayne Boulton of Hope College in Michigan has written: "Schaeffer is less a scholar than a thinker. The scholar," Boulton comments, quoting Harry Blamires, " 'cannot endure exaggeration . . . hesitates to praise or condemn; he is tentative and skeptical . . .' The thinker, on the other hand . . . 'hates indecision . . . is at home in a world of clearly demarked categories . . .' and 'works toward decisive action.' " In saying that, Boulton was right. Not only did Schaeffer have a comprehensive view of truth, but he also believed that it should not merely be studied but also acted upon.

The other defense has been made by people like Michael Diamond as well as by Schaeffer himself. The overwhelming majority of those watching the films have not been specialists, but ordinary Christians who have been confused by what is happening around them. For such viewers, the series have been helpful, introducing them to topics they might not otherwise have considered, and giving them courage they might not otherwise have had. So long as those people do not ascribe to the films attributes they do not possess (the series never claimed to be an exhaustive or definitive history of modern culture), then no harm is done. As for specialists, academics can always be reached by other means such as books, seminars, and so on. Schaeffer could see the validity of many of the criticisms, but he believed that it was important to get his message across to as many people as possible.

Many of the showings have been accompanied by seminars, attended either by Schaeffer himself or by close associates. In them the issues raised briefly in the films could be discussed in greater depth by all present.

The abortion debate

The Schaeffers embarked on a major U.S. tour, speaking in over eighteen cities where the films were being shown. The films were also seen in hundreds of other cities. Francis Schaeffer also spoke to the Biblical Inerrancy Council meeting in Chicago. As he wrote to one of his family, Evangelicals in the United States were "not making a clear line between those who hold the historic view of the

Bible being without error in all that it teaches, and those who are holding the neo-orthodox view in the name of Evangelicalism." He feared that, in order to keep the peace, Evangelicals might compromise—and, by losing the doctrine of Scripture, cease to be evangelical at all. Christians were "in danger of having the ground cut from under them."

Schaeffer then invited Dr. C. Everett Koop, a renowned surgeon, to L'Abri. Koop's talk in Huemoz convinced first Franky and then Schaeffer himself that another series ought to be made, this time on the issue of human life and the attacks that secular humanism was making on its sanctity—especially its promotion of abortion, euthanasia, and maybe even infanticide.

As always, Schaeffer did not deal just with the issues themselves, but with the basic humanist, materialist philosophy behind them. He showed that they were part of a process by which humanism was corroding the basic Christian structure and value system of Western society. Much of the new film series was taken up in expounding purely biblical material (Schaeffer called chapter five of the accompanying book the clearest exposition of the gospel that he had ever made). Those films, entitled, "Whatever Happened to the Human Race?" were also accompanied by seminars, often led by Schaeffer and Koop, one dealing with the basic moral side, the other with the medical.

During the filming of one of the scenes in Israel, Schaeffer felt ill. He returned to Switzerland, and Edith contacted the Mayo Clinic in Rochester, Minnesota. After the filming was finished (autumn 1978) he went there for a checkup. On October 12 he was told he had malignant cancer of the lymph system. Major treatment was necessary, and he underwent chemotherapy.

By May, 1979 the lymphoma seemed to have vanished, and he launched into a new series of seminars. The aim of these seminars was not just to alert Christians to the attack on human life that was spreading in the West, but actually to coordinate action to do something about it. In February, 1980 the cancer returned, as well as water on the lungs, and the lengthy treatment process had to begin all over again.

Despite illness he battled on. He now had a hearing in high places. In Washington, D.C., his seminars were attended by members of Congress and the White House staff. A major L'Abri conference was held in Rochester, Minnesota, with almost two thousand people from all over the United States and other countries.

The debate over abortion began to raise more fundamental issues in his mind. He remembered how Nazi Germany had disregarded the sanctity of life and had developed a system in which arbitrary or purely functional "sociological law" had taken over. He feared lest the same system should start creeping into the United States through the increasing humanist control of medical, educational, legal, and news media establishments there.

A Christian manifesto

Schaeffer's interest in politics was not a new one. But when making "Whatever Happened to the Human Race?" and "How Shall We Then Live?" he found himself thinking about the political implications of his Christian worldview in a deeper way. All his books had centered around the theme that Jesus Christ is the Lord of the whole of life. He had dealt with the implications of that in philosophy, art, music, and so on. But now he saw that Christians ought to start asking the question, "If our country and culture are increasingly dominated by humanist values, what should be the Christian's attitude toward government?" That led him to write *The Christian Manifesto*.

He noted that the great Scottish thinker of the seventeenth century, Samuel Rutherford, had, in his work *Lex Rex*, propounded the view that the law was above rulers, who had no right to ignore its basic principles. Christian commentators of the seventeenth and eighteenth centuries had pointed out that the Bible clearly taught moral absolutes. That climate of thought had a decisive influence on political leaders of the day, in particular those who drew up the American Constitution. If not Christians themselves, they were imbued with biblical thinking and principles. The United States therefore had a Christian heritage based firmly on Reformation values.

In the last forty years, however, America had lost that Christian underpinning through the rising power of humanism, with its base in a godless universe founded on materialism and biological chance. The question was, what should Christians do about it? They had failed to act for too many years, and the rot had now gone a long way through society.

Schaeffer's controversial response was that Christians should, if necessary, engage in civil disobedience, say, for example, on the abortion issue.

> The bottom line is that at a certain point there is not only a right but a duty to disobey the state . . . In almost every place where the Reformation had success there was some form of disobedience or armed rebellion. [Citizens had a] moral obligation to resist unjust and tyrannical government.

Today, he continued, "the whole structure of our society is being attacked and destroyed." The silent majority, asleep in their "personal peace and affluence," failed to see that an "exclusivist, closed system" was taking over. The reality of the situation was that "one either confesses that God is the final authority or one confesses that Caesar is Lord."

Schaeffer was careful to emphasize that Christians should be guarded in their actions: talk of civil disobedience was scary; there were plenty of kooks around. But "if there is no final place for civil disobedience, then the government has been made autonomous, and, as such, it has been put in the place of the living God."

Christians should, however, not act against things without clearly showing an alternative. Schaeffer emphasized that he was not trying to set up a theocracy (Christians "should not wrap Christianity in our national flag"). He was advocating truth, not a spiritualized all-American patriotic program. What he wanted was a return to the openly Christian ethos on which America was founded. Only its firm belief in moral absolutes could provide *true* freedom. In this America there would be "freedom for all religion" (not just for secular humanism). "Reformation Christianity could compete," uncensored by the humanist media, "in the free marketplace of ideas."

Many Christians, who had supported Schaeffer for many years and warmly backed his causes, now found themselves sorrowfully disagreeing with him for the first time. There were two reasons for this. First, there were those, mainly in the United States, who disagreed with Schaeffer's interpretation of history. *A Christian Manifesto* was published in early 1982. In November, a *Newsweek* article attacked it, describing him as the "Guru of Fundamentalism."

The onslaught from humanists was predictable, although the magazine piece was in a way a tribute: He was now seen as an enemy to be reckoned with. Professor Mark Noll believed that the book had not interpreted American history accurately, and because of that, was damaging the cause in which both Schaeffer and Noll believed. Schaeffer replied that Noll and others, by casting doubt on America's Christian origins, were playing into the hands of the humanists who wanted to claim a secular foundation for American values in order to justify the humanist state they were now establishing. In doing this, "the difference between the past and the present was obliterated, and students especially were harmed in not seeing the change which had taken place."

The debate then became semi-public. Correspondence was shared with friends and then with the evangelical press. Much of the discussion was conducted by historians—for example, they discussed the extent to which John Witherspoon (1723-94) was an Evangelical, and, if he was, the degree to which his Christian commitment affected his political thinking. Some, like George Marsden of Calvin College, a Schaeffer supporter since the sixties, felt that Schaeffer was not applying as vigorous a test of orthodoxy to the Founding Fathers as he had done with other thinkers he had examined over the years. The danger in "designating large sections of the American heritage as more-or-less Christian" was that it "helped lower the guard of Christians in distinguishing what is truly biblical from what is merely part of their cultural heritage."

What disturbed Noll was that Schaeffer was "compromising his message . . . that only in Christ and only through a biblical world-and life-view can we truly glorify God in all areas of life." Noll was "especially distressed when an erroneous reading of history takes the place of solid biblical insight in the promotion of political action in the present." He felt that Schaeffer's "impact for the cause of Christ in the twentieth century has been very great" and that he had done "Evangelicals the world of good over the course of his career." He was "particularly impressed with Dr. Schaeffer's willingness to struggle with the major ideas of history" and "of contemporary culture, and with the imperative themes of Scripture." But if Schaeffer built his case on a false historical base, his more important message for today's America could be lost.

The *Presbyterian Journal*, which discussed the correspondence, consulted Professor C. Gregg Singer of Atlanta, a leading church historian. Singer supported Schaeffer's interpretation. On the Founding Fathers, Singer commented: "Although no one has the right to judge these men as to their salvation, there can be no legitimate doubt that they were religiously literate and that the Scriptures made a deep impression on their thinking even if we do not see precise biblical quotations in the political documents they produced." Singer concluded that Schaeffer's basic approach was "firmly based on the most biblical theology available . . . Schaeffer speaks with great force and insight on behalf of the cultural mandate found in our heritage of covenant theology."

Schaeffer's words apply to Christians living in any democracy:

This is our moment of history and our responsibility: not just to write and talk of far-off ideals, but to struggle for scriptural and practical means of what can be done in a fallen world to see people personally converted *and also* [Schaeffer's italics] to see what our salt and light can bring forth in the personal life and the political and cultural life of this moment in history.

To obey or not to obey

Many of those who agreed with Schaeffer over the years fully supported his plea for Christians to be involved in the world in which they live, including the political sphere. But they found themselves disagreeing with him over exactly what the "practical means" should be, and in particular whether civil disobedience is ever justified.

What is appropriate, Schaeffer felt, depends on the circumstances in each place and time. "What would be extreme in one place might not be in another," but Christians should be very careful to guard against what "crazy people" might do. Because civil disobedience can be misused, just as anything in the fallen world can be twisted, it does not mean that Christians should not engage in it. "It is more important to stand by the principle, and then resist the wrong use of it, than to fail to teach, and live, the principle." That failure characterizes most of the church now—not wanting to rock the boat.

Christians should both evangelize the spiritually lost and teach people to live according to biblical teaching, partly for their "individual salvation, but also [because] there can be no solid base for a lasting change in society without a changed ethos which would come from such a base." But Christians cannot wait for such an ideal change to occur. "We are too far down the road" and "must act now and do what can be done now." There should be no tension between evangelism and social action, "between doing both . . . while at the same time not confusing the one with the other."

Debate on this issue continues, and more can be said on both sides. Yet all can agree that it is the Christian's duty to be salt and light in the world, as Jesus commanded.

A personal journey

I went to Swiss L'Abri in January, 1983. Getting off the train at Aigle, I found myself on the bus to Huemoz next to an American student also going there.

I spent most of my first day traveling around L'Abri, now a cluster of chalets spread around Huemoz. The students there were serious, mainly from the United States, although there was a sprinkling of Europeans, Canadians, and Australians. Australians are to the 1980s what young Americans were to the sixties—traveling around the world, staying in different countries often for months at a time, and thus are able to get maximum benefit out of a prolonged stay at L'Abri. The chalet system was now tightly structured; everyone was assigned to one in particular, but visited others for meals and study.

Most of the students were Christians, seeking how to reach young people in their own age group back home, or finding out to what vocation God was calling them. As one of the long-term staff, Ellis Potter (a crew-cut, knowledgeable, articulate ex-Buddhist monk) told me, one of his main jobs is to teach people how to think, so that then they can start to look for answers to their questions.

One of the students I met was Tom, an earnest young American living in Spain. An art history major, he was also a Taoist. Some of the discussions he was able to provoke, in a gentle way, during mealtimes in the different chalets, got many of the other students, not to mention some of the younger workers, tied up in glorious knots. He met his match in Ellis Potter, however. When Tom quoted a poem by Edgar Allan Poe which, he said, expressed much of his own view of life, Ellis quoted the rest of the poem and went on to show how Tom's view was untenable in general and also from the poetic context.

More typical of the students at L'Abri was Becky, a graduate student in physics. She had spent much of her youth in Europe, and was now taking a year's leave there before returning to her research work back home. She was spending some months in L'Abri to think through the relationship between her Christian faith and scientific studies before going on to university in Paris, where she would be helping with an IFES outreach team for overseas students. Her stay in Switzerland was giving her the time that she had lacked in college to think about these matters. Like others at L'Abri, she was in the library every day with headphones, a notebook on the desk, and pencil in hand; she studied in the morning and discussed over meals with her fellow students the issues that had been raised in her mind.

One of the meals to which she and I were invited was at the chalet of John and Priscilla Sandri (Priscilla was naturally interested to meet the grandson of the man who had conducted their wedding service). By now snow had fallen (how no one broke their legs with all the ice I shall never know) and the view of the surrounding mountains was breathtaking. The Schaeffers' youngest daughter Debby lived with her husband Udo just up the valley in Chesieres, where, according to one exhausted student I met, they made everyone in their chalet study and work twice as hard as the others down in Huemoz.

The news came that Schaeffer was ready to see me, so early one morning I braved the heavy snowfall and trudged the thickly covered path from Villars to Chesieres (I was later shown the shortcut, which avoided the main road) to Chalet le Chardonnet, the Schaeffer family's private home. Francis Schaeffer was there to greet me, wearing the Swiss mountain knickers made famous in the films. He looked, as many who had been to L'Abri said he would, both serious and warmly welcoming.

At first, sitting in front of the log fire in the downstairs drawing room, we talked about my grandfather. We ended up spending almost all the daylight hours together as he reminisced about his past, the state of the world today and that of the church, as well as other more private matters. His mind was acute and, although he was evidently not so strong as the Schaeffer of the early days who led treks across the mountains, he would occasionally amble up to the fire, put on a few logs, stoke the embers, all the while discussing some matter of theology or an event from the past.

Throughout he was warm, friendly, and relaxed—serious, but with a sense of humor sneaking to the surface. It was the same a few days later for the famous Sunday lunch, an institution at L'Abri. Students and guests were given a lift up from Huemoz after the Sunday morning sermon (preached by Ellis Potter) to Chesieres. The long table was laid immaculately by Edith Schaeffer, who had also prepared the meal. Schaeffer sat like a paterfamilias at the head of the table, with the students and guests listening to what he had to say.

The food was excellent. The conversation varied immensely, from *The Tao of Physics* to the story of Isaac and Abraham on Mount Moriah. That biblical account had become a major issue for some students, especially after seeing it raised in one of the films. Down in Huemoz everyone involved in the debate had gotten tangled up in existential knots, unsure of why God would ask Abraham to sacrifice Isaac. At lunch the students asked Schaeffer what he thought. Well, he replied, it was all very simple—the story of Abraham and Isaac was a marvelous foreshadowing of the death of Christ for our sins.

Kierkegaard cropped up eventually in the discussion, of course. Questions on *The Tao of Physics,* raised by a young American scientist, revealed how much reading Schaeffer had done on that subject. But the earlier incident also revealed the extent to which the caricatures of Schaeffer were untrue. It showed that if the question had a simple, biblical answer, then that was the reply Schaeffer gave. If, as the *Tao of Physics* discussion made clear, the issue was complex, with a lot of preliminary groundwork needed before bringing in the gospel, then Schaeffer would give a longer answer, using the kind of language he employs in his books. It illustrated the truth mentioned to me by Joe Martin and Os Guinness: Schaeffer always took people where they were, talking to them in a way that met their individual needs.

L'Abri legend proved true—lunch continued until 5:30 P.M. The students returned to Huemoz while I stayed on to conclude my interview. The study at the top of the chalet contained not only books but magazines, some piled neatly on the floor, as well as some of Franky Schaeffer's better-known drawings. We also spent some time talking in the Schaeffers' personal room, with Francis Schaeffer under a warm afghan on the sofa, discussing world politics and the lack of understanding of many Evangelicals about the threat of totalitarianism to our society.

The time came to leave, and he bade me goodbye warmly. Eleven months later, he again became seriously ill—and left Chalet le Chardonnet to live permanently in Rochester, Minnesota, near the Mayo Clinic. My visit thus was more special than I could have known.

After an unexpected recovery from that illness in January, 1984, Schaeffer embarked on a mammoth tour in connection with his latest book, *The Great Evangelical Disaster,* and Franky Schaeffer's film of the same name. When he returned to Rochester, his cancer was worse than before, and after a few weeks he left the clinic for his new Rochester home. He lived there, cared for by his family, who had come over to join him. His frequent words to them were "His grace is sufficient." Francis Schaeffer died, with his family near by, on May 15, 1984. Hundreds attended his funeral in Rochester, Minnesota.

A prophet in space and time

In an age when secular thought seemed to dominate society, Francis Schaeffer fought back. He showed that the Bible has the answers in the twentieth century. When many Evangelicals cowered in the trenches, he moved out to battle in the front line. Others could see only the symptoms of what had gone wrong; they were frightened by what was happening around them. Schaeffer, by contrast, was able to grasp the *causes* of the twentieth-century climate and diagnose its illness.

Beyond that, he provided a framework by which to assess and respond to secular culture, in fields as diverse as art, ecology, theology, and particle physics. Many Christians came closer to God's truth at L'Abri and then committed their lives to its reality and service. The Schaeffers did not just believe in truth as a cause to be fought for. They demonstrated it as something to be lived for as well. Francis Schaeffer was a faithful prophet in our "space and time."

JAMES PACKER

1926–

James Packer

J ames Innell Packer, the theologian, was born in Gloucester in 1926, the son of James Percy Packer, a clerk with the Great Western Railway, and his wife, Dorothy Mary Packer, a schoolteacher. He was an introvert, a bookish, clever child who preferred reading and study to being sociable with other children. His family was originally from Oxfordshire and later moved to the western part of England—his voice today still has the distinctive "West Country burr" for which the region is famous. His grandfather was the keeper of the "New Red Lion," in Chalford, in the Stroud Valley, and his great-grandfather had been an Oxfordshire gentleman farmer who lost all his stock in a terrible cattle epidemic. (The West Country is mainly rural and noted for its picturesque scenery.)

He was brought up in an Anglican home, but as he told me once, "we didn't talk about Christianity." He was not forced to go to Sunday school but attended church with his parents. He was stirred to interest in Christianity by the son of a Unitarian minister with whom he played chess. Although at fifteen he rejected Unitarianism, he nonetheless found himself thinking more deeply. He recalled to me that he "never doubted the reality of God." He read the Bible and other religious works in the local library and defended the historic creeds in debates with atheists at school.

When he was seventeen, he read two of C. S. Lewis's famous

books, *The Screwtape Letters* and *Mere Christianity.* But Christianity remained for him a set of ideas; he had, as he told me, "no personal relationship with God at all." An old schoolfriend became a Christian while at Bristol University (young Packer was still at school, studying to enter Oxford), and though he tried to explain what had happened to him, Packer was in "complete perplexity" over his friend's experience. He did, however, promise to contact the Christian Union when he got to Oxford. In 1944 he entered Corpus Christi College in Oxford.

Conversion and Oxford

"By the time I went up" to Corpus Christi College, he recalled to me, "I wanted reality." He studied Latin and Greek, switching some time later to theology. During his first term he played in a jazz band, the "Oxford Bandits," as their clarinetist. He was a great jazz enthusiast and found making music a very emotionally rewarding experience. He enjoyed King Oliver and Louis Armstrong, Morton, Bechet, and "Bunk" Johnson. Now, as then, he feels that the New Orleans jazz of the 1920s was the most valuable cultural product to emerge from North America in the twentieth century (a view also held by Francis Schaeffer's close friend and collaborator, the art historian Hans Rookmaaker, with whom, in later years, Packer would discuss this common musical interest). Oxford contemporaries felt that being a jazz soloist was more in keeping with his introvert personality than if he had been a violinist in an orchestra, but Packer, like Rookmaaker, especially enjoyed the "fellowship music" of jazz— the "group experience."

Packer did not just play music and work hard in the libraries, however. Keeping his promise to contact the Christians in the university, he attended evangelistic services run by the Oxford Inter-Collegiate Christian Union (OICCU). There, as he recalled for me years later, while listening to a sermon preached by a relatively unknown preacher, Rev. Earl Langston of Weymouth, "the scales fell from my eyes . . . and I saw the way in." It was, he remembers, "an ordinary conversion," nothing spectacular, but it made him realize where he wasn't and where he ought to be.

He gave up playing in the jazz band. He felt that he was not playing well enough. But his new Christian faith also made a difference. He was now "identifying heavily with the OICCU," who met for Bible lectures every Saturday night. This clashed with the band which played at the same time. Lastly, he decided, on the principle of 1 Corinthians 6:12, that while it would be quite lawful as a Christian for him to continue as a jazz musician, it would not be expedient, as he had been very emotionally attached to it. Now his priorities had changed.

He was helped to grow in the faith by C. J. B. Harrison (known to many generations of students as Harry Bean) of the Honor Oak Fellowship, and by his college's OICCU representative, Ralph Hulme. Hulme attended St. Aldate's, a church that was at that time regarded as less reliable than St. Ebbe's, which was not only far more narrowly Evangelical, but also the place where most members of the OICCU worshipped on Sundays. So although Packer was heavily involved in OICCU, his decision to follow Hulme to St. Aldate's on Sundays meant that he was thought of as being "unsound." Consequently, when James Houston (later to be founder of Regent College in Vancouver where Packer is now a professor) proposed him for election to the OICCU executive board, he was rejected as "unreliable," which seems astonishing to us today.

Discovering the Puritans

He had, however, earned a good academic reputation. When Rev. C. O. Pickard-Cambridge, an elderly clergyman who was going blind, gave a large number of theological volumes to the OICCU, Packer was appointed their junior librarian as he was known "to be interested in books." Among them was an uncut set of the writings of John Owen, the great Puritan of the seventeenth century. It included treatises on "indwelling sin," which spoke directly to Packer's needs. This was to be a turning point in his life, one which was to influence the whole of his future, and it was fascinating to hear his account of it as we met one afternoon in the vestry of Dick Lucas's old church in the heart of London.

There was much false teaching in Oxford at the time, including some in the OICCU, which implied that even those who were converted needed a further experience—"sanctification by faith"—after which all struggles with sin would be over. The young Packer knew this to be untrue, both to life and to his own Christian experience. But he was at the time a "very isolated person," and all this wrong doctrine had made him "very anxious." He felt the odd man out. Later he concluded that the followers of these teachings were either very insensitive or, more to the point, "very good at kidding themselves" that they could obey all of God's laws.

Owen, however, he told me, did him good, and in reading Bishop Ryle's great book on holiness he discovered that Ryle based much of his teaching on the Puritans. Their insight into the human heart, he found, was unrivaled and gave him a deepened spiritual interest.

Other students had discovered that the Puritans gave them the kind of solid, biblically-based doctrine for which they were seeking. They included Raymond Johnston (later to be director of CARE Trust), Bernard Gee, and Elizabeth Lloyd-Jones, Dr. Martyn Lloyd-Jones's eldest daughter (my mother). They would meet regularly in the "British Restaurant" to discuss their findings and debate theological issues. They have kept in touch ever since.

The call to the ministry

Packer began to sense that God was calling him to full-time Christian ministry and to a teaching role within that ministry. The idea crystalized over a three-month period, and, as he recalled to me, on "one long Sunday afternoon with the Lord" he decided to enter the ministry. His remaining hesitations were whether, being an introvert, he would be able to engage in pastoral work, but his reading of the Puritans encouraged him in his resolve.

Then, just before he graduated in 1948, an offer came in what he has described to me as "the good providence of God," from the

Anglican theological seminary at Oak Hill, near London. They wanted a classical languages teacher for their intermediate students, as well as someone to teach Greek. Packer had originally intended to go straight to Wycliffe Hall in Oxford to start training in preparation for ordination in the Anglican ministry. But he had begun to feel Oxford getting under his skin and feared that Wycliffe would seem like an airless room were he to go there immediately.

Oak Hill, he knew, would be different, especially as he discovered that he would have to teach some philosophy as well. It was a great year for him. He taught Ephesians to those reading for the General Ordination Examination and all of his students graduated. "I found," he told me, that, "I loved teaching . . . teaching was in my genes . . . nobody ever taught me to teach." At Oak Hill he drew close to Alan Stibbs, a fine Bible teacher and a leading Anglican Evangelical.

After a happy and productive year near London, he returned to Oxford, to Wycliffe. The influences that were to shape his thinking were slowly forming in his mind. First there was the pietistic, evangelistic thrust of OICCU, which emphasized outreach and personal holiness. Then there was the practical, pastoral impact of reading the Puritans, such as Baxter and Owen. (This linked Packer to Free Church circles, including that of Martyn Lloyd-Jones.) Third, there was what he has described to me as the "Protestant evangelical traditional heritage in the Church of England," which he received from St. Ebbe's (where he now went regularly) and from John Reynolds, the OICCU senior librarian.

This heritage, Packer felt, had two strands in it. First, there was the "National Protestant" strand—one which was decisively anti-Roman Catholic and anti-Tractarian (the Tractarians were a faction that tried to restore ritual in the last century). They were pro-1662 Prayer Book and in favor of maintaining the distinctively Protestant worship traditions which that book contained. Packer, however, felt that this group sometimes forgot that the real distinctiveness of the Anglican church lay in its defined doctrines, not in its ceremonies and forms of worship.

The other strand was the "pietistic Evangelical," with its origins in the eighteenth century revival. Such Anglicans concentrated on winning converts and placing them in fellowship groups, but, as he explained to me, "sat loose to Protestant niceties under pressure" if the emphasis of distinctives got in the way of evangelism. Because doctrine was underplayed, many pietists later evolved into theological liberals. They wished to keep the experience, but jettisoned the doctrine on which it was based.

Unfortunately, these two strands of Protestantism and evangelism often failed to intertwine, with the result that churches that were zealously Protestant did not evangelize, and the evangelizing churches neglected Reformed doctrine.

Packer noticed that in the writings of Bishop Ryle, the two strands—Protestant and pietist—*had* interwoven. Ryle's books influenced him enormously and provided him with an Anglican evangelical framework of doctrine, pastoral care, and evangelism upon which to base his own thinking to the present. Because Ryle and the Puritans were Calvinists, Packer also inclined that way. But, as he told me, he preferred to call himself a "Bible Calvinist rather than a system Calvinist." After reading Hebrews several times, he turned to Romans, and it was his study of that great epistle that made him a Calvinist. As another distinguished Anglican of the same age, Dick Lucas, has pointed out, all the problems that people had on this issue were ridiculous—the Bible was clear and simple on that point. Packer also realized at Wycliffe that God was going to make teaching at tertiary level a great part of his career.

Another profound influence was Dr. Martyn Lloyd-Jones, then, in Packer's view, "on a plateau of supreme excellence" that was to continue throughout the 1950s. Packer heard him preach every Sunday evening at Westminster Chapel during 1948–49. He told me once that he had "never heard such preaching, which came to him with the force and surprise of electric shock, bringing to at least one of his listeners more of a sense of God than any other man" he had known. Packer learned through him about "the greatness of God and the greatness of the soul." Dr. Lloyd-Jones's sermons on Matthew 11 helped him understand what preaching was really all about.

Listening to Martyn Lloyd-Jones, he remembers, was like hearing a whole orchestra perform after a single piano.

New horizons

The year 1952 was to be a major one in his life. The first important event was meeting his future wife, Kit, at a conference on the picturesque North Downs in Surrey England. The main speaker had double-booked by mistake. Unable to come, he felt obliged to find a substitute, so he asked the already up-and-coming Packer if he would fill in for him.

Kit was a nurse at St. Bartholemew's Hospital in London—the same hospital where Martyn Lloyd-Jones had trained and where Sir Arnold Stott had been a physician. She was from Llandabie, Dyfed, in South Wales. The two of them were married in 1954, the same year as his Oxford contemporary Elizabeth Lloyd-Jones married Fred Catherwood. The Packers have three adopted children: Ruth, who is married and living in Bristol; Naomi, who is finishing a theology degree at Durham, the famous old University in northern England; and Martin, who is at school in Canada. James Packer comes over at least every second year to see family members, including his sister, who lives in Reading, not far from Oxford, and old friends, including members of the Lloyd-Jones family. He is also constantly meeting new friends from the generation who has been influenced by his many published works—which will be considered later.

He was also ordained in 1952 and became curate to the late William Leathem in Birmingham. In many ways he felt closer to those holding his own Reformed views who were outside the Church of England, in the Free churches. He was actively involved from the beginning with Dr. Lloyd-Jones in the Westminster Conference for the Study of Puritanism and was soon associated with the revival of Reformed theology which Lloyd-Jones pioneered in Britain.

But Packer remained an Anglican because of that church's evangelical heritage and stayed with it in order to work from within for true reformation and renewal. He has never regretted that decision. To him, all Evangelicals, whether Anglican or Free Church, were "concerned about godliness." Apart from his views on ritual, which he now thinks is not as important an issue as he did then, he has observed of his thought in general that "I had it in my mind by 1952, and it's there still."

To some, especially those in the Free churches who deeply admired his exposition of Reformed theology, his arguments for not remaining an Anglican seemed like special pleading. (For many people this may not be an issue; it is important here because it remained a major issue in Packer's life until he came to Canada.) Certainly, he is by temperament more of a Free Church Calvinist than an Anglican one, and his decision may be viewed as a strange one. On the other hand, he does represent the best-argued case for Evangelicals to stay and fight within a doctrinally-mixed denomination such as the Church of England. Whatever the merits of the case (which applies to many other denominations in Britain and the United States that were originally Evangelical in foundation), and whatever loss has been suffered by the Free churches in Britain, it is a valid option and will be examined in more detail later on.

Packer had always recognized that the parochial side of his ministry was not his primary calling, and in 1955 he followed what he told me was his true vocation—teaching. He started as a lecturer (assistant professor in U. S. terminology) at Tyndale Hall in Bristol.

As a clear speaker on theology, he was soon in demand as a conference speaker, including InterVarsity conferences. At the Theological Students Fellowship Conferences, where he often took over for Martyn Lloyd-Jones, he was able to influence generations of future church leaders and teachers. Robert Horn, now editor of the *Evangelical Times* in Britain, has explained the reason for this.

Until the 1950s, Horn told me, Evangelicals were wary of theology (this has been seen in the chapters on Martyn Lloyd-Jones and on John Stott, both of whom helped to change this attitude). This was partly because so many young evangelical students seemed to lose hold of their distinctive beliefs when they studied theology at a university or seminary. Consequently, Evangelicals had felt it necessary to withdraw into a pietistic, protected, nonintellectual world of their own, and the major issues raised by liberal theologians had been dealt with only in a piecemeal fashion by the small number of evangelical scholars then writing and teaching.

Martyn Lloyd-Jones did much to dispel this evangelical inferiority complex, and Packer complemented him by inspiring younger theologians and ordination candidates with a new sense of intellectual integrity and confidence in the face of liberal theology. That one could be fully Evangelical, hold a conservative view of Scripture, and remain intellectually defensible all at the same time came, as Horn pointed out to me, as "an absolute revelation to a lot of people," who listened to Packer's carefully-prepared overall exposé of liberalism. He presented an integrated, systematic defense of evangelical, biblical truth, which, until then, students had had to ferret out for themselves from many different sources in order to form their own cohesive system of belief.

Evangelicalism and the Word of God

The book that established his reputation, and which, as his old Oxford contemporary Raymond Johnston once told me, has been the key to his high standing in evangelical circles, was *Fundamentalism and the Word of God*, published in 1958. The word "Fundamentalism" has been taken to mean different things on opposite sides of the Atlantic; consequently, Packer's own definition of the term at the time is important. By Fundamentalism he meant evangelical obscurantism—a theme he enlarged on in the book's first two chapters. In the words of an eminent former Oxford theologian, Fundamentalism was seen in those days as a coarsened mutation of the kind of Calvinism embraced by Packer and other Reformed thinkers. Though representing one version of it, it was by no means the whole story.

It could be claimed that the theme of the book is really "Evangelicalism and the Word of God," as it is in essence a defense of the *evangelical* position against attacks from liberals. The Billy

Graham crusades of 1954-55 had aroused within the population a new awareness of Evangelicals, as had the rapid growth of Christian unions in the universities. The resulting panic and sense of hostility that emerged from the ranks of the now-threatened ecclesiastical establishment and its allies within the church tarred all Evangelicals with the brush of obscurantist, anti-intellectual American Fundamentalism (in the sense of the word as defined above).

The Evangelicals' sharpest critic was Michael Ramsey, a former Cambridge professor, at that time bishop of Durham, and later to be archbishop of Canterbury and spiritual leader of the Church of England. He wrote an article entitled, "Our English Fundamentalism," which contested the holding of a John Stott mission at Durham University. Other attacks on IVF followed, attempting to show that evangelical doctrine was a new phenomenon, a reaction against modern biblical scholarship and scientific discoveries. Packer, invited initially by the IVF graduates' fellowship to give a talk rebutting this kind of reaction, realized that a larger reply was needed; the book *Fundamentalism* was the result.

The book did not merely show what Packer believed to be the folly of the liberal position. It also demonstrated to Evangelicals that their faith was intellectually tenable. Indeed it was this aspect of Evangelicalism that differentiated it from the anti-intellectual Fundamentalists and showed up the liberal portrait of Evangelicals as a ludicrous caricature. Packer aimed to make a constructive restatement of evangelical principles in the light of the controversy and to "fix the right approach to the Bible, to the intellectual tasks of the faith, and to the present debate."

He showed that Evangelicalism, unlike ecumenical liberalism, was not a "loosely linked collection of isolated insights" but a "systematic and integrated whole, based on a single foundation." The real split between liberals and Evangelicals was on the "principle of authority," a point which the liberals had totally missed or ignored. "Authentic Christianity is a religion of biblical authority," explained Packer. Where Roman Catholicism had placed tradition above such authority, liberalism had placed fallible human reason. He saw both as perversions of the truth.

For Packer, Evangelicalism was "in principle nothing but Christianity itself." Fundamentalism, as it had now developed, had forgotten this, and in its fear of the human intellect had lost Evangelicalism's intellectual virility. "All truth is God's truth," he stated, "and right reason cannot endanger sound faith . . . A confident intellectualism, expressive of robust faith in God, whose Word is truth, is part of the historical evangelical tradition." He advised Evangelicals to reject the fundamentalist label and simply call themselves Christians.

The liberals, in failing to recognize authority as the key issue, simply did not know what they were talking about. Authority was important because "Christianity is based on truth . . . on the content of a divine revelation" revealed to us by God's Word—Scripture. Evangelicals held the "original Christian position": that Scripture was both complete and comprehensible and that it was all one piece; Old and New Testaments must be taken together. One implication of this authority was that "the Bible itself must fix and control the methods and presuppositions with which it is studied." The liberal position was totally subjective, based entirely on human reason and analysis. (This debate foreshadowed the later inerrancy discussion in which Packer has become an especially well-known participant in the United States in recent years.)

In Packer's assessment, the liberals also failed to see that the Bible was simultaneously "a fully human and a fully divine composition." The Scriptures were the "oracles of God," not merely a random series of books containing trace elements of the truth. The Bible was propositional truth from God that was infallible—and, to use the word that later became a key to the whole issue—inerrant. For Packer, it was the "infallibility of God speaking." Christ himself believed this, he said, and such a view was far more edifying to the church than was the liberal position.

Further, the liberal claim that Evangelicals were obscurantist and irrational was false; rather, it was the liberals who were refusing to face the facts by rejecting Christian reason. Christ told an enquirer in Matthew that he should "love the Lord thy God with all thy *mind.*" True Christians should be guided, Packer felt, by "reasoning faith." It was "reasonable" to believe and receive the teaching of

God. Proper reason, whether scientific or otherwise, was to "appreciate objects for what they are" and to analyze Scripture as being something other than it really was would therefore be unbelief.

Another function of reason in Packer's view was to apply the teaching of God to life, a theme also stressed by Martyn Lloyd-Jones and Francis Schaeffer. Packer reminded his readers that God "forbade Christians to lose interest in his world." Reason was also used in communicating the gospel to others. It was not therefore a clash between faith and reason that was being waged, as many well-meaning Christians wrongly supposed, but a battle between "a faithful and a faithless use of reason," between authority and subjectivism.

The mind of liberalism had been permeated by contemporary secular thought which had resulted in a warped view of Scripture. This was true even of the "New Liberalism," which recognized Christ and the reality of the supernatural, but, unwilling to accept the logic of its position and become Evangelical, was still stuck in the rut of the old methodology and its subjectivism. True Christians recognized that they know God and his truth only through his testimony to himself—the Word of God in Scripture. (Packer would probably say today that while his understanding of some of the issues—such as rationalism versus rationality in theology—is deeper now than it was then, his view of the whole subject has not changed substantively.)

Controversialist for the gospel

Many of the views which Packer espoused in *Fundamentalism* might strike us as commonplace today, but this only shows the vast influence he and some of his contemporaries brought to bear on the Christian mindset. For the fifties generation, still suffering from a siege mentality, the book came, as Robert Horn reminded me, as a tremendous shot in the arm. It brought a "distinct feeling of lifting up drooping heads," for Packer had not only taken on the enemy, but had done so in a way which gave Evangelicals a "whole rounded view of Scripture," expressing what young evangelical theology students knew they believed, but in a sound, doctrinal, and systematic way.

The book, Robert Horn told me, combined with Packer's lectures at conferences, changed the mood of a whole generation of students, and, through the prominence and influence they later achieved as church leaders and seminary teachers, altered the way that Evangelicals think today. (There were many candidates for the ministry at that time, thanks to the numbers converted in the Billy Graham crusades.) People learned that they could trust Scripture and had no need to fear reason. Packer had made doctrine exciting, contrary to the popular view that it was a boring subject best avoided. The truths that Packer made clear in the 1950s are as relevant today as ever.

He was an effective lecturer at Tyndale Hall too. Dick France (R. T. France), later a New Testament scholar and writer, commented to me on his lectures, "We really felt that we were getting the goods." Packer taught historical theology, and students discovered that if they took notes rapidly enough, they could obtain a crystal clear, lucid outline of theology that made much further reading redundant. He would walk into the classroom, look across it, and start at once. In discussion, he could be ruthless with those who wandered from the point and showed great skill in his handling of difficult questions.

Because he is an introvert, Packer was not felt to be at his strongest on the pastoral side of college life, one of his former pupils told me. He was not always an easy conversationalist over meals—he had little use for small talk—and he never publicly played his jazz clarinet during that student's time at Tyndale. But he had, like Martyn Lloyd-Jones, a phenomenal memory for names and faces.

He was also popular as a speaker at Christian student meetings. Dick France described to me a visit he made to OICCU. As expected, on Saturday night he gave a solid Bible lecture, but then on Sunday, he delivered a powerful gospel message that was "attractive and not at all egg-headed," which, given his cerebral reputation, was not what many expected. In all his talks, Packer taught people to think for themselves—perhaps one of his most important contributions.

Evangelism and God's sovereignty

In 1960 a London university mission nearly collapsed, and Packer was sent in to rescue it. "Missioning," he recalled to me, was "not really my thing," but the talks that he gave on the subject to the students produced a remarkable book: *Evangelism and the Sovereignty of God*. Under the influence of Martyn Lloyd-Jones and the Banner of Truth publishing house, Reformed theology had once again become popular, especially among students. To such readers the book was a godsend. It was extremely useful, Dick France recalled to me, and gave Packer prominence as a champion of "Reformed Evangelicalism."

The book clearly demonstrated that the Calvinists' belief in divine sovereignty regarding salvation did not prevent them from being truly committed to a evangelism, and that, by contrast, it was precisely because they believed in it that they could evangelize most effectively. Packer wrote that his aim was "to dispel the suspicion . . . that faith in the absolute sovereignty of God hinders full recognition and acceptance of human responsibility, and to show that, on the contrary, only this faith can give Christians what they need to fulfill their evangelistic task." He showed that it was nonsense to believe anything else. Since everybody believes in God's sovereignty when they pray, it clearly was "not true that some Christians believed in divine sovereignty while others hold an opposite view. What is true is that all Christians believe in [it] but some are not aware that they do, and mistakenly imagine and insist that they reject it."

The reason for this "error" was "rationalistic speculations . . . a reluctance to recognize the existence of mystery and to let God be wiser than men, and a consequent subjecting of Scripture to the supposed demands of human logic." Such human logic was not content to let the two truths of divine sovereignty and human responsibility "live side by side by side, as they do in the Scriptures." Packer demonstrated that much of the problem was the modern failure to see that the proclamation of the message, not its effect, constituted true, biblical evangelism, a case he clearly made from the career and writings of the apostle Paul.

Sadly, Packer reflected to me, Christians still mistakenly insist on defining evangelism institutionally or organizationally. He has occasionally called for a stop to all big meetings and jamborees so that the local evangelical churches can simply get on with their biblical task in their own areas, instead of relying on outsiders to come in and do it for them.

Part of the problem, Packer still believes, is that the Christian church has lost confidence in the power of the Holy Spirit to save, a confidence that characterized the early church. As he points out in his book, the "sovereignty of God in grace gives us our only hope of success in evangelism"—those who believe in it are therefore actually better evangelists, as they receive from it a "certainty that evangelism will be fruitful." As Paul wrote, man in sin is naturally dead so that humanly speaking, evangelism is a hopeless task. We can, Packer continues, "organize special services and distribute tracts, and put up posters, and flood the country with publicity—and there is not the slightest prospect that all this outlay will bring a single soul home to God."

Packer felt that many wrongly attributed the malaise in evangelism to Reformed teaching. He, however, diagnosed the real problem as a "widespread neurosis of disillusionment" arising from the failure to see that evangelism as a *human* activity must fail. Evangelicals had come to see it as a "specialized activity, best done in short, sharp bursts," and had fallen into the way of assuming that evangelism was sure to succeed if it was regularly prayed for and correctly run (i.e., if certain well-defined techniques were used). Churches presumed that intensive evangelistic mission backed up by a routine of prayers would do it, even though "well-planned evangelism" had not succeeded in the way that they had hoped.

As Packer put it, "Paul's confidence should be our confidence too . . . There is no magic in methods, even theologically impeccable methods. When we evangelize, our trust must be in God who raised the dead. He is the almighty Lord, who turns men's hearts, and he will give conversions in his own time. Meanwhile our part is to be faithful in making the gospel known, sure that such labor will never be in vain. This is how the sovereignty of God's grace bears upon evangelism."

It is easy to see why Dick France called this an extremely useful book. On the one hand, it showed people that belief in the sovereignty of God actually helped evangelism by giving confidence to those practicing it and by making them more committed. (As Packer reminded me once, Whitefield, the great eighteenth-century evangelist, with his Reformed views, preached no fewer than ten sermons a week on the average throughout his career.) The book was also important because it made clear to Reformed Christians that they were to get on with the task of evangelism with the application and urgency that Scripture commanded.

New battles

By this time, Packer was fighting new battles. *Evangelism* had made him one of the leading exemplars of the Reformed position in Britain, and he was still active, along with Martyn Lloyd-Jones, in the Westminster Conference for the Study of Puritanism. It was precisely his awareness of the Puritan tradition that led him to remain within the Church of England. He had written his doctoral thesis (he gained an Oxford D. Phil.) on the great seventeenth century Anglican Puritan, Richard Baxter. In order to defend Puritan doctrine from within, Baxter had remained in the Church of England even when others had left it. Baxter was then, as Packer is today, an exponent of the Westminster Confession of Faith, the famous Puritan basis of faith drawn up by a body that included the Anglican Puritans.

Roger Beckwith of Oxford told me that for Packer, Anglican Puritanism was genuine Evangelicalism. Packer saw himself in the Puritan tradition and thus argued that his position of staying within the Anglican fold was perfectly defensible from an evangelical point of view. And if to be an Anglican was right, it followed that the true, evangelical foundation of the Church of England had to be defended, especially since it was now under attack. (Its spiritual head, Archbishop Fisher, and others were seeking to undermine what Packer felt to be its essentially Protestant base by altering canon law, worship, and even the founding Thirty-nine Articles themselves.) To the delight of Anglican Evangelicals, but to the sorrow of some of his Free Church brothers who felt that he could be devoting his talents to wider issues, Packer decided to help organize the defense of the Anglican church's evangelical base.

John Wenham, a leading Anglican evangelical New Testament scholar and then vice principal of Tyndale Hall, was worried by the trends and approached Packer after a debate in Oxford in 1958. He proposed the founding of an institute in Oxford to continue the fight against theological liberalism. Soon, Packer and Beckwith recalled to me, a list of supporters was drawn up and the sum of £18,000 raised. The committee decided that rather than founding another theological research center on the lines of the already existing and successful Tyndale House in Cambridge (run interdenominationally by the IVF), the institute should be a specifically *Anglican* center, to help Evangelicals in their fight against liberalism within the Church of England. It was named Latimer House after the great reformer and martyr.

One of its aims, according to the present warden, Roger Beckwith, was to revive evangelical Anglican scholarship and thus provide back-up support for those in the front line. Originally, the staff was to consist of the eminent Anglican theologian Philip Edgcumbe Hughes, one of Martyn Lloyd-Jones's closest friends, and another Anglican, Richard Coates. But difficulties arose and, to the immense loss of British Evangelicalism generally, Hughes went to the United States where he taught with distinction at several seminaries, including Westminster Theological Seminary in Philadelphia. Coates therefore began the work alone. Then in 1961 Packer was persuaded to leave Tyndale in Bristol to join Latimer House as librarian. Coates later left, and Packer remained alone until Beckwith came over from Bristol to Oxford as his assistant in 1963.

One of their main tasks, in which they were successful, lay in preventing the unifying of the Church of England with the Methodists. While many Anglicans opposed the scheme because Methodists were not episcopally ordained, Packer and other Evangelicals were against it not only because the Church of England could not fully acknowledge Methodist orders as valid but because Methodism had become so permeated with theological liberalism that the defense of the clear, evangelical foundation of the Church of England would become even more complicated once the Methodists were included. In all the debates, Packer raised the doctrinal issue, making clear in the process that true unity was on the basis of faith, love, and common commitment to the gospel.

The Evangelicals found new allies in defeating the scheme. Packer and two other Evangelicals, Colin Buchanan and the well-known writer and evangelist Michael Green, worked closely with two Anglo-Catholics, Canon Mascall and Graham Leonard, now bishop of London and a leading member of the intellectual Right. From the common ground on which they found themselves standing, Packer, Buchanan, Mascall, and Leonard wrote a book entitled *Growing into Union*, published in 1970, outlining areas where they thought such growth was possible.

All four authors declared their concern "that unity should exhibit and retain diversity. If the body of Christ has many differing members, our church life should do justice to that. No doubt there are differences among members in which one is right and one is sinful. The nature of church life must promote the healthy living together of such members (with a view to a better mind prevailing). But there are also differences simply deriving from the fact that God by nature and by grace has given different gifts to his different children, and he desires his church to conserve and exploit the rich variety of abilities contained within it."

This view was natural to someone in a church as varied in its doctrinal emphases as the Church of England. But to many outside, in the Free churches, Packer had gone overboard in his search for ways to accommodate the Anglo-Catholics. He had conceded too much, they felt, on the issue of authority. To many Reformed men, the Anglo-Catholics were little different from their Roman Catholic brothers. Free Church Evangelicals had retained their links with Packer after the split of 1966 (outlined in earlier chapters), and even after the Anglican Evangelical Congress at Keele in 1967—when evangelical Anglicans met to try to work out their future in the Church of England—despite the fact that he had played a key role in its proceedings. But the book marked the parting of the ways, and Packer's involvement with Reformed Free Church Evangelicals ceased for some time.

Although both sides would disagree, what the split showed was the difference in mindset between the minister and the scholar. To the scholar, discussion is a vital part of the creative dialogue that contributes to new knowledge. To the minister, the truth is an entity to be fought for and dialogue seems to ease the way down the slippery slope to compromise, or worse. It was also the old historical battle all over again—between those who felt that it was worth trying to remain in a group in order to effect change from within, and those who felt that the poison had spread so far that further discussion was meaningless, and that withdrawal was the only viable option for true Christians to take. Unfortunately for Packer, the Reformed Evangelicals with whom he had had such close fellowship over the years decided to reconstruct both the Westminster Ministers Fellowship (run by Martyn Lloyd-Jones) and the Puritan Conference on lines which effectively excluded him and all others like him who had opted to remain within their doctrinally-mixed denominations.

The whole debate proved the point made by Francis Schaeffer, based on his own experiences of the bitter split in American Presbyterianism in the 1930s. On the one hand, Schaeffer argued, in order to maintain a tenable foothold within their denomination, those who remain within often have to concede too much. (Packer had a problem over his membership in the Church of England's Doctrine Commission, which published a radical report on "Christian Believing" with which he and other Evangelicals took strong issue.) Schaeffer felt that although such people may never have to compromise their own doctrinal stand, they find that the line beyond which they will not go is continually being shifted by the non-Evangelicals who control the denomination.

On the other hand, according to Schaeffer's thesis, those who pull out are marked by an increasing intolerance towards those who wish to stay in. They cut themselves off from fellowship with evangelical Christians who share the same gospel. Thus the true church is split, and the separatists cease to be able to help or influence their fellow Evangelicals.

As Packer told me, a gathering such as the Puritan Conference seemed to him to be a wonderful opportunity to draw together *all* Evangelicals who longed for spiritual vitality and better preaching. Many now feel it would have been better if he and other Reformed Anglicans had been allowed to stay within the Conference. Free Churchmen would then have had opportunity to discuss the issues lovingly with their brother, and would perhaps have been able to persuade him to devote his efforts to what they felt were more important issues.

Knowing God

But if Packer was losing one constituency he was gaining another—the international readership of his highly-acclaimed best seller, *Knowing God*. By 1983, the book had sold over half a million copies, which, as one Reformed American pastor learned from its author, ushered Packer into new financial security. Published in 1973, it influenced many younger Evangelicals, especially in the universities, and was used by many churches in discussion groups and other meetings.

Part of the reason for such popularity was that it was not a heavyweight theological tome but an eminently practical book which enabled its readers to grasp many complex truths, sometimes for the first time in their lives, by seeing them logically developed and explained in one volume. Packer has said of himself that he is "Packer by name and packer by nature"; it was this trait of his that gave the book the conciseness and cogency which allowed those who studied it to cover a lot of biblical ground in a short space of reading.

The book showed that, in an age in which the importance of doctrine is often forgotten, the study of God is as relevant as ever. It dealt not just with the attributes of God, but went on to outline their practical implications in the daily lives of Christian people—a kind of applied theology. Having started out as a series of magazine articles, the chapters were not written with a purely academic audience in mind. This was especially true of the chapters on God as Father (the doctrine of adoption), inward trials (where much of what Packer wrote tied in with his own undergraduate experiences at Oxford), the "adequacy of God," and Christian assurance.

Many hoped that *Knowing God* would be a foretaste of a theological *magnum opus* that would summarize the evangelical position in one systematic volume. But it is perhaps typical of its author that when this work does finally appear, it will not be just a learned academic treatise, but also a practical book to help students in theological colleges. Many have lamented the fact that he has not yet produced such a volume. But since the 1950s he has devoted a considerable part of his energy and his literary output to helping the soldiers on the theological front line. His friends hope that his new book, when it is eventually published, will be one that, while not written for the officers, will at least be a work that influences in a lasting way the thoughts of the commandants of future generations.

Beyond the battle for the Bible

One of Packer's constant refrains in *Knowing God* was that God spoke to people through his Word—the Bible. The "Battle for the Bible," as it became known in the United States, thus had very considerable implications. For, if the Bible were known to contain mistakes, then how could it be trusted? Much of the *spiritual* teaching within it might also be mistaken. The defense of Scripture was thus an urgent priority, which Evangelicals such as Schaeffer and Packer clearly recognized.

By 1971 Packer was back at Bristol, at the newly formed Trinity College (with which Tyndale Hall, to which he had returned, had now merged). Although he was cold-shouldered by some in his own country, including Anglican Evangelicals who did not share his concern for reformation and renewal, Evangelicals in North America were turning to him with increasing regularity. In the United States the debate over the inerrancy of the Bible reflected an urgency that had never developed in Britain. As a leading North American theologian told me, it demonstrated the greater strength in the United States and Canada of the aggressive Baptist and Presbyterian theology, which was, this theologian felt, far from content with the sort of pietistic theological blur that seemed to satisfy many English evangelical clergy.

Furthermore, many seminaries and other colleges in North America were making inerrancy a key issue—a foundational issue—which was not the prevailing attitude in Britain. As one theologian told me, more North Americans saw that ideas have legs and that theology matters, than was the case in England. Packer, with his strong instincts for championing inerrancy, found such interest appealing.

British Evangelicals had made ecclesiastical unity the major issue, but for North American Evangelicals it was not just a simple matter of insisting that all Evangelicals stick together. The problem went deeper; there were now many who claimed the evangelical label in one form or another, yet who rejected what had hitherto been one of Evangelicalism's most basic tenets—the infallibility and inerrancy of all Scripture as originally given.

These neo-Evangelicals taught that Scripture was certainly infallible in all spiritual and moral matters, but when it came to historical and scientific matters it was possibly in error—i.e., that the Bible was *not* in fact inerrant. According to Harold Lindsell, much of this teaching came either from Fuller Theological Seminary in the United States, or from those individuals influenced by Fuller thinking.

In 1965 a conference was convened in Wenham, Massachusetts to try to deal with the problem of this ideological drift. Packer addressed it but discovered, as he recalled to me later, that the polarization between the different views was exacerbated by the conference format, so that nothing constructive resulted.

Then in 1973 a Presbyterian named R. C. Sproul called a conference for the defense of inerrancy. This time the gathering yielded positive results in the shape of a book entitled *God's Inerrant Word*, to which Packer contributed two chapters. At a subsequent gathering, Packer and others, sensing that something more permanent was needed, founded the International Council for Biblical Inerrancy. It was to have, as Packer told me, a two-pronged strategy designed to combat anti-inerrantist teaching. As well as organizing creative scholarship at appropriate academic levels, it would initiate an educational program for use in churches.

Major conferences were convened in Chicago in 1978 and in San Diego in 1981. Inerrancy was tightly defined at Chicago, and its relevance made clear in San Diego: the Bible could be trusted. A further meeting, for scholars, took place in Chicago in late 1982, on hermeneutics. Packer was a major draftsman of all the statements issued—the most important of which forms the appendix to his book *God Has Spoken*.

In his essay, "Freedom, Authority, and Scripture," Packer makes the point that inerrancy is a most practical issue. "It is," he writes, "really about knowing, trusting, obeying, and proving God as a way of life. It is an illusion to think that differences of opinion about the meaning and trustworthiness of the various strands of biblical instruction make no difference to one's thoughts about God, one's relationship to him, and one's moral practice. What is actually at stake is whether, or how far, we learn the secret of supernatural living and of pleasing God."

Entry into such a life comes, in Packer's view, through accepting and obeying the teachings of God revealed in Scripture. "True freedom," he writes, "freedom from sin, freedom for God and for righteousness, is found where Jesus Christ is Lord in living personal fellowship. It is," he continues, "under the authority of a fully trusted Bible that Christ is most fully known, and this God-given freedom most fully enjoyed. If, therefore, we have at heart spiritual renewal for society, for churches, and for our own lives, we shall make much of the entire trustworthiness—that is, the inerrancy—of Holy Scripture as the inspired and liberating Word of God."

New pastures

As seen already, Packer was back in Bristol when the inerrancy debate took off in earnest. He was associate principal of Trinity College—the institution which resulted from the merger of three colleges by the local bishop. Packer, who had been principal of Tyndale Hall for a year, was now working with Alec Motyer, principal of the new college. He found that in this larger body he did not have the scope that he had enjoyed at Tyndale, where, as he told me, he had been able to revise the syllabus into a more organic teaching pattern in which the interconnections between academic and pastoral training studies could clearly be grasped by the students. At Trinity such linkage had become impossible. He soon found he was putting in at least ten hours a week in administration on top of his already arduous teaching duties and tutorials.

Time to sit back and think was scarce. He thought Nottingham '77, the follow-up to Keele '67, was a "non-event." He had argued against holding it, but when it went ahead anyway he contributed a chapter on "Christology" to the symposium. The exclusion order placed on him by many of his former Reformed colleagues meant that he was unable to pursue his bilateral course of remaining an Anglican while continuing close cooperation with Free Churchmen who shared his Reformed views.

Increasingly he felt that revival was what mattered, as he told me, yet he saw the opportunities for it in the Church of England ebbing away, as many of his fellow Anglicans expended their energies in meetings and congresses. Those people who shared his passion for revival were often precisely those Free Church Evangelicals who had severed contact with him. It was a frustrating situation.

In 1978 he published a pamphlet entitled "The Evangelical Anglican Identity Problem." Although Packer would strongly disagree, many who knew him felt that the problem he was describing was in fact his own. He reminded readers that it was the gospel that was the true basis for evangelical unity, and with this many Free Church Evangelicals heartily agreed. Where they differed from him was over the portions of his statement in which he tried to make the case for being an Evangelical in a church as doctrinally pluralistic as the Church of England. As one long-time Free Church admirer of Packer told me, whereas *Knowing God* had been timeless in its scope and style, these arguments for pluralism seemed like "special pleading." Other Free Church Evangelicals, who similarly supported Packer's Reformed beliefs and his stand on inerrancy, became concerned that his "Anglicanness" prevented people from listening to him who ought to be doing so.

In the United States and Canada, however, such problems did not arise. A leading North American Evangelical confided to me that Christians in this continent found in Packer a combination of clarity, vigor, insight, practicality, and compassion, plus, as he mischievously added, the charm of an English accent. As concerned as Packer was over the vitally urgent issue of defending Scripture, American Evangelicals were increasingly inviting him over to North America as a guest lecturer on many subjects including biblical inerrancy, an issue whose importance they saw with crystal clarity.

While Packer was being stymied in Britain, these Americans were asking him to do things which, as he told me, "seemed to me significant." Then Regent College in Vancouver, Canada, a transdenominational evangelical college, asked him "out of the blue" to join their faculty. He would have no administrative duties, they promised, and a lighter counseling commitment with the students than he had had at Trinity.

What Regent really offered him was plenty of time for writing and for reflection, as well as a secure niche on the side of the Atlantic where his talents were better appreciated. (As one young North American evangelical theologian pointed out to me, Regent is, however, not as well-placed geographically for widespread travel in the United States as, for example, the cluster of well-known evangelical theological seminaries in the Midwest.) The offer, he realized, would make him a "perfectly square peg in a perfectly square hole."

All the frustrations he had been suffering in England would be over. He had wanted churches in Britain to get on with their proper biblical task of ministering to the needs of their own areas, instead of losing themselves in a multitude of meetings and jamborees. Too many of his fellow evangelical Anglicans, he felt, had settled for being a wing of the Church of England with views of their own. They did not share his yearning for reformation and renewal, he thought, but were interested merely in being tolerated and allowed to get on with their own task undisturbed.

He found North American churches to be very different—far ahead of anything in England in terms of local organization (though much of this was because local Christians were both more affluent and more conscious of the need to support the church financially). Parachurch bodies, of which he encountered plenty, were being run by enthusiastic and gifted young people who were not at all moth-eaten, to use the phrase privately coined by a leading Anglican Evangelical. Such bodies, he noticed, would evaluate themselves, and if they were not making any progress in their specialized form of ministry, would ask why. To them, maintaining the status quo was not enough to justify their continued existence.

He found that as a foreigner he was judged purely on the content of what he was saying and did not experience the kind of cultural or cultic prejudice he had increasingly encountered in England. When he spoke here, the fact that he was an Anglican was not even a factor; he was judged by his views alone. He found Americans expressing their enthusiasm in a way that the English, with their more reserved nature, did not do. He was, in the opinion of one professor at Regent, an example of Mark 6:4—a prophet not without honor except in his own country. (Ironically, he was invited to Britain in 1983 by a group anxious to achieve a gospel-centered unity by bringing together Evangelicals from all denominations, Free Church and Anglican alike. He spoke at some of their meetings which were organized by Francis Schaeffer's son-in-law Ranald Macaulay, along with the minister of a church in which Martyn Lloyd-Jones often preached, Roy Clements of Cambridge.)

He is currently involved, when at home, in the team ministry at St. John's Anglican Church in Vancouver, where he preaches most of the Sundays that he is in town. (He preaches once or twice on Sundays in most of the many places he visits.) He also leads a weekly Bible study and has informal pastoral commitments at Regent.

In the United States he is an adjunct or visiting professor at two other seminaries besides Regent and has lectured at many more. He tours for four or five weekends a year with the Philadelphia Conference on Reformed Theology and has ministered frequently in the summer at Laity Lodge in Texas and at Pensacola Theological Institute in Florida.

As his lifelong friend, Raymond Johnston, told me, Packer's eminence among Evangelicals is primarily due to the "quality of his mind." He gave a coherence to evangelical doctrine at a time when beleaguered theological students needed it most. Books such as *Knowing God* have, by providing a "total architecture to Christian belief" provided the same help to students—and to Christians generally—of subsequent generations on both sides of the Atlantic. Theological students no longer have so much to fear from liberalism—Packer has demonstrated its bankruptcy to them.

He showed in theory, as Martyn Lloyd-Jones had in practice, that Reformed people were not only as committed to evangelism as those who held different views, but were in fact able to evangelize from a more secure base. Although many disagreed with his decision to remain an Anglican, he was able to give a solidly evangelical rationale to those who followed his example of staying within a doctrinally-mixed denomination.

Above all, in an era when the gospel has been under attack, and at a time when Scripture has been assaulted not just from outside but from within, he has demonstrated that the evangelical position is the truly Christian one, and that part of the defense of the message of Jesus Christ has been to affirm the total inerrancy of the Bible in all that it states and teaches. He has shown that theology is no sterile science when practiced by people whose commitment is to revival in the church, and that doctrine, far from being dull and boring, is the key to the full experience with God that should be the joy of every Christian.

BILLY GRAHAM

1918–

Billy Graham

Willliam Franklin Graham—"Billy"—was born on November 7, 1918, the son of Franklin and Morrow Graham. The Grahams were of old Confederate stock and farmed just outside Charlotte, North Carolina. His parents were active church members, but their commitment to Christ actively increased in 1933 after Frank Graham suffered a serious injury. Then in the fall of 1934 Billy's life was altered too, when the fiery evangelist Mordecai Ham came to town. Until then, Billy had been a typical country boy—doing average schoolwork, always ready for fun. At first he thought Ham was a "wild fanatic." Then slowly but surely, he became convicted of his own sin. He discovered that one could "know Christ personally," and near the end of the crusade he went forward to commit his life to Christ as Lord. Although, as childhood friend Grady Wilson recalls, Billy was "by nature very shy" he soon found himself speaking in public. In 1936 evangelist Jimmy Johnson persuaded him to give his testimony to some prisoners, and thus, without his realizing it, his career as an evangelist had begun.

Billy originally intended to attend the University of North Carolina. But his mother had been impressed by evangelist Bob Jones who had started a college in Tennessee, and so Billy decided to go there instead, joining his friends Grady and T. W. Wilson. To fill in time, he and the Wilson brothers sold toothbrushes. Billy was so sincere, Grady recalls, that he believed his own sales talk and nearly ruined his own teeth on the brushes. Bob Jones College turned out to be a mistake. It was not academically accredited and far too strict for Billy's liking. So he transferred to another school his mother had found—the Florida Bible Institute near Tampa.

There he spent three-and-a-half very happy years. By 1937, thanks to his tutor, John Minder, he was given his first preaching engagements. He was gradually changing from a carefree country boy to a serious preacher. Two Christians he admired were found guilty of grave moral failures which made him realize the need to depend on God for strength. He was influenced both by visiting speakers and by his then girlfriend and fellow student Emily Cavanaugh. To be a pracher, he now saw, would demand his total commitment. In March 1938, at a place near his institute, called the "18th Green," he decided to become "an ambassador for Jesus Christ."

His ministry is born

He began preaching with a new vigor, undiscouraged by Emily's final rejection of him. He participated in street services in the rougher parts of Tampa, and at the Tampa Gospel Tabernacle, making up in zeal for what he would later say he lacked in quality. The Baptists especially liked him, and although he had originally been a Presbyterian, in 1939 he was ordained a Baptist minister. The following year he moved to Wheaton, Illinois, to study anthropology at the well-known Christian college there. One of his fellow students was Ruth Bell, the daughter of the famous missionary to China, Dr. Nelson Bell.

By 1941 Billy Graham and Ruth Bell were engaged. Ruth, a Presbyterian from a more sophisticated background, helped to broaden his horizons. Her sound common sense (revealed most charmingly in her book, It's My Turn Now) and deep spirituality were to prove of immense help to him in the years to come. She provided him with the devotion and security he needed, but also gave him well-thought-out advice. She has been a model of what a Christian wife should be, and the Graham's marriage has been an example and encouragement to many. The wedding took place in 1943, just as his ministry was gaining momentum.

Graham's first pastorate was in Western Springs, near Chicago, but his ministry soon widened. He was asked to take over the weekly radio broadcast "Songs in the Night." The soloist he hired was a popular Canadian-born singer, George Beverly Shea. Thus began an association that has lasted ever since. He also spoke, at the request of Rev. Torrey Johnson, at a successful Youth for Christ rally in Chicago. Graham had decided to enter the Army chaplaincy, but he fell ill, and rather than accept a desk job, resigned his commission in order to concentrate his efforts in Youth for Christ instead. He made a series of short tours around the United States and Canada, then in 1946 visited Britain with Youth for Christ. The team members committed several social blunders, including that of staying in an expensive hotel at a time when many British people were short of food. Graham learned quickly and realized the need for cultural sensitivity, an asset that has been a major factor in his later highly successful Third World crusades.

His career took another turn in 1947, when William Bell Riley, the octogenarian head of the Northwestern Schools in Minneapolis, asked him to succeed him. Graham was reluctant at first, but he reconsidered when Riley died within months of making the offer, and was appointed president with childhood friend, T. W. Wilson as his deputy. The motto he chose for the school was "Knowledge on Fire." But he soon felt that he was not cut out for the frustrations of administrative life, and while retaining his post, set off again on evangelistic meetings around the country.

He also revisited Europe where he met Dawson Trotman, the founder of the Navigators. This greatly influenced him, for Trotman enabled him to see the crucial importance of following up the converts made at rallies, a policy that had until then been sadly lacking in mass evangelism, including Graham's own. He attended the World

Council of Churches Congress in Amsterdam in 1948. His biographer, John Pollock, has commented that by so doing "he showed that he would not hesitate to break the taboos of his circle in order to further the gospel." This view differed from that expressed by his fellow Evangelicals, Martyn Lloyd-Jones and Francis Schaeffer.

Some time after his return from Europe, Graham had a spiritual crisis that greatly helped his subsequent evangelism. He had never been to seminary and felt the need for a deeper level of knowledge than he then possessed. A friend of his, Chuck Templeton, had, like himself, become dissatisfied with a certain superficiality in Youth for Christ and had gone to Princeton Theological Seminary to remedy the lack. But the prevailing liberal atmosphere there had caused him to doubt Scripture's authority. They argued the case together, and slowly doubts began to enter Graham's mind too. Was his faith as simplistic as Templeton maintained?

He went to a conference in California and decided to pray to God for guidance. As he did so, he realized that he could not answer many of Templeton's intellectual queries. But he also knew that from that moment on he would accept the Bible by faith as the Word of God. The phrase "the Bible says" has become one of his best-known expressions. He has never had any doubt that his unashamed faithfulness to the Word of God, coupled with his totally sincere belief in its truth, has been perhaps the major factor under God in his success as an evangelist. To walk in integrity before God and his Word has been his "greatest desire." As he has said, "I really mean what I'm preaching." His simplicity and clarity when speaking may in no small measure be due to the fact that he never had his theology complicated by a seminary education.

The "most successful evangelist" in America

This transparent conviction and trust now helped him to become, almost overnight, the best-recognized evangelist in the United States. Even more important, he was also the most respected. The Los Angeles Crusade started in September, 1949 and was initially carried on without any drama. Billy Graham was already known in the Christian world as a man with a "quick mind, facile tongue, and a magnetic platform personality" and a "spiritual punch which has merited him unusually wide acceptance in different religious groups all over America." He was well aware of his limitations and told the magazine *Christian Life* in July, 1949 that he "prayed years ago not to be a great preacher but a great soul-winner."

But it was his decision to extend the Los Angeles Crusade that lifted it from being just another event into a nationally-known success. A popular radio personality, Stuart Hamblen, who had one of the rowdiest shows on the air, was converted. His broadcast testimony created a stir, as did the conversion of criminal Jim Vaus. Such dramatic transformations gave Graham and his team new incentive to go on. William Randolph Hearst, the newspaper magnate, instructed his reporters to "puff Graham," and the North Carolina evangelist became an instant national celebrity.

As the magazine *Illustrated* noted on December 31, 1949, a "wave of religious revival," led by "hot gospel" men, of whom Billy Graham was the "most flamboyant," was sweeping America. In the Los Angeles tent, it observed, "he hypnotizes the six thousand nightly by a blend of good showmanship, common sense, and a fine voice." The publicity preceded him to Boston, an area of the United States usually thought of as hardened against the gospel. Yet, as Grady Wilson recalls, the visit brought "the closest thing to revival that I've ever seen." He ended up preaching, the *Reporter* commented in its article "How Beulah Land Came to Boston," to a total of over 100,000 people in seventeen days, including a one-day record 16,000 on January 16, 1950.

New invitations for him to preach poured in. In Columbia, South Carolina, he spoke to the state legislature, and the crusade was attended by the famous Henry Luce, owner of *Time/Life*. As the *Christian Herald* noted, these three crusades meant that in "west, east, and south, America was responding en masse to the old-time gospel."

A leading secular magazine, *Newsweek*, commented on May 1,

1950 that Graham had "clinched his title as America's greatest living evangelist." The article was not sympathetic to his evangelical Christianity. But it highlighted two key reasons for his success. Evangelism had become discredited in the eyes of many Americans—the "Elmer Gantry image" (after the ficticious evangelist in the novel). Many evangelists would question the work of local ministers, then alienate the audience further by blatant appeals for money, euphemistically called "love offerings." "Mr. Graham," noted *Newsweek,* "unlike many evangelists, will not visit a town unless invited by local ministers . . . Also . . . Mr. Graham doesn't emphasize love offerings. His salary at Northwestern Schools is $8,500 a year—his main source of income." The local committees guaranteed his expenses only, and those which "lose money from his visits are reimbursed by those which profit."

The secular picture journal, *Look,* observed on June 14, 1950 that another reason was the "impeccable behavior of his revivalist team . . . Acutely aware of the sometimes shady reputation of revivalism as an occupation, Graham has struggled to keep his ministry clean." His team, which now included the popular Cliff Barrows, was, like Graham himself, always smartly dressed. As *The Pathfinder* commented, his "spellbinding oratory is as colorful and up-to-date as the flashy ties he wears." To Graham, "Christians are the only people in the world who have anything to be happy about" and evangelism ought to project an attractive image that helped win people.

T. W. Wilson, Graham's long-time chief of staff, has stated that part of the team's success has been the providence of God at work. Even the secular press acknowledged that something special was happening. In an article in January, 1951, *Look* noted that it was "doubtful whether, in any other age, Graham would have enjoyed his enormous success of the last two years." The United States was being "stirred by a religious consciousness the like of which it has not felt since the turn of the century." It was "Moody's old revival message warmed over the fires of contemporary events . . . All the substitutes for religious faith seemed to have failed when he [Billy

Graham] appeared. The scientists had to confess that though they could control the atom, they couldn't control human beings. Communism and fascism, which purchased human freedom with promises of security and happiness, gave neither in return. The failures of these ideologies sent people searching for a personal faith."

Furthermore, it was evangelical Christianity that the masses were turning to, not the liberalism that had prevailed between the wars. Noting the growth of Christian belief on the university campuses, the magazine went on to observe, "In the present revival, the influence of the modernists is almost nil. Once again, emphasis is on the Gospels as the Word of God, rather than the mortal records of a period in history." Remarkable opportunities were occurring. Revival was surmounting all class and racial barriers. In the segregated South, Southern Baptists were beginning to treat black believers as equals for the first time.

Graham on his own success

Billy Graham was being hailed as "the most successful evangelist in the world today." Americans, as distinguished evangelical theologian Lewis Drummond has commented, "love a hero," and Graham had become one. But he himself had no doubts as to the real cause. He told *Christian Life* in January, 1951 that "all the glory and the praise and the credit must go to God the Holy Spirit. It is the Holy Spirit that convicts, the Holy Spirit that regenerates, and it is the Holy Spirit that carries on the work after we've gone. It is actually all a supernatural performance and a supernatural process. All we are is witnesses to the saving grace and power of the Lord Jesus Christ. And I sincerely believe that any man preaching a simple gospel message in the power of the Spirit can expect results if he is speaking to unconverted people."

Follow-up, especially by the local churches, was essential, he maintained, as was solid doctrinal teaching to build up the new converts in the faith. When it came to the invitation at the end of each message, he made it clear that "I'm very much opposed to general invitations that call people forward for anything in order to get a move. We try to make our invitations straightforward, so that a person knows he is coming for conversion and salvation." The real work was that of the Holy Spirit, and, through him, the local churches, in salvation and follow-up. It was these emphases that made Billy Graham different, and, under God, gave him the power that astonished even the most cynical of hearers.

The ministry expands

His ministry was expanding rapidly. In order to cope with this and to keep the financial side of his work indisputably clean, he established the Billy Graham Evangelistic Association. No "love offerings" were ever to be taken. Graham was to be paid a regular salary, at the same rate as ministers of big city churches, as a paid employee of the association. The team would be paid in the same way. All their income would come from central funds, so that they could offer their services free to those who invited them. (The costs of each crusade, such as publicity and rental of conference halls, etc., would be met locally.) One of the new, centrally-supported ventures was the nationally broadcast "Hour of Decision" evangelistic program. Graham was initially reluctant to begin such a series, but the necessary funds arrived before the deadline he had set for guidance. The programs, soon to be broadcast over 150 stations, began November 5, 1950.

The Graham team also altered the terminology of evangelism. From then on, "revivals" were given the more appropriate name "crusades" and "personal worker" was replaced by counselor—terms that have stuck ever since. His other innovation, cooperation across denominational lines, had the beneficial effect of bringing Christians together in the common cause of winning lost souls for Christ. But his desire to have a broad base of local support before coming to a town sometimes meant that liberal churches who did not stand behind the gospel he proclaimed also took part. The policy, as it was applied in some towns, had the unfortunate result of alienating evangelical churches who were warm to Graham and his presentation of the gospel, but whose leaders felt unable publicly to sit on the same platform as the leaders of the liberal churches participating in the crusade.

One of the greatest contributions made by Graham to the cause of Christianity in the United States has been the promotion of genuine reconciliation and integration between blacks and whites. His continued activity in this area (often at the cost of losing considerable support from white Americans) has been a major factor in the immense success he has enjoyed in Third World countries generally and in Africa in particular. The South, where he was raised, had a terrible record of racial prejudice, and it was not until he came to the North and studied anthropology at Wheaton College that he came to see that black people were his full equals as human beings. His Southern background proved, however, to be of immense value when his crusades began in the South. Southerners resented interfering liberal Northerners ordering them to integrate with the blacks. But Graham was a white Southerner like themselves and when, at the Chattanooga Crusade of 1953, he demanded racially-integrated seating, his opponents could not accuse him of being a meddlesome outsider. In the Dallas Crusade, the local committee tried to enforce segregation. Graham, seeing a Negro aide in his hotel lobby, made his views clear by openly taking him up with him in the elevator instead of making him climb up by the back stairs.

After the Supreme Court decision of 1954 in which segregation was declared illegal, Graham was legally able to insist that all crusades be fully integrated. His stand on racial issues was warmly appreciated by President Eisenhower. It also had the effect of bringing him into close contact with Senator Lyndon Johnson, who was vigorously campaigning in Washington for equal rights.

Billy Graham also took steps to improve follow-up at his crusades. He persuaded Dawson Trotman of the Navigators to take charge, and a counselor-training program was established. Those coming forward at the meetings would be counseled by qualified Christians, many of whom were lay people, on a one-to-one basis. Counselors

were to see themselves as "spiritual obstetricians." They were to
remember that it was really "Christ that saves" and that "the great
follow-up agent is the Holy Spirit." All those who made decisions
were to be referred to local churches. At the same time, Graham's
first best-selling book was published—*Peace with God*. He also began
writing a regular, syndicated column for the newspapers, as well as
branching out into film-making (though he refused offers to star in
Hollywood productions).

The international evangelist

Many evangelists successful in the United States have failed to
achieve fame beyond its borders. In 1954 Billy Graham showed that
he had the ability to reach people in cultures quite different from
his own—a major achievement. In 1952 he had been asked by the
British Evangelical Alliance to conduct a crusade in Britain. A venue
was arranged—the Harringay arena in north London. Prayer meetings were set up worldwide. Much of the fund-raising for the team's
flight and accommodation expenses was done in the United States.
Unfortunately the team did not then have the superb knowledge of
other countries that was later to be a hallmark of their overseas
successes. As a result, the publicity brochure they produced created
a storm of controversy that nearly overshadowed the crusade itself.

The final brochure read, "The England of history has been an
England whose life, both national and individual, was ever centered
on the things of God"—the recent coronation having reinforced this
emphasis. Nazi bombing had leveled many churches, and a disillusioned atmosphere now prevailed. "What Hitler's bombers could
not do," the brochure stated, "secularism with its accompanying
evils has accomplished." Hyde Park was filled with orators who
spoke on many topics, "but most forcefully they speak for communism." Over ninety percent of Britons had no church connection.
"Only a religious revival," wrote Graham, "can give the English
people the moral integrity and stability necessary to stand with us
in the days to come." Unfortunately, in the original brochure, the

word "socialism" had been used in place of "secularism" and the press created an outcry when a *Daily Herald* reporter discovered this.

As a result, Graham's visit got massive publicity, not all of it sympathetic or welcome. He had to spend some time on arrival explaining that he did not intend to be political, but had agreed to preach in England at the express invitation of local Christians. The crusade opened on March 1, 1954 with a sermon by Graham on John 3:16. The numbers attending slowly grew. A regular participant recalls the "absolute thrill" that pervaded English churches as the audiences multiplied.

British evangelist Tom Rees had held many crusades from the 1940s, many of them fairly successful. They had paved the way for the kind of event that Graham was now holding. But as the number of people converted steadily increased, it soon became obvious that Britain had not seen anything like it since Moody's visit decades before. Graham's preaching had a "certain gospel simplicity at heart" that many found refreshing. It was, as a close Graham associate has said, "a remarkable experience." John Pollock has written that Billy Graham "had released Britons from their reticence; it suddenly became easy to talk about religion."

Not all evangelical churches took part, for the reasons mentioned earlier. But many of them, such as Westminster Chapel, were happy to nurture their share of the new converts. Martyn Lloyd-Jones, while sorry that Graham had liberal churchmen on his platforms, was quite happy to see Graham privately in Westminster Chapel, and, when on one occasion Graham fell ill, took him to see a specialist he knew in Harley Street.

Billy Graham has always understood that non-participation in his crusades does not necessarily mean lack of commitment to evangelism, but rather a difference among believing Christians as to the *methods* of proclaiming the Good News. As a close associate, Maurice Rowlandson, has pointed out, wise supporters of crusade evangelism never make the claim that their method is exclusively the best, but recognize that it is one of the methods that God has blessed. Non-participating churches such as Westminster Chapel proclaimed the gospel faithfully every week and saw many conversions. When Harringay converts arrived on their doorstep, they were warmly welcomed.

By the end of the crusade, over 1,869,000 people had heard Graham preach, and 37,600 had inquired about becoming Christians. He told the *Daily Sketch* that he hoped many of them would be "those who will make an impact in years to come in London, the nation, and the world." But what had thrilled him most, he added for the *Daily Mirror*, was "the support given by the churches." After trips to Europe, he returned to Britain in 1955, for a crusade in Scotland. Here an important system was used for the first time that has been an integral part of his work ever since. Operation Andrew, named after the apostle, was a plan whereby local Christians pledged themselves in advance to pray for and interest non-Christian friends, whom they must then bring along to the crusade meetings in order to be admitted themselves.

As at Harringay, many of the converts went on to become church ministers. There are those who feel that the major long-term impact of these crusades has been the number of present-day clergy whose spiritual lives began in 1954 and 1955.

Evangelist across the globe

Two less successful English follow-up missions, at Wembley and at Cambridge, were succeeded by a highly profitable and fruitful visit to India—the first major tour to the Third World that Graham had made. He realized, as had Martyn Lloyd-Jones in IFES, that people are often best evangelized by those of their own culture and nationality. The gospel should be seen to be true because of its claims and relevance, not muddied by Westernism or anti-imperial resentment. The fact that he himself was from the affluent West makes his sensitivity and his Third World popularity all the more impressive. At the Henry Martin School of Islamics he met Dr. Akbar Haqq, whom he persuaded to become an associate and evangelist to Asia.

Back home . . . and away again

Meanwhile, his organization had expanded still further, moving to new premises in Minneapolis. In spite of much criticism, he installed the latest labor-saving office machinery, made even more necessary by the founding of the magazine *Christianity Today*. This journal, under the distinguished editorship of Dr. Carl Henry, the systematic theologian, was independent of the Billy Graham Evangelistic Association, but strongly supported by it. The staff and contributors have been called the "intellectual vanguard of the Billy Graham movement." Its establishment showed that Graham, though no intellectual himself, recognized the significance of the deeper issues including the need to combat theological liberalism in a cogent manner.

Two successful crusades followed—in New York and in Australia. In New York Graham found himself attacked by liberal theologian Reinhold Niebuhr for his lack of social concern Graham replied that such issues were always vital, but that the deepest need was the same as ever—for sinners to find salvation in Jesus Christ. Nearly two-and-a-half million heard him preach in sixteen weeks, but perhaps some of his greatest impact was in Harlem, where many poor black people lived. He had, for some time, felt the need for a fully racially-integrated team in order to "take a strong stand on race relations" in practice as well as in theory. The director of the missionary organization, "Word of Life," introduced him to Ohio pastor Howard Jones, a black preacher who had had experience evangelizing in Africa.

Jones had long felt that Graham was "something else" and had been "impressed with him straight away." He agreed to work on the team initially for five weeks, but ended up staying for ten. Many whites resented Jones's presence, but Graham insisted on his full participation, stating, "I don't care how many stop supporting me." Jones persuaded several black pastors in Harlem to cooperate, and when he and Graham arrived one Sunday at Salem Methodist Church the place was packed—3,000 inside and 1,000 downstairs, all of whom had come despite the rain. When the sun appeared, they flocked outside, and by the time Billy Graham began his appeal, there were 8,000 listening, as well as a further, uncountable number watching from the balconies. As many as 10,000 heard him in Brooklyn, and many blacks decided to make the journey to the main crusade in Madison Square Garden.

Howard Jones was asked by Graham to join his permanent team, which he did a year later, in order to help coordinate the work in Africa. There, in 1960, Graham and Jones undertook a major tour. Billy Graham, Jones recalls, made a "tremendous impact" on the Africans. His sincerity impressed them, and they also noted his refusal to visit South Africa because Howard Jones would not have been admitted there. In 1972 Graham accepted an invitation to speak in Durban and Johannesburg provided that the audiences were racially integrated. The South African government disliked this and only reluctantly agreed. Many black South Africans told Jones that they "thought they would never see the day when people could mix together without racialism." Billy Graham's meetings had shown it could be done.

Political connections

In the early fifties, many had considered Graham to be promising senate material for his home state of North Carolina. He had refused, but there remained those who wished to use his personal charisma for their own political ends. In 1960, an American presidential election year, he tactfully stayed out of the country as long as possible. He wrote a noncommittal article on Nixon for *Life*, but his Democrat friends begged him to withdraw it. In the end he submitted a piece on why Christians should vote. At his friend Lyndon Johnson's inaugural in 1965, he said, on the topic of social issues, "our problems are basically spiritual." He felt that if "the church went back to its main task of preaching the gospel and getting people converted to Christ, it would have more impact on the social structure of the nation."

On one issue he continued to be active—that of race. He had held crusades in Little Rock in 1959 and one in Birmingham, Alabama in 1964, not long after the racial tensions had erupted there again. Graham and Martin Luther King were friends, and Howard Jones recalls King telling Graham, "Your crusades have done more to help race relations than anything else I know." When Johnson launched his campaign to help poor blacks in the 1960s, Billy Graham enthusiastically supported him. No President had done so much since Roosevelt, he felt, and what impressed him most was that Johnson "really believed" in the program. He was, he later remembered, "with LBJ more than any other President." He often stayed in the White House during Johnson's presidency (far more than when Nixon held office) and preached there several times.

More expansion in the ministry

In 1960 Billy Graham founded a mass circulation magazine—*Decision*. The "Hour of Decision" broadcasts and the now frequent televising of many of the crusades had shown him that a popular journal was necessary. *Decision* was an instant success. Another innovation was the school of evangelism attached to every crusade. Seven theological seminary students attended the 1961 Philadelphia Crusade, and in 1962 twenty-seven were paid to join the one in Chicago in order to see evangelism in action. By the November, 1962 El Paso Crusade, a school of evangelism to teach seminary students (and later ministers as well) had become a fixture. Initially the team doubled as its staff, but later on distinguished outsiders such as Kenneth Chafin and Lewis Drummond (now Billy Graham Professor at the Southern Baptist Seminary in Louisville, Kentucky) were brought in as guest lecturers, in order to give the program greater scope and depth.

The aim of the schools was to make local churches realize the importance of evangelism and how to approach it. But, as Graham told ministers in Los Angeles in 1963, it was fully realized that humans could not organize spiritual revival. "The longer I work in crusades," he said, "the more I am convinced that salvation is of the Lord." This emphasis is, and has been, one of Graham's greatest strengths. Similar emphasis is made today by Drummond and by Joseph Aldrich at the schools of evangelism.

The BGEA also engaged in film-making in a bigger way than before. The film "Man in the Fifth Dimension" became very popular, as did two films made with Cliff Richard: "Two a Penny" and "His Land." All these activities were a heavy financial investment, but even though millions of dollars were now needed, the BGEA carefully kept its fund raising low-key. Billy Graham himself maintained his clean image by rejecting any salary increase for a long time and by continuing to live a relatively modest life in his family home in Montreat, North Carolina. (Os Guinness has described it as a large log cabin). Team members such as Grady Wilson increasingly conducted smaller crusades of their own, especially after Graham fell ill for a while in 1963.

Britain—and Berlin

The years 1966 and 1967 saw new crusades in Britain. For that of 1967, the modern technological device of cable relay was used, so that people could see Billy Graham on screen at relay points all over Britain. Coffee-bar evangelism was also initiated—an art that was perfected by the New York Crusade of 1969. Many of the counselors were converts from the 1954 Crusade, which proved that the oft-quoted criticism of his crusades—that few of the converts lasted—was demonstrably false.

There were also smaller evangelistic events in Turin, and in Zagreb, Yugoslavia. The Zagreb visit was Graham's first preaching trip to a communist country (though Yugoslavia is not an iron curtain nation), and enthusiastic crowds listened to his sermon in an open field in the pouring rain.

But by far the most significant event was the October, 1966 "World Congress on Evangelism" in Berlin, sponsored by *Christianity Today*. Over 1,200 delegates from more than 100 countries met with the theme of "One Race, One Gospel, One Task." Christian leaders from every kind of background were present, and the congress received substantial coverage in the secular press. The church was *visibly* becoming international and multi-racial and, paradoxically, it was an American, Billy Graham, who was helping speed up the process— a fact often ignored by the near-sighted U. S. secular critics of his ministry, who still insisted on seeing him only in American terms and as a product of southern U. S. Christianity in particular.

The Christians, Carl Henry reminded the delegates, were a new race of people, a fact that the church ought never to forget. They were, as Billy Graham pointed out in his address, "ambassadors under authority." The gospel was relevant to all the needs of modern man and its only hope. On Reformation Sunday, Graham, the delegates, and 10,000 West Berliners celebrated that great event in the Wittenbergplatz church. The congress showed Graham as moving into the role of the evangelical world statesman that he has since become.

God's ambassador

His new status was recognized by the Berlin regional follow-up conferences—in Singapore in 1968, Bogota in 1969, and Amsterdam in 1971. At Singapore, where twenty-five nations met with the theme "Christ Seeks Asia," Graham kept a low profile. The congress established a permanent coordinating office for Asian evangelism, with Bishop Chandu Ray of Pakistan as its first secretary. Graham spoke at Amsterdam and was, as will be seen, the originator of the idea that led to the Lausanne Congress in 1974, arguably one of the most influential Christian gatherings since the Second World War.

But it was in the crusades conducted outside the traditionally Christian countries that he showed his truly international stature. As Henry Holley, the director of international crusades at the time, has remarked, "Billy has an amazing credibility and acceptance" outside the United States. In sixteen years of crusades in Third World and similar countries, Holley found "an amazing amount of cooperation." Indeed the crowds that came to hear Graham in such lands usually exceeded by far those he drew in America.

In Seoul, Korea, in "five days he spoke to 3,200,000 people." Furthermore, he always had to speak through an interpreter. How many Americans, Holley has speculated, would turn out to hear a Japanese evangelist, preaching in Japanese, being translated into English? In terms of locally-raised financial support, "we've over-subscribed every budget," Holley recalls. The response to the message has, in percentage terms, been "greater than in the United States," and this in countries like Japan, where only one half of one percent of the nation is Christian.

Some reasons why

Henry Holley has listed the reasons, under God, for this success. The first is that, as in the United States, the local Christians "know that he'll proclaim a message without compromise"; that, as anywhere in the world, "penetrates the hearts and minds of the people that are prepared for it." Graham has a financially spotless image too—all the funds for the crusades are raised locally. Then the fact that he is so famous makes "his presence . . . an encouragement to the local church" and can give Christians in that country a status that they might not hitherto have enjoyed. This has been especially true since 1974, when Graham, in his overseas visits, deliberately stopped identifying himself with the United States.

But perhaps the main reason has been the considerable effort made by Graham and his associates to be sensitive to local feelings. "Unfortunately," Holley has pointed out, "Americans do not always enjoy a good reputation." Frequently in the past U. S. missionaries have imposed American methods on places to which they are wholly unsuited, and have thereby alienated local listeners from the gospel. "Each culture is different," and the Graham team has been very careful to find out exactly how different each one is.

"I have a philosophy," Holley has said. "We look at everything through their eyes." The team therefore never gives a package deal that local Christians have to accept or reject in order for Graham to come, but instead offer suggestions based on tried and tested methods that have proved successful in a variety of countries—and which have often first been used outside the United States. The local Christians are then asked to adapt these to the particular circumstances of their own culture.

"How would I react," Holley asks his fellow Americans, if a Japanese evangelist was coming to the United States? The team must never have a "made in America label" on arrival and must always adopt a "very, very, low profile." Holley feels that the Chinese sage Lao-tzu voiced a good principle. "The best leaders' work is done," he used to say, "when it's over and the people say, 'We did it ourselves.'" If the national churches can say this about themselves, in human terms, when the Billy Graham team has gone, that is the team's "best contribution." Above all, both Holley and Graham believe that "the Holy Spirit is the constant factor" in every crusade and that he is the one who achieves "all the goals."

Japan, Nagaland, and Korea

In 1966 the Japanese churches invited Graham to come to preach in Japan. He accepted, and the Tokyo Crusade took place in 1967. On the first night all 1,500 seats were filled; by the last, 36,000 were cramming in to hear the message. A total of nearly 16,000 enquirers came forward during the whole period. But more important was the impact on the local churches. They engaged in massive preparatory activities before Graham arrived, and this had the crucial long-term effect of not only boosting their morale, but of showing to their fellow Japanese the existence of an autonomous Japanese church, uncorrupted by Western influence.

The visits of the Graham team have produced similar results in other countries, and, if the crusades there have helped kindle the kind of growth that has gone on to become self-supporting, they have, for this alone, been worthwhile. The greatest revival of this century has been taking part in the Third World nations, where leadership has been local. Billy Graham has seen this, and his encouragement of the church in these areas (in the same way as Martyn

Lloyd-Jones's through IFES) could turn out to be a far more major contribution to the spread of God's worldwide kingdom than anything he has accomplished in the United States or Europe. As Henry Holley has said, Graham's epitaph should read: "Billy Graham— Evangelist to the World."

His continuing impact can be seen in two further crusades which he conducted in Third World countries. The first, in Nagaland, in North-East India, in 1972, has been described by biographer John Pollock as the "Kohima Miracle." The area was one of massive political unrest and violent conflict. The Indian federal government was initially reluctant to grant visas to Graham and his team, but eventually allowed them entry. Tribes from six Indian states converged on Kohima for the crusade meetings. At one stage the political tensions grew so high that the team suggested cancellation, but Naga Christians flew to see Graham in Bangkok and persuaded him to come. Over 100,000 people greeted him on his arrival in Kohima on November 20, 1972, and more than 4,000 professed conversion during the crusade. For the local church, this was like revival.

The Korean Crusade (in Seoul, in June, 1973) was entirely run by local Christians. It was also the biggest event in which he had ever preached. Over 500,000 heard him the first night, and on June 3 the audience numbered more than one 1,120,000. Graham decided in his appeal to stress more than usual the cost of becoming a Christian, in order to ensure that those going forward truly grasped the implications of what they were doing. In spite of this, no fewer than 120,000 responded to the gospel during the course of the crusade.

Characteristically, Graham and the team realized that these astounding results were not, even in human terms, their own doing. They were the product of patient sowing by the local Korean Christians among their own people; the team was merely reaping the results. This truth about so much of the success is strongly emphasized to ministers by members of the Billy Graham team. Inviting Graham, observed Sterling Huston, his director of U. S. crusades, to a group of American ministers in 1983, is no short cut to outstanding results unless the local churches have done their work first. Over eighty percent of those converted at crusades were brought there by believing Christian friends. This had been the case in Korea and everywhere else Billy Graham has been. A Graham crusade can never be a substitute for evangelism done by local Christians in their own areas, and both Graham and his team continue to emphasize this wherever they go.

Watergate

One event was still to occur before Billy Graham would become a truly international evangelical statesman—Watergate. As John Pollock has commented, the temptation to be deflected from his main task and enter the political arena had nudged at Graham for a long time, and it took the trauma of Watergate finally to rid him of it. Billy Graham had many qualities that would have made him an excellent political leader; the attempt mentioned earlier to persuade him to run for the Senate showed this.

Senior politicians such as President Eisenhower regarded him highly, and he enjoyed his conversations with them, especially if he felt he could influence them for the gospel. President Johnson, who shared his vision of a genuinely multi-racial America, encouraged Graham to use the crusades as a means to unify blacks and whites. But Graham refused to participate in secular activities, and turned down Johnson's request to be involved in implementing civil rights programs, even though he believed in them. Johnson was warmly welcomed when he attended one of Graham's crusades, which he did more than once.

With Nixon, however, Graham found himself politically ensnared. He first met Nixon in 1954—the senior Mrs. Nixon was a keen Graham supporter. Graham, as has been seen, withdrew from endorsing Nixon in 1960 (and indeed became friends with some of the Kennedy family). But in 1968 he felt, as did numerous other American Evangelicals, that Nixon had the moral character and strong family life to make an excellent President. It must never be forgotten that all that is now known about Nixon was completely hidden then.

Although Graham did not publicly endorse Nixon, it soon became news that Nixon had offered Graham the vice-presidential slot on the ticket and that the two men were close.

After Nixon's victory in November, 1968, *Time* magazine wrote that "Billy Graham's spirituality pervades" the White House. The Nixon-Graham relationship received huge press publicity, even though it was not as close as Graham's had been with Johnson (nor was Graham's influence with Nixon anything like as great). Graham's statement to a friend (quoted by Pollock) that Nixon had "brought a sense of ethics to the Presidency . . . largely derived from the Christian faith as believed and practiced by his parents" showed his own feelings quite clearly. Nixon paid a visit to the Knoxville Crusade, and when Graham was honored by his old home town of Charlotte, Nixon was there to see him accept the award. Graham, although an internationalist in outlook, was also a strong patriot, and so to be honored by the President's attention, regardless of who was President at the moment, was something he esteemed highly.

In 1972, Graham, along with the overwhelming majority of Americans, voted for Nixon—who therefore won by the greatest margin in U. S. history. But unfortunately, in the light of future events, Graham made his support for Nixon public. His participation with the President and other American celebrities in the patriotic "Honor America Day," which Nixon used for political ends, enabled hostile critics unfairly to tar Graham with the right-wing brush of pseudo-Christian American civic religion. Not only had he denounced such false belief, but his Third World success showed that his message was truly international. Nevertheless, his identification with Nixon and Middle America in the popular mind meant that commentators could dismiss him as a purely American cultural phenomenon and totally ignore his activities elsewhere.

In many cases during this period, it was not Graham as a person who was being attacked, but his faith. Those who wished to deny true evangelical Christianity used Nixon against him, especially once the Watergate scandal had broken open. Initially, like many Americans, Graham and the team thought the affair was a "political frame-up" against Nixon by the Democrats. Graham, as the revelations piled up, came to see it as a "symptom of a deeper moral crisis" facing the United States. In reply to hostile questioning, Grady Wilson pointed out that there was "a little bit of Watergate in all of us . . . Watergate is sin."

Graham loyally refused to condemn Nixon outright, as he still sought to influence his friend for the good. This was misunderstood, and criticism of Billy Graham mounted, as it had done over his refusal to oppose the Vietnam war. As a senior team member recalls, "we got our fingers burned" over Watergate. It was not until May, 1974, when he heard the White House tapes and realized the full moral duplicity of Richard Nixon, that Graham finally saw that he had to speak out. He had been deceived by Nixon, who had portrayed to him a very different image from the real, inner Nixon so shockingly revealed by the tapes. Graham's statement urged prayer, a lack of hypocrisy in the media, and the need to turn to God for forgiveness.

People now saw, as John Pollock has written, that Graham was human. His true gifts, his spiritual ministry, would now shine through more clearly, and, with the temptation to be involved in American politics now banished, he could concentrate more effectively on his God-given task of proclaiming the gospel to all the nations. Unfortunately the press failed to realize this. Marshall Frady, then a *Newsweek* journalist, wrote a hostile biography implying that after Watergate Graham was all but finished. Even ten years after Watergate, questions put to Graham at press conferences are often primarily political, ostensibly to find out whether Graham will endorse a certain politician or policy, but often really to find a means of tripping him up so that his Christian message can be discredited.

On the one hand, therefore, one must sadly conclude that regarding Nixon, Billy Graham was well meaning, but unintentionally naive. He had abandoned the neutrality that had until then been one of his major strengths and thereby allowed himself to be manipulated for political ends by politicians who did not have his sense of integrity and honesty. On the other hand, he swiftly learned the lessons. He ceased to permit himself to be identified with any political leader or cause in domestic politics and stopped identifying himself abroad with America and U. S. interests. This gave him greater credibility in the Third World where his ministry was increasingly to be focused, and also meant that he was less distracted at home, in the United States. As should happen with a Christian leader, a mistake had led to self-examination, and reflection had led to renewed strength. For those who were unprejudiced enough to see it, Billy Graham had now become a truly international evangelical figure.

Lausanne

This new role emerged most forcefully at the Lausanne International Congress on World Evangelization, held in Switzerland in July, 1974, with over 2,700 delegates from more than 150 countries. Fifty percent of those present, including half of the key planning committee and the speakers, were from Third World countries. *Time* described it as a "formidable forum, possibly the widest-ranging meeting of Christians ever held." Various congresses had been held after Berlin, but Graham felt the time had come for another truly international gathering, and in 1971 he convened an informal group of leading Evangelicals, including the late Stacey Woods of IFES and Bishop Dain of Sydney, Australia.

The issues they had to discuss were vital for the future. Many Third World churchmen had called for a ban on any future Western missionaries in their countries, a deep concern to someone as evangelism-minded as Graham. There was also a concern that the World Council of Churches had become "bankrupt of any real spiritual leadership" on the issue of the gospel. On the other hand, Graham was aware of the true Third World church and of the enormous revival spreading right through it. New and significant figures were emerging among the Third World Christians with immense potential. A positive congress, that would not be merely a center of opposition to the WCC, but would also show that evangelical Christianity was both alive and growing, seemed an excellent idea. Stacey

Woods and others agreed in principle, but successfully argued that the time was not yet ripe.

By August, 1972, at the Los Angeles consultation, everyone agreed that action should be begun. Billy Graham was chosen as honorary chairman of the planning committee, Bishop Dain became executive chairman, and Don Hoke the executive director. The late Paul Little was made program director, and Leighton Ford chairman of the program committee. The main committee met six times in three years, and an office was established in 1973. Graham, Dain recalls, did not involve himself in the day-to-day details, but was "constantly available" to give advice if asked. At meetings, he was "never intruding," but "always helpful." The committee ran on consensus, voting only once in its history.

"Lausanne," Dain remembers, "would never have happened but for Billy Graham." He ensured that the congress would be grounded on a sound doctrinal basis, and that the delegations from each country represented a genuine cross section of Evangelicals even in matters such as age and professional status. It would "relate the changeless gospel to a changing world." The theme would be "Let the Earth Hear His Voice," especially the 2.7 billion who had "yet to be evangelized."

The congress itself, Dain has said, represented a "wide span." There was a basic theological unity common to all delegates, but a broad spectrum of background. Some were from wholly evangelical denominations such as the Australian Baptists; others were from doctrinally-mixed churches such as the Anglicans. There were radically "angry young men" demanding political action in their Third World homes on the one hand, and wealthy, conservative Christians from the American Midwest on the other.

Yet, as Dain has pointed out, they had all chosen to come. When, at the planning stage, Graham wrote to many leading Evangelicals to find out if they wanted such a congress to be convened, the "overwhelming response" was favorable. Those opposed had been those who hoped that Lausanne would be primarily negative in emphasis, an anti-WCC caucus rather than a positive rallying cry to

Evangelicals to engage in world evangelization that Graham had intended.

The congress was a major landmark, in that it officially marked an international recognition that the majority of evangelical Christians were from the Third World. It was a watershed—an acknowledgment that Western domination of the church had ended. This change was embodied in the covenant, a document drafted from many congress resolutions by John Stott, whose genius for diplomacy enabled him to produce a document agreeable to all the very different groups there.

Lausanne showed that evangelism and social concern were not incompatible, and that Evangelicals could once again engage in both without compromising either. Billy Graham spoke twice, but played a low-key role throughout. The congress, he felt, "accomplished far more than I had ever anticipated." It is a tribute to his vision that a congress such as Lausanne, which put the Third World on the map of the Christian world, should have owed its origins to an American. As John Pollock has written, Billy Graham had now publicly become "a world Christian statesman."

On to Brazil, Africa, East Asia

More successful Third World crusades followed. In the autumn of 1974 Graham went to Brazil, where he had been in 1960 and 1962. Now the Protestant church was growing faster than the population, and the Pentecostals probably faster than any other major denomination in the world. There were 125 Christian life and witness classes for trainee counselors in Rio alone before the Brazil Crusade even began; the average for most Graham crusades is ten. Although initial attendance was lower than expected, by the last two nights there were over 200,000 crowding into the Maracana stadium. A year after the end of the crusade, Brazilian pastors had been requested by local believers to provide over 100,000 New Testaments. The already expanding church had been enlarged still further.

At the Far East Crusade—in Taipei in October, 1975, and in Hong Kong in November, 1975—many young people professed conversion.

More important, the crusade proved a massive incentive to local evangelists, whose own crusades reaped even more bountifully than Graham's own—much to his delight, as that was just the kind of effect he hoped for. In December, 1976 he addressed the Pan-African Christian Leadership Assembly in Nairobi, Kenya. Then in late 1977 he conducted crusades in Metro Manila in the Philippines and again in India. In the Philippines he was given a banquet by President Marcos, whose wife addressed the School of Evangelism.

In September, 1977 Graham went to Hungary at the request of its Free Church council. In Budapest he preached to 30,000 young people, including many from surrounding East European countries. He also attended a reception given in his honor, as an "ambassador of good will," by the American Embassy, at which several senior Hungarian state officials were present. Then in October, 1978 he preached, at the invitation of the local Baptists, in Poland. Once more, he was also regarded as an international goodwill ambassador. He visited the Roman Catholic shrine of the Black Madonna at Czestochowa in order to bring Catholic, Orthodox, and Protestant churches together.

Moscow

In 1982, Billy Graham accepted an invitation to Moscow, the Soviet capital, to address a conference of "Religious Workers for Saving the Sacred Gift of Life from Nuclear Catastrophe," made up of Christians, Buddhists, and other delegates from around the world. His visit, which will be examined later, caused immense controversy. Graham had been worried about the nuclear issue for some time. But he also felt that the invitation was "a God-given opportunity for me to proclaim the gospel in a country where I have not had this privilege before." He would see top religious leaders and Soviet government officials. He concluded: "My purpose in going to the Soviet Union is spiritual, and it is not my intention to become involved in political or ideological issues."

He spoke at the Baptist church in Moscow to an audience all of whom were there by special admission tickets. There was a demonstration by several local Christians, some of whom had unofficially managed to get in. (Fifty Baptist families had been raided just before his visit and their Bibles confiscated. Twelve of them had been imprisoned.) Unfortunately Graham was not able to see the prisoners. At the conference itself, he made a biblically-based plea for peace. He did not however join in a walkout led by a Dutch delegate on the refusal of the conference organizers to discuss solidarity, or Charter 77—the Czech freedom group. Graham stated that he did not wish to enmesh himself in politics—he was an observer.

He did however visit the "Siberian Seven," the Pentecostal group who were still refugees inside the U. S. Embassy. Later, he claimed to be one of those who had helped in their eventual release. (The reaction of the Seven will be discussed at the end of this chapter.) Graham took immense care to do nothing to offend his Soviet hosts, partly because he hoped it would be possible for him to return to the USSR at some stage in the future in order to conduct a crusade there. (In fact, as a direct consequence of this 1982 mission to Moscow, Graham was invited to return to the Soviet Union in September, 1984 for an extended preaching ministry in four major cities.) Needless to say, his decision to maintain a low profile caused considerable discussion among Evangelicals concerned about Eastern Europe, not all of whom agreed with his approach.

Czechoslovakia and East Germany

Graham's visits to East Germany and to Czechoslovakia in late 1982 proved less controversial, however. Rolf Damman, general secretary of the East German Baptist Union, commented that Graham's visit to the German Democratic Republic "resulted not only in many conversions and rededications, especially among young people, but it has also given us a feeling of unity with other Protestant churches."

A sympathetic account of Graham's trip to Czechoslovakia in the autumn of 1972 has been given by his interpreter for the visit, Stanislav Svek, the general secretary of the Czech Baptists. Graham was invited by the Baptist Union shortly after his Moscow trip, and he agreed to come if he could combine the timing with his East German trip. Official government permission was granted for him to come (Czechoslovak authorities had been impressed with his views on the peace issue). In Prague he preached in the Baptist and Czech Evangelical Brethren churches, in a Hussite church in Brno, and in Bratislava, the Slovak capital, where his sermon was relayed to the Baptist church nearby. He met with the heads of the Bohemian Protestant churches in Prague and with Slovak leaders in Bratislava, as well as with Cardinal Tomasek at a party held in the U. S. Embassy. He talked with Christian Peace Conference delegates (including many non-Czechs) and with Deputy Premier Mattei Lucam.

Both with political leaders and at official functions such as laying a wreath for the victims of the Lidice massacre, he made it clear that his main reason for coming was to "preach the gospel." He even managed to do so on television, to everyone's amazement. He also emphasized the issue of peace. In his address in Bratislava at the memorial to Soviet troops who died in the war, he stated that the sacrifice of the blood of American and Russian soldiers to set people free from Nazism was a picture of the greater sacrifice made on the Cross by Jesus Christ to set sinners free. Peace, he said on several occasions, had three dimensions—between neighbors, between nations, and between man and God. He preached regularly on all three.

Home again

Graham's overseas crusades turned him into an international figure of far greater stature than many evangelists whose only appeal was to a home-grown audience. Some more radical commentators have tried to show that his influence in the United States has declined. The Moral Majority, they say, has appointed Jerry Falwell, not Graham, as America's leading Evangelical. This is partly because Graham has avoided U. S. politics in a way that Falwell and others have not—no bad thing, as it has given Graham and the gospel a credibility in those countries in which evangelical Christianity is growing. This might not have happened had he remained a purely parochial figure over-familiar with White House officials.

His decision to oppose the arms race has, as veteran political commentator Henry Fairlie has pointed out, reduced his following among more politically conservative Christians, as has his decision not to make abortion the priority issue in determining for whom to vote. But this means that he is now seen increasingly as an evangelist first and foremost—which is what he had always meant to be since the time he dedicated himself on "the 18th Green" to be an "ambassador for Jesus Christ."

Crusade evangelism—biblical or human?

Crusade evangelism has had a bad name in many Christian circles. It has been viewed as a phenomenon wholly alien to the New Testament. In non-Christian circles too, it has often had overtones of emotionalism or of the kind of ruthless exploitation embodied in the famous fictitious character Elmer Gantry, who preached for profit. As seen earlier, Graham's scrupulous methods and transparent honesty banished the Gantry image in secular eyes. In cleaning up evangelism he gave it a new, and welcome, respectability.

But the question still arises: even though Graham has made mass crusade evangelism something which Christians need no longer be ashamed of, is it really a biblical approach to conversion or merely a human one, given a clean bill of health by Graham's honesty and straightforwardness?

Those against mass evangelism point out that it is clear from Scripture that there was no evangelism conducted in New Testament times apart from the local church. Evangelism was carried on by local Christians sharing the Good News of Jesus Christ with the people with whom they were in regular, daily contact. Not only was evangelism local, it was built into the everyday lifestyle of each individual Christian. The idea of "meeting" evangelism—the notion that non-Christians should hear the gospel primarily through listening to it at specially held meetings—is also foreign to the New Testament pattern.

The missionary journeys of the apostle Paul, they add, were also church based. He was always commissioned by a local church and spent his time planting local churches wherever he went. Far from hurtling into a place for a week of meetings, he would often remain in a city for months or even years and keep in close personal contact thereafter.

On this score, they argue, the very basis of mass evangelism is false. Anything that is not in the Bible must be rejected if the church is to be truly loyal to Scripture. Certainly, crusade evangelism does not appear anywhere in Scripture. But arguments from silence are always dangerous. Because a method is absent, it does not follow that it is necessarily *wrong*. (Nor, however, can it therefore be claimed as the best by its supporters; if it were the *best* way of doing things, surely God would have included it in the Bible.) Many of the churches that oppose Graham use organs for congregational singing (one of their criticisms of the crusades is that they use modern musical instruments such as guitars). Organs appear nowhere in the New Testament. Does this mean, therefore, that organs are unbiblical, even *wrong*? The silence of Scripture can be interpreted either way.

The defense of Graham's method of mass evangelism (as opposed to mass evangelism in general, which may often be quite different) is precisely that he bases it in the context of local church ministry. The revolution that he created in crusade evangelism is not simply that he cleaned its image up, important though that was. It is that he entirely altered its nature. Before Graham, as seen earlier, itinerant evangelists would often attack local ministers. Graham, by contrast, always insisted on working through them and with them and would not come to their area unless they invited him to do so. The local church is as much the center of God's strategy as it has ever been— and it has often taken mass evangelist Billy Graham to say so.

Crusade evangelism as redefined by Graham is therefore a parachurch organization running closely in parallel with local churches, not a rival to replace them or supplant their God-created role. As he himself has said, one of the reasons that mass evangelism came into being was that the churches were failing to fulfill their clear biblical duty to proclaim the gospel. It was only natural that

Christians who had a burden for the lost should seek to do something about this sad state of affairs. But, as Graham also pointed out, should the churches once start to carry out their duty and become effective ambassadors for Christ, then parachurch organizations such as his own would cease to be necessary.

However, Graham's biblical emphasis on the local church has led him into an area which prevents many Bible-believing churches that fully share his zeal for evangelism and his Christ-centered message from cooperating with him. His policy has been to invite all the local Protestant churches—and Roman Catholic in some countries—to participate in the crusade in their particular city or region. In the past, this has meant that many liberal churches have taken part. Often, eminent clergy whose views are far from evangelical, and whose gospel seems very different from the one which Graham proclaims, find themselves as honored guests on his platforms to the consternation of many local Christians, who have frequently had bad past experiences with these very people. This problem has grown with Graham's fame; appearance on his platform confers a considerable degree of respectability to those concerned.

To the Graham team, the fact that a liberal church wishes to participate means that it can be influenced for the gospel. Similarly, if an eminent liberal theologian lives in the area, it is only courteous to invite him. Furthermore, as he is present on the platform, he is hearing the truth and may be gained for Jesus Christ.

To some, these views, while well motivated, miss the point. To have liberals involved, many Evangelicals feel, creates confusion. The essence of the evangelical message, the one that Graham himself preaches, is that it is the only truth, the only truly *biblical* message for today. Evangelicals therefore carefully differentiate themselves from those in their locality who proclaim a compromised, watered-down version of the gospel. When a crusade is organized, local non-Christians, whose conversion is the whole purpose of the crusade, see Evangelicals and liberals working together, side by side, as if there were no difference in the doctrine of salvation proclaimed by the two. Then, in the crusade meeting, the non-Christian sees evangelical leaders sitting with well-known theological liberals, who, as in the case of the Harringay Crusade of 1954, are sometimes known to be opposed to the evangelical position.

The Graham team argues that it is the liberals who are compromised by their public appearance in company with Evangelicals. But others feel that for liberals and Evangelicals publicly to cooperate only creates confusion in the minds of non-Christians and new converts and is therefore best avoided. This is not to say that liberals should be ostracized, but that Evangelicals should collaborate only with those who preach the biblical gospel. Unfortunately, many liberals, unable to fill their own churches because of the way in which they have diluted the message, take part in crusades in order to gain the converts they cannot attract themselves.

Graham always emphasizes that new converts should go to Bible-believing churches; he is right to do so. Many Evangelicals who love him and his message wish that he could apply the same rule for those who take part in his crusades. It is felt that he only gives ammunition to his enemies, who frequently lack his charitable spirit. They are able, unfairly, to claim that he himself is a compromiser because he associates with liberals.

Going for decision

According to John Pollock, Graham is out to get decisions in his crusades, using the same words and phrases from year to year. Many of Graham's fellow Evangelicals feel that the method he uses, coupled as it is with choirs, solo music, and other well-known formulas, is putting too much pressure on the human will, and relying on man-made methods instead of on the almighty power of the Holy Spirit. The "altar call," they argue, is a nineteenth-century invention (made famous by the evangelist Finney) unknown to the New Testament.

Others, more sympathetic to Graham, have another objection. Billy Graham is, they point out, undoubtedly anointed by God for the task he has carried out over the years; there is no human explanation for the success that he has had. They note too that Graham has consistently claimed that it is the power of the Holy Spirit at work that is the key to the whole enterprise: unless he is present, no amount of human organization will make the slightest difference. God has ordained Graham to preach the gospel, and this he has done without compromise.

If this is so, they feel, and as Graham has the view of the Holy Spirit that he does, together with a total reliance on God and upon the power of answered prayer, then why has he used methods that, to them, smack so much of strong human pressure? Since over eighty percent of converts came as a result of being brought by Christian friends, human methods to attract people—rock groups, superstar testimonies, and so on may be unnecessary. In addition, since the Christians will have been praying for their unconverted friends for some time (especially if they have been active in one of the "Operation Andrew" clubs), it does not matter so much if the non-Christian does not go forward *that* night—his or her Christian friends will not only continue to pray but also insure that Graham's clear gospel message is not forgotten.

Graham team members such as Roger Palms point out that it helps many people to be able to identify a specific moment when they became a Christian. This is undoubtedly true. But if Graham is truly anointed by God, which his career would seem to indicate that he is, then two interesting queries arise. First, it is the preaching of the message that people have really come to hear, and through which, in God's power, they are saved. In some countries, Graham has had to dispense with the long preliminaries—even with the altar call. Yet the response has not been diminished for lack of those two items. In other words, if Graham simply preached his message, without the preliminaries, the same number of people would attend and go forward because God would bless the faithful proclamation of his Word.

As has been shown, argument from silence is dangerous. The fact that music, testimony, and so on were methods entirely absent from the early church is no reason for saying that such modern methods are wrong. Yet many people feel the simple reliance on the preaching of the message, the witness of obedient Christians, and total dependence on the Holy Spirit—all methods of the New Testament—are still valid today, and if a mass evangelist were to rely on them alone, the God who so singularly blessed them in the days of the apostles would do so again in our day.

Perhaps the best example is set by Martyn Lloyd-Jones during the Harringay Crusade. He was profoundly unhappy with many of Graham's methods (which he felt placed too much pressure on the will) and by the fact that many liberal clergy appeared on the platform. Yet he prayed regularly every Sunday that many would be born again through Graham's faithful proclamation of the gospel and welcomed all the converts coming to his church.

Above all, Lloyd-Jones himself preached the gospel to unbelievers every Sunday evening, and although he never had any altar calls he saw conversions every week. He showed that the only people who have the real right to criticize are those who share Graham's zeal for the lost and his desire to see God's kingdom grow. Because of this, Graham today speaks very warmly of Dr. Lloyd-Jones, despite their differences. It is a shame that Graham's critics have often overlooked the good Graham has done and in their stridency and lack of love have only attacked him.

Moscow . . . or how far should one go?

The main difference that many Christians have with Graham is not so much with his method, or with what he preaches, but with his underlying theology of salvation. A vivid illustration of this was Graham's trip to Moscow, described earlier in this chapter. The question boils down to this: people come to hear Billy Graham because he is a world-famous evangelist. They are born again at one of his meetings. Suppose, instead, that Graham had not been able to come to the meeting that night (if he had a cold or had been prevented by the authorities from coming). Would those who were saved in the first instance not have been in the second? Suppose the crusade had been cancelled—what difference would this make to the eternal destinies of those who would have been saved at the crusade had the cancellation not taken place?

Graham said of his own success in 1951 that all "the glory and the praise and the credit must go to God the Holy Spirit. It is the Holy Spirit that convicts, the Holy Spirit that regenerates, and it is the Holy Spirit that carries on the work after we've gone. It is actually all a supernatural performance and a supernatural process. All we are is witnesses to the saving grace and power of the Lord Jesus Christ."

Thirteen years later, he told students in 1964 at Harvard Divinity School (as quoted by Pollock), "I used to think that in evangelism I had to do it all, but now I approach evangelism with a totally different attitude. I approach it with complete relaxation. First of all, I don't believe that any man can come to Christ unless the Holy Spirit has prepared his heart. Secondly, I don't believe any man can come to Christ unless God draws him. My job is to proclaim the message. It's the Holy Spirit's job to do the work."

When in 1982 he was asked to go to Moscow, his reaction was that "it was a God-given opportunity to proclaim the gospel in a country where I have not had this privilege before." As the article in *Christianity Today* of June 25, 1982 noted, he "hoped to be permitted eventually to hold preaching missions in large cities throughout the Soviet Union," though "this goal did not loom as large for Graham as it did in the public news media." He wished to plead the case of persecuted Christians with the authorities (Henry Kissinger, Vatican leaders, and many leading Evangelicals advised him on this) and to state his case (at the conference) for nuclear disarmament and an end to the arms race. As the article states, "Certainly these are worthy goals. No fair-minded person—let alone any evangelical Christian— could object to them."

The issue is whether Graham paid too high a price to achieve these goals, and thereby tragically discredited the cause of the gospel he was so anxious to proclaim.

The secular press was unremittingly hostile. *Newsweek* felt that he was being totally naive. He was, it commented, "manipulated by practiced Soviet hands" from the moment he stepped off the plane. Its reporter, Andrew Nagorski (who was later expelled by the Soviet authorities for his rather too accurate portrayal of the truth about life in Russia), felt that "throughout his six-day visit, Graham gave no hint just how limited a view of Soviet life his hosts were permitting him." News of his activities was censored but, Nagorski wrote, "Graham proved to be his own most effective censor."

At the Baptist Church, admission was by invitation only—most of the people hearing him were either Christians already or KGB staff. (Roger Palms has pointed out that KGB people need to hear the gospel too.) Throughout the nuclear conference, although Graham implicitly criticized the Soviet handling of freedom and justice, he took no part in activities which attacked the government's handling of human rights. The *Times* correspondent felt that Graham "felt obliged to go out of his way not to offend his hosts by speaking out against religious repression."

According to *Christianity Today* Graham regretted that he did not put some things more clearly, in a way that could not have been mishandled by an unsympathetic press. It pointed out that he is an evangelist, not a diplomat, and that much of what he said was quoted out of context. Much of the secular press coverage was unfair, written by people who did not share Graham's love of the gospel, and who could not therefore understand his motives in visiting the USSR. So it is worth examining what authoritative Christians had to say on the matter.

The best-informed source about Christianity in communist countries is Keston College in London, which has countless sources among Christian believers behind the Iron Curtain and a knowledge of persecution there that is unsurpassed. The Keston spokesman felt that the "Soviet authorities were obviously very anxious that Dr. Graham should attend the peace conference; he was therefore in a very strong bargaining position. He could have made one of the specific conditions of his attendance the release . . . of the Siberian Seven." He could also, in asking governments to abide by agreements on religious freedom, have requested the Soviets to "comply with these agreements in the form of one specific gesture." As the propaganda value of his attendance was very high, he could probably have achieved these things—yet he did not even ask for them.

Graham is one of the people who claims some credit for the release of the Siberian Christians. Yet one of them, Liuba Vaschenko, told a Keston College source that this "could have been any man of God visiting us. If we had some hopes of Mr. Graham's chances of helping us, all has turned to disillusionment." Indeed, Keston College noted in its bulletin that the reactions of most of the Russian believers whose views reached them "have, to date, been unfavorable. Believers express no animosity to Dr. Graham personally but feel he was used by the Soviet authorities." A Baptist elder wrote, "We understand Billy Graham has been deceived. We pray for him and hope that he will allow God to open his eyes to the truth."

According to *Christianity Today*, the "question of whether Graham did the right thing in going to Moscow depends on how highly a person values the proclamation and power of the gospel. Only time and eternity" it commented, "will reveal the full answer. But at this point we are not prepared to condemn him." Certainly, Christians should be very careful before they level criticisms at a fellow believer. How many of the critics have the level of concern for the unsaved, in Russia and elsewhere, that Graham has?

But the real issue was revealed in the article's subheading: "Billy Graham presented the claims of Christ to many who had never heard before *and might never hear again*" (author's italics). This is the nub of the issue. Suppose Graham had refused to come, or agreed to come only under the preconditions Keston College suggested, and been rejected as a result? What if he had succumbed to severe illness and been forced to cancel the trip? Would those people who heard the gospel clearly spelled out by him in Moscow then never have heard it?

Or, as many feel, would the loving, sovereign Lord who wished to see them come to true salvation through his Son have sent them another messenger, one less controversial, and one who would not have had to make the compromises that Graham undoubtedly thought right to make for the sake of the gospel?

If the people who heard the gospel in Moscow would otherwise *never* have heard again—and suffered eternal perdition as a result—then one can easily argue that Graham was right to go. Embarrassment and misunderstanding from the secular press are a small price to pay for saved souls. But as a secular journalist, William Safire of the *New York Times*, has pointed out, the gospel is today being proclaimed all over the Soviet Union, often at great personal risk and sacrifice, by Russian Christians.

Some of Graham's fellow Evangelicals feel that God can surely raise up his messengers in the USSR today and indeed is doing so with much power. It is not, therefore, a question of whether one believes in the proclamation and impact of the gospel or not, but how people will hear it, and through whom. Surely, they argue, if Graham had not gone, God would have ensured that those who missed him would still have heard the Good News of Jesus Christ through other channels.

Graham has rightly stated that we live in one of the most significant moments in history—one in which the gospel has been preached as never before in countries that have lain in spiritual darkness. One of God's greatest instruments in this has been Graham himself. The crusades in India, Korea, South America, and other places demonstrate without a doubt the role under God that he has played. On the other hand, there have been mighty revivals in recent years in countries to which Graham has never been.

A good example is China. In 1951 all foreign missionaries were expelled from its borders. In the years 1966–1976 the church underwent savage persecution in which many were martyred. But the local Christians continued to evangelize quietly but faithfully. The church, estimated at two million in 1951, now numbers at least fifteen million (according to the Chinese Church Research Center in Hong Kong the number if fifty million). This growth is almost unprecedented in the history of the Christian church. Yet since 1951 there have been no crusades, no mass evangelism, no visits by Billy

Graham. The same is true on a smaller scale of a country such as Romania; Hungarian Christians estimate there are more Christians in the Hungarian minority in Romania than in Hungary itself, a land which Graham has visited.

Graham has summed it up correctly and put it in its true perspective in a statement appearing in Pollock's book. He feels that "with all my heart as I look back on my life, that I was chosen to do this particular work" of evangelizing "as a man might have been chosen to go into East Harlem and work there, or to the slums of London like General Booth was. I believe that God in his sovereignty—I have no other answer for this—sheer sovereignty, chose me to do this work and prepared me in his own way."

This is surely the biblical way of looking at things. If Graham had not gone to Moscow, God would still have been glorified in the Soviet Union and other messengers found. But in other places, Billy Graham was without doubt God's chosen herald, bringing the Good News. Graham has said, "I have that confidence every time I preach," that the Holy Spirit will convict and save the lost. God can bring revival either with or without Billy Graham. Either way God is glorified and his kingdom increased, something for which all Christians can rejoice.

A call for peace

One of the major issues in which Graham has become involved is the debate on nuclear weapons. There has been, he has said, a "quantum leap in technology" resulting in a "quantum leap in our ability to destroy our entire planet," which would result in the end of human life. "The whole human race" he told the Moscow peace conference, "sits under a nuclear sword of Damocles." While many political issues are involved, the "nuclear arms race is primarily a moral and spiritual issue that must concern us all." Humankind has new technology, but it is morally unchanged. It is here, Graham feels, that the real change is needed.

Life, he points out, is sacred. But man has rebelled against God and created a world of sin. Therefore the "problem is in the human heart, which God alone can change." The hatred that could propel humanity into nuclear war is a direct result of sin. Graham is "not a pacifist," nor a supporter of unilateral disarmament—he agrees with legitimate defense in a fallen world. But he feels that the "unchecked production of weapons of mass destruction" threatens to "destroy the sacred gift of life." The nuclear arms race therefore "is not God's will."

To him, there are three kinds of peace—spiritual, between man and God; personal, within a human being; and relational, between human and human. Christians should work for peace in all areas, but it is made possible only by Jesus Christ at Calvary. The question arises—what can Christians do to advance peace on earth? According to Graham, "we must be realists, but we must also be optimists." God is sovereign, as shown by history; "We do not live in a world of blind chance." God will accomplish his will for the world which he created. Christians should be at the forefront of the movement for peace.

Graham, in his address in Moscow, outlined various practical suggestions. He made clear that his views were not political or nationalistic. Christians should "call the nations and leaders of our world to repentance" (no nation is exempt from blame) and "to a new and determined commitment to peace and justice"—a "disarmament race" that would be "equal on both sides, verifiable, and lead to at least a few generations of peace." While true peace will not come until God's kingdom prevails, over ninety-five percent of people would, Graham feels, vote for peace.

Graham urges deeds, not words. But he would ask all leaders to start the disarmament process by a "moratorium on hostile rhetoric" to lessen tensions. Positive steps to increase trust, such as international exchange between peoples, would help, as would a recognition by all governments "to respect the rights of religious believers as outlined in the United Nations Declaration of Human Rights." (*Christianity Today* noted that the Soviet bloc delegation listened to this part of his speech in stony silence.) World leaders should also get to know each other "simply . . . as human beings."

World leaders should, he stated, take steps to begin real talks aimed at "major arms reductions," with the "ultimate goal of eliminating all nuclear and biochemical weapons of mass destruction"—what Graham has called "SALT 10." This may, he admits, "be impossible to achieve, but it can be our ultimate goal." All Christians should pray for peace and dedicate themselves to the task of being peacemakers on earth. Both the superpowers face a "common enemy"—the "threat of impending nuclear catastrophe."

These views have proved highly controversial. While no one can actually speak out *against* peace and *for* nuclear war, some have wondered whether Graham, in his legitimate desire for world peace, is being sadly naive. The reality of the situation, they feel, is that the West is faced by a power of total hostility to justice, liberty, and human rights, and that the existence of nuclear weapons has proved an effective guarantor against takeover of the free West by the Soviets. Graham, they think, has failed to take the inherent evil of the Soviet regime into account. Any pleas from him will fall on stony ground, however well-intentioned.

Others, as seen in the chapter on John Stott, have also come out against the use of nuclear weapons on moral grounds, while emphatically rejecting the total pacifist option. Certainly this is an issue on which Christians may profoundly disagree in practice while being united in principle. It may be that Graham is over-optimistic in his views on the chances of the Soviet Union consenting to eventual total nuclear disarmament and has not been as outspoken as he should have been against the violation of human rights in the Soviet bloc. (Christians in the Philippines have said the same about his silence over the abuse of civil liberties by the right-wing government during his crusade there.) But he has shown that Christians are capable of serious thought on the major issues of the day, and that they are aware of the world in which God has placed them. Even if one disagrees with his "SALT 10" idea, he has at least caused Christians to think more deeply about the most serious secular issue of our day.

Above all, in an age where many people fear the future and doubt the survival of the human race, he has made clear his belief in the sovereign Lord. Even as God destroyed the armies of the Assyrians before Jerusalem (as recorded in 2 Kings 19), so he is still powerful to act today. Furthermore, the nuclear issue has encouraged many to think about eternity.

Graham has been the evangelist to the world in the age of the bomb, and the sober effect that the threat of nuclear holocaust has created has helped many to listen to him with a renewed sense of seriousness. It may well be that God has allowed the threat of nuclear conflict to hang over the nations of the West to bring them to their senses, even though he does not intend to allow such a final catastrophe to happen. Billy Graham has played his part in reminding the world of its fallenness and need of a Savior, and the possibility of mutual annihilation of the human race is a vivid illustration of the biblical picture of the true nature of sinful man.

Billy Graham—God's ambassador

In the official Graham literature of the awards and distinctions that have been bestowed upon him, much has been made of his consistently high ratings in the opinion polls, and of the contacts he has made with the great and famous. In many ways, this is on target. Graham has given a respectability to the Christian faith that has helped to spread it. It is good that an evangelical Christian has been able to share the gospel with people at the top of society, with the decision makers who determine how ordinary men and women live. It is often forgotten today that such rulers need the gospel too—the Bible enjoins Christians to pray for them, and Graham's status has given him a unique degree of access. Similarly Graham has been seen by millions on television news bulletins and popular talk shows, and he has taken full use of the opportunities thus given him to proclaim the gospel to this vast audience.

Graham has made the gospel credible, and in an age of doubt this is far more important than respectability gained by chats in the White House, vital though that is in giving him a unique platform from which to proclaim the Good News of Jesus Christ. His transparent sincerity has convinced thousands that Christianity is no longer something that they can afford to ignore or reject. The straightforward, uncomplicated style of his preaching makes it understandable by people of all kinds of ability and background—from academics to illiterates and from royalty to peasantry.

Much of this can be attributed to the decent, honest, natural virtues that are the hallmark of the part of the United States from which Graham comes. Such characteristics may have been rejected in a so-called sophisticated urban age, but to the majority of those who have heard Graham around the world they are traits with which his listeners will readily identify. The same refreshing innocence (a marked feature of many major American stories in rural settings, such as "The Waltons") that led Graham to be deceived by Nixon has been one of his greatest strengths in reaching out to the millions of the Third World.

For, as noted earlier in this chapter, perhaps the most remarkable feature of Graham's ministry has been the fact that in the post-imperial age, one which has often been marked by strident anti-U. S. feeling, Billy Graham (in many ways the embodiment of the white Anglo-Saxon Protestant American) has been the most successful mass evangelist to the world in this century. Many Americans have succeeded in their home territory only to fail miserably abroad. Graham, on the other hand, is now almost more successful in other countries than in his own, and some of his greatest results have been seen in nations whose culture and thought patterns are about as far removed from those of the United States as it is possible to imagine.

It is perhaps no coincidence that when he began to think of himself not just as an American but as an evangelist to the world, his most significant ministry began. He has had the wisdom to do what many have failed to do: to keep the message of the Good News of Jesus Christ totally unaltered and uncompromised, while at the same time adapting to different cultures and international situations. He has also found an utterly dedicated team of godly men and stuck by them, thus providing a valuable degree of continuity.

Above all, Graham has been faithful to the gospel. Surely God has used and blessed this. People who invite Graham know that they can trust him fearlessly to proclaim the truth. His career, as T. W. Wilson has so rightly said, is proof of the sovereignty of God to save the lost. The church of Jesus Christ has seen an unprecedented growth in the last forty years, especially in countries where the gospel was either unknown or believed only by a tiny handful. In such an age, one in which God has been seen to be alive as never before, Billy Graham has been his ambassador to the nations. Surely no higher tribute could be paid to a man than that.

Other biographies of Christian leaders

Bursting the Wineskins, by Michael Cassidy. Cassidy, a respected South African leader, is a bridge-builder. In this autobiographical account of the working of God's Spirit in his life, Cassidy bridges the barriers of race, culture, and those created by the charismatic movement, and demonstrates the radical power of God to change human lives. "His work is one of the strongest current witnesses joining spiritual nurture, evangelism, social concern, and ecumenism"—*Richard Lovelace.*

George Müller: Delighted in God, by Roger Steer. The definitive life story of the man who lived by prayer and faith alone, housing and feeding thousands of homeless children in England, advertising his financial needs to no one but God. "A miraculous witness to the power of faith"—*George Verwer.*

The Price of Success, by J. B. Phillips. The autobiography of the man whose translation of the New Testament has spoken powerfully in the twentieth century. "I have seldom been as deeply moved as by J. B. Phillips's own description of his euphoria of success, followed by his plunge into deep depression. Yet, in the end, triumph prevailed"—*Kenneth N. Taylor.*

You Are My God, by David Watson. In this moving account of his own spiritual pilgrimage, Canon David Watson, one of the best known clergymen in England, is unsparingly honest about himself, his family, and the struggles and exhilarating rewards of his ministry. "David Watson's book is personal, honest, winsome, instructive, and inspiring. All who are open to the power of the Word and the Spirit will be enthralled and enriched by this record of his pilgrimage"—*David A. Hubbard.*

Available from your favorite bookstore, or from **Harold Shaw Publishers,** Box 567, Wheaton, Illinois 60189.

Date Due

Code 4386-04, CLS-4, Broadman Supplies, Nashville, Tenn.,
Printed in U.S.A.